Praise for
NOBODY'S FOOL

"*Nobody's Fool* is science writing at its best. A must-read for anybody who loves reading about fascinating social-science studies and compelling stories—or just wants to get tricked less."

—Seth Stephens-Davidowitz,
New York Times–bestselling author of
Everybody Lies and *Don't Trust Your Gut*

"This book is worth vastly more than its purchase price. It shows, in rich detail, that con artists around the world use strikingly similar tactics to ensnare their victims. Daniel Simons and Christopher Chabris offer an engaging master class in how to foil purveyors of false promises." —Philip E. Tetlock, author of *Superforecasting*

"Whether you are wondering how frauds like Enron, Theranos, and FTX managed to fool so many people for so much of the time or just want to know how to protect yourself from the Next Big Fleece, Simons and Chabris have got you covered in this tour of how con artists, hoaxers, and troll farms prey on human cognitive weaknesses."

—Gary Marcus, author of *Guitar Zero*,
Kluge, and *Rebooting AI*

"In an era when more information is available to us than ever before, when claims of 'fake news' might themselves be fake news, Simons and Chabris offer a vital tool to not only inoculate ourselves against getting infected by misinformation, but also prevent us from spreading it to others."

—David McRaney, author of *How Minds Change*

"The vast menagerie of scams detailed in Nobody's Fool makes for entertaining—albeit frightening—reading. Thankfully, Simons and Chabris excavate the inner workings of con-artistry and explain in great detail why we fall for it, again and again, and how we can stop. This book is an inoculation for your brain."

—David Epstein, author of
the New York Times bestseller *Range:
Why Generalists Triumph in a Specialized World*

NOBODY'S FOOL

Also by the Authors

The Invisible Gorilla: How Our Intuitions Deceive Us
by Christopher Chabris and Daniel Simons

NOBODY'S FOOL

WHY WE GET TAKEN IN
AND WHAT
WE CAN DO ABOUT IT

DANIEL SIMONS & CHRISTOPHER CHABRIS

BASIC BOOKS

New York

Basic Books
Hachette Book Group
1290 Avenue of the Americas, New York, NY 10104
www.basicbooks.com

Printed in the United States of America

First Edition: July 2023

Published by Basic Books, an imprint of Perseus Books, LLC, a subsidiary of Hachette Book Group, Inc. The Basic Books name and logo is a trademark of the Hachette Book Group.

The Hachette Speakers Bureau provides a wide range of authors for speaking events. To find out more, go to hachettespeakersbureau.com or email HachetteSpeakers@hbgusa.com.

The publisher is not responsible for websites (or their content) that are not owned by the publisher.

Print book interior design by Amy Quinn.

Library of Congress Cataloging-in-Publication Data
Names: Simons, Daniel J., author. | Chabris, Christopher F., author.
Title: Nobody's fool : why we get taken in and what we can do about it / Daniel Simons and Christopher Chabris.
Description: New York, NY : Basic Books, [2023] | Includes bibliographical references and index.
Identifiers: LCCN 2022049503 | ISBN 9781541602236 (hardcover) | ISBN 9781541602243 (ebook)
Subjects: LCSH: Deception—Psychological aspects. | Swindlers and swindling.
Classification: LCC BF637.D42 S55 2023 | DDC 177/.3—dc23/eng/20230322
LC record available at https://lccn.loc.gov/2022049503

ISBNs: 9781541602236 (hardcover), 9781541602243 (ebook)

LSC-C

Printing 1, 2023

CONTENTS

INTRODUCTION

"Once in a while, we can all be fooled by something." That is how James Mattis, a former US defense secretary and Marine general, explained why he vouched for Elizabeth Holmes and her company Theranos, served on the firm's board of directors, and gave glowing endorsements of her character to journalists and others.[1]

Theranos claimed to have developed revolutionary miniature medical testing devices that used just a few drops of blood from a finger prick to perform dozens or even hundreds of different assays, most of which traditionally required a tube of blood drawn from an arm. After they told Mattis these devices would work on the battlefield, he ordered his military subordinates in Afghanistan to test the technology. But no tests were ever run, and when Theranos did start offering services to consumers, they mainly used bulky equipment made by other companies rather than their buggy new machines. The company ultimately collapsed, and Holmes was tried, convicted, and sentenced to more than eleven years in prison for defrauding investors.[2]

Admitting you've been fooled is not easy, and Mattis is right that it can happen to the best of us. But there's a lot more to it than that. The world is filled with people who want to fool us. From Wall Street Ponzi schemes to Nigerian email scams, from chess cheaters with hidden computers to bridge cheaters with covert signaling systems, from psychic mediums preying on credulous audiences to scientific fraudsters making up results their colleagues will believe, from art forgers to deceptive marketers, traps abound. And all successful deceptions have one thing in common: They take advantage of how our minds work.

The *Saturday Night Live* characters Hans and Franz famously said, "Hear us now and believe us later." The irony of their catchphrase is that by default, we don't wait until later to believe. Humans operate with a "truth bias"—we tend to assume that what we see and hear is true until and unless we get clear evidence otherwise. We hear now, believe right away, and only occasionally check later.

Truth bias is a feature, not a bug. Most people tell the truth most of the time (or at least they do not lie deliberately), making a bias toward truth both logical and reasonable. Without a shared assumption that people generally speak the truth, we'd be unable to live together in communities, coordinate our actions, or even hold simple conversations. But truth bias is also an overarching factor that plays a critical role in every con, scam, and fraud. It is a prerequisite for almost any act of deception, and when it impairs our otherwise rational decision-making, we refer to it with terms like credulity, naivete, or gullibility.[3]

In the "president scam," an audacious con made famous in the 2000s by the French-Israeli fraudster Gilbert Chikli, a midlevel manager receives a call from someone claiming to be their company's president or CEO, who then weaves a story to talk the manager into transferring corporate funds to some plausible destination—when in fact it goes straight to the scammers. The entire trick hinges on the manager's willingness to believe—if you don't accept that it's the president on the line, you'll never fall for it. But if you start with a truth bias, a fast-talking scammer can ensnare you before you think to check.[4]

We're left with a conundrum: We need to believe others, but if we trust too much, we're in trouble—especially now. Given the ever-multiplying demands on our attention and the growth of deliberate attempts to misinform us, defaulting to belief puts us more at risk than ever. So what can we do, short of cynically and exhaustively questioning everyone and everything? Luckily, we can do a lot.

It can be tempting when learning about a simple con to think that you would never have fallen for it—or to assume that only less intelligent, less educated, or more gullible people can be victimized. But the fact is that everyone can be fooled, even the best and brightest among us. In this book, we reveal how people exploit our bias for truth—our inclination to accept too much and check too little—and we propose concrete steps we can take to bolster our defenses. We don't offer a compendium of scams and scammers or a treatise on the history, economics, or sociology of deceit. We also don't delve into the motivations, incentives, and emotional makeup of con artists and their victims. Rather, we explain the cognitive psychology of the cheated—the patterns of thinking and reasoning that make us all vulnerable.[5]

We wrote this book for several reasons. We are cognitive scientists who study what people notice and miss, what they remember and forget, and how they make decisions. In our previous book, *The Invisible Gorilla*, we wrote about the consequences of our mistaken intuitions about how our own minds work. As professors, we have had firsthand experiences with students who cheat on papers and exams. As researchers, we have dealt with fraud and deceptive practices within our own academic communities, even cases involving our own friends and colleagues. Because we are human beings, we have been fooled many times ourselves. Because we are psychologists, we have reflected on how it happened.[6]

As we immersed ourselves in this topic, we came to appreciate how widespread deception has become. Frauds of many sorts are growing in terms of both dollars stolen and victims scammed. But the story goes beyond crime. Businesses have adopted more deceptive techniques as standard operating procedure, blurring the line between legitimate and illegitimate commercial tactics. In the 2000s, for example, some hedge funds and mutual funds tolerated or even encouraged gathering and trading on inside information, sometimes using systems and codes designed to give their principals plausible deniability. Many online vendors routinely manipulate their product and business ratings on Amazon, Yelp, and other sites. Companies worth millions or billions of dollars sell nothing but tools for cheating—from bots and cheats for online games to prewritten papers and test answers for college courses. And around the world, political campaigns increasingly traffic in fake news and conspiracy theories or at best do not care whether their claims are true or false.[7]

Over the course of writing *Nobody's Fool*, we studied hundreds of examples of deception of all sorts and applied our understanding of cognitive psychology to identify recurring features and emergent patterns. In so doing, we also considered strategies that may help people get fooled less. A critical first step, one that counteracts truth bias and is at the core of the more concrete suggestions we make throughout the book, is a simple one to remember: **Accept less, check more**. The challenge comes in realizing when we need to check more and figuring out how to go about it. Here's a straightforward example of how it works.

SUPREMELY FAKE

"It's not the tweets, it's the retweets that get you in trouble.... You see something that looks good and you don't investigate it." In a social media world of fake news and political disinformation, those are wise words (and ironic ones, considering who said them). Political disinformation goes nowhere unless its recipients spread it to their friends, and they spread it to theirs, and so on—which makes it critical to short-circuit this process when it reaches us.[8]

One of Donald Trump's first acts on assuming the presidency in 2017 was to nominate a successor to Supreme Court justice Antonin Scalia. He selected Neil Gorsuch, a federal appellate judge from

Colorado and a longtime favorite in Republican legal circles. Within days, a friend of ours shared on Facebook a bombshell news story: "JUST IN: All 8 Supreme Court Justices Stand in Solidarity Against Trump SCOTUS Pick." The article stated that the eight remaining justices "agree that President Trump is completely wrong in choosing Neil Gorsuch" and that "Chief Justice John Roberts penned a letter from the Supreme Court that addressed the issues with Gorsuch's 'approach' being 'the law of the land.'"⁹

When we first saw the post, we were shocked by this story. A single sitting justice publicly denouncing a nominee would be unprecedented, and this article claimed that all eight of them had done so in unison. The person who posted it is, to our knowledge, intelligent and well-meaning, and we had no reason to distrust their judgment. But before clicking Like or Share, we decided to check.

The article on Neil Gorsuch, which originally appeared on BipartisanReport.com, was a typical example of what is now called "fake news." In reality, Roberts and the other justices said nothing publicly about Gorsuch after he was nominated. But like many such stories, this one wasn't entirely fabricated. It quoted lines from a recent Supreme Court opinion that had reversed a decision from a lower court, one that had cited one of Gorsuch's opinions from nine years earlier. The Supreme Court often reverses lower court decisions, and doing so is not a condemnation of the judges who made them—often a reversal rests on a genuine difference of opinion or interpretation, and at worst, it is a correction of error.

We knew that the Supreme Court would not have done what the post claimed, but we felt ourselves briefly accepting the claim as true ("Wow!") before increasing our uncertainty ("Is that really true?"). Only then did we check to make sure that we were correct in our conclusion ("No way!").

In this case, the checking part was easy. For a claim of this magnitude, sites such as Factcheck.org and Snopes.com usually post investigations (they did), and if it were true, major news outlets on both the political left and right (*New York Times, Wall Street Journal*) would cover it (they didn't). And any lawyer, no matter how partisan their politics, could have told us that the Supreme Court doesn't work the way the Gorsuch piece said it does.

By one prominent account, truth bias exists because evolution left a quirk in the design of our minds: We automatically tag all incoming information as true, and it takes an effortful, extra step to remove that "true" tag or to replace it with a "false" tag. Had we seen the Facebook post while distracted, or without time to reflect on it, there's some chance we might have skipped that second step and carried around a false belief, perhaps long enough to spread it to someone else.[10]

REMAINING UNCERTAIN

Outside the legal system, we rarely ask other people to affirm that they are telling the whole truth and nothing but the truth—and doing so would be decidedly antisocial. But asking ourselves whether a key piece of information is unquestionably true, or whether we should withhold judgment until we can verify it, can save us from the consequences of acting on a falsehood. Making a deliberate choice to remain uncertain restrains truth bias.

Scientific experiments on truth bias often take the form of a game of lie detection. Participants watch videos in which actors tell stories that are either true or false and then decide which ones they believe. In a typical experiment by the cognitive psychologists Chris Street and Daniel Richardson, for example, the participants watched eighteen videos of different people telling stories about their travels, half of which were true and half of which were lies. The results revealed a truth bias: The participants judged 65 percent of the speakers to be truthful rather than the 50 percent who actually were. However, when the participants were given a third option—to say that they were unsure—they rated just 46 percent of the stories as truthful.[11]

Remaining uncertain can be aversive and does not necessarily come naturally, but it is a habit we should cultivate whenever we can. We don't need to distrust everything we hear, but we should make a practice of taking a beat, remaining uncertain, and asking ourselves, **"Is that really true?"**

Sometimes, simply reminding people to consider whether what they read or posted online is true can help stanch the flow of falsehoods. The psychologist Gordon Pennycook and his colleagues sent direct messages to over five thousand Twitter accounts that had recently tweeted links to stories on two partisan "news" sites. The messages presented a single headline and asked the recipients to evaluate how accurate it was—that is, they drew the recipients' attention to the possibility that online stories might be false. The day after receiving the direct message, these accounts tweeted fewer stories from sites that fact-checkers regard as untrustworthy than they did on other days.[12]

Remaining uncertain can take many forms. During the 1980s, the rock band Van Halen included a curious rider in their tour contract: Each venue had to provide a large bowl of M&M's containing a mixture of every standard color but brown. Before each show, lead singer David Lee Roth went backstage and personally checked the bowl to make sure it contained no brown M&M's. His logic was that if the organizers failed to follow such a simple instruction, they shouldn't be trusted to have safely installed all of the rigging, wiring, staging, lighting, and pyrotechnics for a complex show. If the organizers failed the M&M test, the band paid more attention to the staging, and in Roth's words, "We'd line-check the entire production. Guaranteed you're going to arrive at a technical error."

Van Halen's rider was what scientists might call a positive control, an extra experiment that checks whether everything is working as it should. The M&M test checked whether the local stage crews were sufficiently conscientious and attentive to detail. Of course, it wasn't foolproof—a crew could have thrown out every single brown

M&M and still made a serious mistake elsewhere. The band members couldn't exhaustively inspect every stage detail by themselves, though, so the test was an improvement over taking the local crew's assurances that all was well. Simple checks are never perfect, but blind acceptance is a terrible alternative. This book will help you learn to apply similar checks in your daily life to alert you to possible deception and the need for further scrutiny.

Spot-checking someone's work before assuming that it is correct is like looking both ways before crossing the road or asking "Is that really true?"—it's a step to help counteract truth bias. If we take note of the times when something we once accepted as true turned out to be false or misleading, we can learn when it will help to remain uncertain. Nothing will permanently immunize us against being taken in. But as with any new skill, practice gradually tunes our deception radar to alert us when we are in danger.

WHAT MAKES US ACCEPT TOO MUCH

Trying to remain uncertain can help dampen our risk of accepting too much, but just as pouring gasoline on a fire makes it burn faster, several factors act as accelerants for truth bias. In particular, the qualities of the messenger—or at least how we perceive them—can make a message unduly persuasive.

When a source presents itself as objective and fair (like faux-centrist BipartisanReport.com, which first posted the Gorsuch story), we're more susceptible to deception. Anything presented by an authority—assuming the recipient recognizes and respects the source—has a head start on being accepted as true or worth obeying. This is one reason why a common "call-center scam" involves telling victims that they owe money to a tax authority (such as the US Internal Revenue Service), immigration agency, or other government entity and that law enforcement will come right away to serve an arrest warrant unless the bill is paid over the phone.[13]

The power of the source in amplifying our truth bias is even more potent when we find the storyteller to be sympathetic. That's why people aiming to deceive us work so hard to make themselves and their stories appeal to our emotions, desires, and identities. The memoirist Binjamin Wilkomirski spun a compelling tale of surviving Auschwitz as a child that was hailed by the *Guardian* as "one of the great works about the Holocaust," but it was later discovered that he had lived in Switzerland during World War II—and was not even Jewish. Similarly, a twenty-three-year-old Australian woman called Belle Gibson started a natural healing business based on her claim to have cured her own brain cancer. She had not had cancer, let alone cured it by eating the right foods, but enough people accepted her tale that she racked up over $1 million in smartphone app and book sales. Even the most sympathetic characters can be liars.[14]

We should be especially wary when a story is conveyed with utter certainty, because the confidence of con artists can accelerate our tendency to accept without checking. Bernie Madoff cheated investors out of tens of billions of dollars in an infamous Ponzi scheme. During the more than fifteen years that the scam was in full swing, he was questioned several times by authorities and journalists who had been tipped off to his dubious activities. According to one postmortem analysis, Madoff explained his investing success to US Securities and Exchange Commission (SEC) inspectors by saying "he could actually sit on the trading room floor, and 'feel the market' and know exactly when to buy and exactly when to sell. And Madoff always bought at the right price, and always sold at the right price, day after day, year after year. Inexplicably, the SEC just accepted these answers and went on." The SEC accepted Madoff's fatuous claims in part because of the palpable confidence with which he made them. When the financial journalist Michael Ocrant questioned Madoff about the growing suspicions about his business, he found him surprisingly forthcoming and recalled later that "there wasn't even a hint of guilt or shame or remorse." Just a year before his scam collapsed, Madoff calmly told a public meeting, "In today's regulatory environment, it's virtually impossible to violate rules. It's impossible for a violation to go undetected, certainly not for a considerable period of time." All else being equal, the more confidently a statement is made, the more likely it is to be believed. Paradoxically, the more convincing a speaker seems—the more correct and self-evident their arguments feel—the more we need to investigate further.[15]

EVERYDAY DECEPTION

Like the intricate rigging of Van Halen's stage shows, the scams depicted in movies like *Ocean's Eleven* and series like *Money Heist* typically involve criminal masterminds orchestrating conspiracies in secret locations with parts that must come together like clockwork to succeed. But in reality, complex, sophisticated, long-running cons like Madoff's fake hedge fund are the exception. Most of the deception we encounter is simple and opportunistic—closer to misleading headlines than to masterful hoaxes—and it often happens in plain sight.

The nationwide college-admissions scandal in the United States, known by the code name given to the FBI's investigation, "Operation Varsity Blues," is a case in point. Over a period of years, a consultant named Rick Singer promised to get the children of wealthy clients and celebrities admitted to prestigious universities that might otherwise have rejected them. He bribed athletic coaches or directors to use their influence to get his clients admitted, and he fabricated credentials by Photoshopping the student into an image of someone else rowing, swimming, or playing lacrosse or by paying a stooge to take the admissions tests for the applicant. This series of simple frauds— no hidden cameras or stage sets, spy-world dead drops, or computer hacking—went undetected for years and had dozens of victims, including not only the colleges that were deceived but also the students who lost places at good schools to the children of Singer's clients.[16]

Many deceptions require no conspiracy at all. One of the most infamous scientific fraudsters of all time, Dutch social psychology professor Diederik Stapel, created datasets from scratch and passed them off to his unwitting students and coworkers, who then "discovered" results supporting the hypotheses that they and Stapel had collectively developed. Stapel later confessed—and an official investigation confirmed—that he had acted alone in faking the data. When the stakes are higher—as in clinical trials of potentially lifesaving medicines for cancer, Covid-19, and other diseases—such scientist-on-scientist frauds pollute the medical literature that doctors and the rest of us rely on to make health decisions.[17]

Unethical journalists engage in one of the simplest forms of deception. After coming up with a good story idea—a normal step in journalism—they skip the steps of gathering information, finding sources, conducting interviews, and checking facts and just write the finished story as though they had done all those things. For a skilled writer, fake stories are not only easier to craft but often more engaging and convincing than true ones. After all, in fiction, an author can assign each character just the right traits, perfect the plotline and conflicts, and eliminate inconsistencies to make a story a little more elegant and memorable than a real one.[18]

Even when telling a true story, unethical writers sometimes polish the rough edges to give it a more attractive and convincing gloss. The prominent science writer Jonah Lehrer altered the facts of historical events and fabricated quotations. For example, regarding his early career struggles, the magician Teller had said, "I'd always assumed I'd spend my life happily performing in artsy-fartsy little theaters," but Lehrer magnified Teller's concerns into an existential crisis in the false version he published in his book *Imagine*: "I was definitely on the verge of giving up the dream of becoming a magician. . . . I was ready to go back home and become a high-school Latin teacher." When Lehrer related the story of how pioneering social psychologist Leon

Festinger infiltrated a 1950s doomsday cult that expected aliens to arrive at a particular date and time, he wrote, "When the clock read 12:01 and there were still no aliens, the cultists began to worry. A few began to cry. The aliens had let them down." What Festinger actually observed, though, was entirely different—and more surprising: "One might have expected some visible reaction. Midnight had passed and nothing had happened. . . . But there was little to see in the reactions of the people in that room. There was no talking, no sound. People sat stock still, their faces seemingly frozen and expressionless." Where Festinger described signs of confusion and uncertainty, Lehrer reported anxiety and distress.[19]

This type of cheating is less dramatic than a con that empties your pockets or bank account. But when these sorts of minor deceptions become business as usual—when millions of people are exposed to made-up quotations, distorted history, or fictitious scientific results—our collective trust in what should be nonfiction declines, and that adversely impacts our ability to reach rational conclusions.[20]

Even schemes that do take our money can be surprisingly banal at their core. FTX was a popular trading platform for cryptocurrencies like Bitcoin, and it was backed by top-tier venture capitalists and attracted users with celebrity endorsements and Super Bowl ads. Its customer agreement said, "Title to your Digital Assets shall at all times remain with you." But when FTX filed for bankruptcy in November 2022, it was discovered that it had been sending customer deposits to a sister company called Alameda Research, which used them to fund its own trading and investment activities—that is, FTX was simply making promises and doing the opposite.[21]

Examples like these show that knowing when we should pause to check and what we should check for are not obvious. We can't distrust everyone and still function in society, and we can't personally investigate every detail. The challenge is in striking a balance. We must believe in and trust others enough to go about our lives while suspending just enough judgment to recognize when we could be fooled—when checking things out is likely to pay dividends.

HABITS AND HOOKS

Deception works when it feels like truth. In this book, we'll argue that all successful deceptions exploit features of human thinking and reasoning that normally serve us well. Those looking to fool us don't usually craft their plots with knowledge of cognitive psychology in mind, but the tricks they play and the scripts they follow are effective because they point directly at our weaknesses. Understanding these tendencies is central to developing our own skill at recognizing and avoiding deception.

We begin with chapters on four key cognitive *habits* that we all have, crucial features of how we think and reason that unfortunately can be weaponized by people who want to fool us. They include our ability to *focus* on the information we care about—often the information right in front of us—while ignoring distractions or irrelevant information. With experience, we develop expectations for what should happen or what incoming information should look like, and we use these expectations to automatically make *predictions* that are accurate much of the time. Our abilities to think and reason depend on our making fundamental assumptions about ourselves, other people, and the world around us; when these assumptions are strong enough, they constitute *commitments* that we rarely question or even realize we are making. And as we become practiced at any task, we increase our *efficiency*, meaning we develop routines, rules of thumb, and shortcuts that save us immense amounts of time and effort in making decisions. We will show in detail how each of these habits creates fertile ground for deception to take root.

The remaining chapters explore four *hooks*: features of the information we encounter in our daily lives that we find attractive but that can snare us. Like a compelling trailer for a movie, an enticing elevator pitch, or a musical earworm, hooks snag our interest and bias us toward accepting claims without checking them. Hooks are neither inherently good nor bad, and most things that grab our attention deserve at least some of it. But when we're being deceived, one or more hooks are almost always misdirecting us. When the information we encounter matches or resembles what we already know and trust, we use *familiarity* as a signal of its truth. We rely on the *consistency* of information we encounter as evidence of its veracity. We associate great *precision* in predictions or evidence with the accuracy and truthfulness of the ideas that gave rise to them. And we are attracted to stories of *potency,* in which small causes have large consequences for our lives and society as a whole.

Our habits and hooks make it possible for others to deceive us (as well as for us to deceive ourselves). Most frauds, especially long-running and complex ones, exploit multiple habits and hooks and also rely on a degree of self-deception by their victims. In fact, many frauds succeed because those of us most likely to be deceived identify ourselves to the scammers, making their task easier (a point we return to in the conclusion of the book).

In each chapter, we relate stories of crimes, cons, and scams—some famous, others obscure, and a few from our own experience—that illustrate how deception capitalizes on our cognitive habits and hooks us into accepting when we should instead have checked. Some of these scams are funny. Others are poignant. Some are victimless. Others harm us all. Some are even ironic—like a deceptive study of dishonesty, a psychic who did not predict their own downfall, or an American who was scammed into helping run a "Nigerian prince" scam.[22]

Throughout the book, we draw upon classic and current research in cognitive psychology and the social sciences to explain why all of us are fooled at least some of the time. We describe the science behind our cognitive habits and hooks, discuss how they usually help us, and illustrate how they can be exploited. Each chapter includes maxims that encapsulate our advice for spotting those times when we should be more vigilant, along with specific questions we can ask to help detect deception before it's too late. We hope that by learning about cognitive habits and hooks and seeing many different examples of how deception works, you'll gradually come to accept less, check more, and avoid being fooled.

PART 1
HABITS

CHAPTER 1

FOCUS—THINK ABOUT WHAT'S MISSING

We tend to make decisions using the information before us, ignoring irrelevant or distracting information. That habit of focus means we tend to neglect the importance, or even existence, of information that is absent. A tool known as a possibility grid can help us notice when we're being misled by the information we aren't considering.

JOHN EDWARD IS ONE OF THE MOST FAMOUS PSYCHIC MEDIUMS working today. At the height of his popularity in the mid-2000s, he hosted *John Edward Cross Country*, a show on the WE tv network. It opened with Edward offering a caveat: "Mediumship is not a cure for grief. It can be very therapeutic, healing, and very helpful. It can be extremely empowering when you understand the process, but if you're looking for a reading to *fix* your grief, it does not. I want to be very, very clear."[1]

Edward is a stocky man with close-cropped hair. On the show, he wears a black leather blazer and blue jeans. After his preamble,

Edward paces a small stage holding a microphone and begins to work his magic.

"I am ready to go. . . . There's a younger male energy in this section," he says from the right of the stage, looking at the people directly in front of him. "They make me feel like this would be son, nephew, grandson. There's a cancer connection that comes up here." The camera shows Edward from behind and his audience in front of him. "Does this make sense? Where's Robert, Robby, Rob? Where's the R?"

A woman in a middle row with dark hair and a gray sweater shoots up her hand. She's attending the taping in a group with some of her relatives. Edward asks for a microphone to be given to her.

"Robert?" he asks.

"My father," she says.

"Passed?"

"Yes."

"OK. Cancer?"

"No."

"Where is the bone issue?"

"There's two. There's my grandfather," she says, and then, gesturing to a man next to her, she adds, "and his mom."

"Somebody had something that affected their bone," asserts Edward. He is speaking directly to the woman, pointing with the same hand that holds the mic.

"His mom," she repeats. "Bone cancer," says the man, off mic. Now he is given a microphone of his own.

"She had bone cancer?" asks Edward.

"Yes," says the woman.

After ascertaining that the man's mother died of bone cancer, Edward reveals that he's made contact: "She's making me feel like when she passes, she passes either around or on a governmental holiday or something that would be celebratory, but for the country."

"Um, my, my father," stammers the woman, with a hint of a Boston accent.

"I'm seeing the American flag, so when I see that, it lets me know that we're talking about, like, either July 4th, Veterans Day . . ."

"September 11th," she interrupts.

"Did he pass in *the* September 11th?"

"Yes. He was a fireman."

"Your dad is Robert; we already addressed that."

"Yes."

"Are you the baby girl in the family?"

"I'm the oldest."

"OK. He's making me feel like you're the baby girl, like that's how it's coming across to me." The woman nods. She looks like she is about to cry.

"He's also making me feel like . . . is his mother still here?"

"Yes."

"He's telling me to acknowledge his mom. We need to make sure his mom knows that he came through. She needs a *big hug*. A huge hug." The woman is now wiping away tears as they stream down her face.

"OK."

"I always say that, as mom, there is no greater loss than the loss of a child. Don't lose sight of that as a feeling, OK?"

Heads nod in the audience. The woman still has her tissue in hand.

This is powerful television. So powerful that it has built an empire for John Edward—books, series on multiple networks, a Las Vegas stage show, national tours, and private consultations with celebrities. Even Kim Kardashian was ecstatic to secure a few minutes in Edward's busy schedule. With the medium's help, she ostensibly made contact with her late father, and days later, she famously split with her second husband (after seventy-two days of marriage). But Edward's fame has come at the price of public ridicule. The animated series *South Park* devoted an entire episode, titled "The Biggest Douche in the Universe," to mocking him and debunking his claims of psychic powers. Most of you likely do not believe Edward can commune with dead people, but millions of people do believe in psychics.[2]

The exchange that took us five hundred words to describe lasted less than two minutes on TV. Reading through it here, you have time to think critically about what's being said, as well as not said, and to seek alternative explanations for Edward's professed powers. If you're skeptical about psychics, you were probably thinking along these lines already. Yet faced with a charismatic performer in real life and made vulnerable by hope, Edward's audience members were in a poor position to resist. We start with this "easy" example with the goal of honing your ability to spot such deceptions. Let's look more closely at Edward's performance.

First, most of Edward's audience members want to believe in his abilities because he gives them the false hope that they might actually be able to communicate with a lost loved one. Their expectations, coupled with his ability to form an emotional connection with individual audience members, make it hard for them to think of the most logical explanations for what Edward does. Second, like many "psychic" performers, Edward likely gathers information about some of his audience members in advance or plants a few stooges in the seats. He can use these plants to guarantee a number of "hits" in his performance. Third, Edward is a master of the techniques magicians use when performing cold-reading mentalism demonstrations, especially the use of rapid banter. He makes his statements and decisions appear authoritative and precise by quickly discarding false leads and misstatements, giving his audience little time to ponder his mistakes and leaving them remembering only the examples and information consistent with his supposed abilities.[3]

Edward peppers his cold readings with vague descriptors that audience members can interpret in many different ways. He then treats their interpretation as if it were what he meant all along. He says, "She passes either around or on a governmental holiday or something that would be celebratory, but for the country," and then treats the response of "September 11th" as if it's consistent with his statement, even though it's neither a celebration nor a government holiday. But it feels consistent to the person who comes up with the response. Moreover, "around a holiday" or "something that would be celebratory" covers most of the calendar—whenever their family member died, it would have been near some important date. In the moment, though, people think only of the timing of the death of their family member and not how Edward could have connected it to something else meaningful.

It's surprisingly easy to get taken in when our attention is focused too narrowly. For example, CEOs who spend a lot of time posting about their companies on social media deflect the attention of unsophisticated investors away from other sources that might contradict their claims. In our talks and classroom lectures, we often demonstrate this idea using a much-simplified version of magician Harry Hardin's classic Princess Card Trick. We introduce it as an example of mentalism or of the ability to read body language, but that's just a cover story. First, we show a slide with six playing cards:

Then we turn our backs and ask a volunteer to use a laser pointer to select one of the cards. Next we blank the screen and ask the audience to concentrate on the volunteer's card. You can do that now. Pick one of the cards and focus on it. We turn around to face the audience, and after making a show of staring closely into the eyes of the volunteer, we say, "Now we're going to remove your card." We advance the slide and your card is gone:

Impressive, right? Not if we tell you that we could not possibly remove the wrong card. We don't really know what card you picked.[4]

The trick relies on the same failure of imagination that Edward exploits. When audience members focus on only the selected card, they are virtually guaranteed not to think about the other cards. Having ignored the unselected cards, they don't realize that we've replaced *all* of the original cards, not only the selected one. They're left only with the evidence they still have in mind, not the evidence they're missing.

Edward succeeds because his audience members focus on the volunteer's father, Robert, a firefighter who died on 9/11. They do not consider how easily Edward could have accommodated a different holiday, a different first name, or a different relationship in his act—just as we could have handled a different card choice.

Edward capitalizes on the difficulty we have in imagining missing alternatives and in thinking about the probability that some of his guesses will be right merely by chance. If someone died of a "bone issue," what are the odds that it was cancer? Probably high—are there any other deadly bone issues? Yet when he says "cancer," it seems insightful. What are the odds that someone attending his show has a dead relative named "Robert, Robby, Rob? Where's the R?" Most attendees will have some dead relatives to whom they were close—after all, the primary purpose of his show is to commune with the dead, and the audience is self-selected. Robert is a relatively common name with many variants, but he could have worked with any "R" name (as well as Bob, Bobby, and other variants), and he fires off the options so quickly that the audience doesn't have time to consider how many possible answers would work; instead, they focus on the one name someone actually mentions. Giving yourself hundreds of ways to be right is a great way to seem like a preternatural guesser.

People are bad at reasoning about the likelihood of seemingly rare events. Imagine you're sitting in a meeting when you learn that you have the same birthday as one of your coworkers. Remarkable co-incidence, right? Not really. If there are twenty-three people at the meeting, the odds exceed 50 percent that a pair of them will share a birthday. Yes, any individual's birthday could be any one out of 365 days. But with twenty-three coworkers in the room, there are 253 pos-sible pairings of two people ($23 \times 22 \div 2$). Given those numbers, it doesn't seem quite as amazing that one of those pairs would match. With a group of fifty people, you'll find at least one match more than 95 percent of the time. Yet, as with Edward's audience and the name that begins with "R," when we identify a pair that happens to share a birthday, we focus on that pair and forget about all of the other poten-tial pairs that did not result in a match.

It's relatively harmless for Edward to affirm, under false pretenses, that people's loved ones loved them back, but psychic claims can sometimes be insidious and harmful—which is why some critics refer to mediums as "grief vampires." In early 2013, three women escaped from captivity in a derelict Cleveland house after having been impris-oned there for nearly a decade. Louwana Miller, the mother of one of the women, had appeared alongside the celebrity psychic Sylvia Browne on *The Montel Williams Show* in 2004, shortly after her daugh-ter had disappeared. Browne told Miller that her daughter Amanda was dead and that she saw Amanda "in water." Browne told a devas-tated Miller that she would meet her daughter "in Heaven on the other side." Miller died two years later, believing her daughter was dead.[5]

Psychics like Browne and Edward promote their successful predic-tions but rarely mention their failures. When they do mention failures, it's with a purpose. Psychologist Matt Tompkins, who is also a profes-sional magician and an expert on the history of magical mentalism, told us that some psychics deliberately call attention to one of the many failures in their performance. By emphasizing that one failure and showing their frustration at it, they mold a narrative about their honesty and the accuracy of their performance. Audience members tend to remember that one inaccurate statement—"I can't believe he only missed that one guess!"—and forget the many unmentioned mistakes.

HOW FOCUS LEADS US ASTRAY

People who attend a John Edward show are mostly believers, not skeptics or deniers. But any of us can be as credulous as a John Edward fan at a *Cross Country* taping if we find ourselves in a setting that doesn't immediately trigger skepticism. That's because we all tend to believe more than we should if we focus only on the information we have.

The phrase "willing suspension of disbelief," which many of us learned when studying literature in school, refers to a suspension of critical thinking or doubt, an acceptance of a speculative premise that we would ordinarily reject, in order to understand and appreciate the rest of a work of fiction. When the narrative and the production are compelling, we don't stop to ask why a hacker could access an alien ship's computer using a MacBook or how changing the DNA of one animal will wind up exterminating its entire species. We don't willingly suspend disbelief when viewing a documentary because we don't see a need to; we expect documentaries to document, not fabricate. The same is true in everyday life. We don't suspend disbelief because there is none to suspend. Our default stance is belief—we accept what we are told, we do not immediately disbelieve it, and we rarely if ever check it out. In our daily experiences, it is the certainty of our beliefs that we must work to suspend, not disbelief.

Many businesses and certain entire industries take advantage of this tendency, perhaps unwittingly in some cases. They release "demos" conducted in tightly controlled conditions that make their new technologies and products seem more capable than they actually are. When these demos appear to work—which they almost always do—they provide a compelling signal of truth to their viewers; it's hard to question something you've seen with your own eyes. Thanks to our truth bias, we trust that what we are seeing is at least a close approximation of reality and that we're not being deliberately misled.

For example, the robotics firm Boston Dynamics (once owned by Google) regularly releases videos of its humanoid robots doing incredible stunts, such as performing parkour moves, but no video can tell us whether the robot would succeed on an obstacle course it had never seen with objects it had never encountered. Maybe it would, but in the face of a compelling demo, we tend to assume that the performance we're seeing is generalizable to similar settings even when we have no direct evidence, at least from the demo, that it does.[6]

The practice of developing computer systems capable of performing with apparent intelligence in highly constrained situations and either claiming or implying that they would work just as well in a broad range of contexts goes back at least fifty years. Sometimes the developers are not deliberately deceptive—they're just overly optimistic about how easy it will be to improve their own technology so that it works in more situations. For decades, computer vision and robotics experts assumed that if a robot could understand a scene containing regular geometric solids (cubes, pyramids, cylinders, etc.), then the hard work would be done, and it would take just a small step to generalize that capability to natural scenes. But time after time, artificial intelligence (AI) systems fall short when making the jump from an optimized "microworld" to the real world, much as potential medicines can perform well in laboratory experiments with animals but fail in human trials. Sometimes a change as minor as tweaking the color of a single pixel in a digital image can make an object-recognition system label a ship as a car or a deer as an airplane. Demo pushers rarely acknowledge that achieving robust, reliable performance in the face of real-world complexity often requires an approach completely different from the one that worked wonderfully in the tightly curated demo environment.[7]

Fraudsters capitalize on this tendency to accept what we've seen in a short, curated experience as representative of a larger reality. Theranos put a special demonstration mode called the "null protocol" into their miniaturized blood-testing machines and used it during investor pitch meetings. After taking a tiny blood sample from a visiting dignitary, placing it in a cartridge, and inserting it into the device, the Theranos representative would tap the screen as though it were operating normally, but the device merely emitted a series of noises without actually carrying out any medical assays. The sample then was spirited away to a traditional laboratory for analysis while the marks—the investors—were taken to lunch or given a tour (which skipped the location where their blood was actually being analyzed). The entire procedure was discussed and rehearsed ahead of time. Like magicians, the Theranos executives manipulated the attention of their audiences, leading them to think they had seen something that never really happened. Even the venerable automaker Volkswagen did something similar: It programmed its cars to minimize emissions only during testing so that they would meet the required standards, a deceptive practice that led to about $40 billion in government fines.[8]

WHERE'S WALD?

Unlike in psychic performances or corporate presentations, most of the time we don't need to be manipulated into paying attention to the wrong thing—we naturally focus on what's in front of us rather than fretting about what's not. If you spend time on social media, you will eventually come across a schematic drawing of an airplane covered with dots. Although it is often posted as nothing more than a flex to signal, "If you know this image then you're smart like me," when used appropriately, it is an icon that represents a basic error of reasoning. Once you know the story behind it, it can help you avoid being fooled.[9]

October 14, 1943, was the date of one of the more successful Allied air raids on German factories during World War II. The US Army Air

Forces targeted ball-bearing factories in Schweinfurt in an attempt to disrupt the Nazi war effort. The raid, on what is now known as "Black Thursday," achieved its goals, but at a great cost. Of the 291 B-17 bombers taking off from Britain, 77 were destroyed and only 33 returned undamaged. More than 600 of the 2,900 soldiers involved in the mission were killed or captured.

The B-17 was the most heavily used bomber in the US war effort in Europe, dropping more ordnance than any other plane, but the losses were staggering. Fortunately, the damaged planes that returned provided a rich set of data for the air forces to study in the hopes of increasing survival rates. Reinforcing the entire plane against antiaircraft fire would be infeasible—the added weight would reduce the range and cargo capacity too much. But perhaps parts of the planes could be reinforced. If the damage to the planes was random, there would be little benefit. But if the damage was systematic, affecting some parts more than others, then the army could fix the vulnerable sections, strengthen the planes, and possibly end the war sooner.

To help with this problem, the army found Abraham Wald, a Romanian-born statistician working with the Statistical Research Group at Columbia University. Wald's work remains influential, with some of the statistical techniques he developed commonly used in psychology, economics, and other disciplines today. At the time, he was developing methods in the field of "survival analysis," and he conducted a systematic study of the damage to B-17 planes. If the damage was entirely random, the odds that a part of the plane would be damaged should scale with the size of that part; bigger parts should be hit more often than smaller parts. The pattern Wald found was likely encouraging to the army: Some parts of the plane were disproportionately more likely to be hit than would be expected by chance.

Now, imagine that you are in charge of B-17 safety. How would you use Wald's results? The most obvious plan would be to bolster the surfaces that take a disproportionate amount of damage—for example, adding steel plating wherever the planes are most often hit.

If that was your conclusion, congratulations! You made a possibly disastrous—if common—choice. Why? All you need to do is think about the evidence that is missing. Wald's analyses of damage were based on the planes that managed to return. The areas more likely to have been damaged on the planes that returned were in fact *less likely* to be critical to a plane's survival. What was missing is what happened to the planes that did *not* return. Presumably, if those undamaged areas were unimportant, you would see damage to them on the planes that returned. And if those areas were crucial to a plane's survival, planes hit in those areas would be less likely to survive.

Wald understood this, of course. His analysis of the B-17s helped lay the groundwork for the concept now known as survivorship bias. We tend to devote more attention to cases that are still around, neglecting those that are not. That bias leads to a systematic misunderstanding of success and failure, one that is especially prevalent in business writing but that plagues many other consequential decisions. You should now be able to see the logical flaw in this statement about coronavirus vaccination by the podcaster Dave Rubin: "I know a lot of people who regret getting the vaccine. Don't know anyone who regrets not getting it."[10]

Remember the bullet-ridden airplane meme whenever you hear someone discuss what they concluded from the information they *have*. It should cue you to wonder about the information they're missing, because what's present is rarely representative of what's not.

WOULD HUSH PUPPIES ON ANYONE ELSE'S FEET STILL SELL AS SWEET?

We all want to succeed, and emulating the habits and strategies of successful people intuitively seems like a good idea, but focusing exclusively on success stories can mislead us about what really causes success. A time-honored technique in business writing is to search a database for companies that have performed well over time and then to identify and describe characteristics those firms have in common. In fact, many business schools structure their curricula around the analysis of case studies of successful companies, leaders, and decisions. But this practice is much like studying only the planes that returned.

A particularly prominent example is the story that begins Malcolm Gladwell's bestseller *The Tipping Point*. Gladwell recounts that the Hush Puppies brand of casual shoes had been languishing until 1994, when it was adopted by an influential subculture in lower Manhattan and suddenly became trendy. Annual sales jumped from 30,000 to 430,000 between 1993 and 1995. This story has been taken to show that companies can capitalize on known "influencers" to promote their brand. It seems reasonable that some consumers are more influential than others, but does it follow that successful marketing requires nothing more than providing your product to a select few who will then advertise it to the masses on your behalf?[11]

The Hush Puppies story actually provides no compelling evidence that hipsters who bought them drove the brand's sudden explosion or that putting "influencers" on the payroll is a winning strategy. Determining the basis for success requires considering all underlying factors, not just one tidy possibility.

Maybe companies with better products, higher sales, and more profits are simply more likely to try the newest marketing ideas. (That is why all the breathless anecdotes about how Google pampers its workers, how Amazon runs its meetings, how Finland's teachers plan their lessons, or how the US Navy Seals operate will tell you almost nothing about what it takes to become an elite performer in the first place.) To show that hipster marketing causes success, you'd need to conduct the business equivalent of medicine's clinical trials by gathering a set of similar firms, randomly assigning them to adopt hipster and nonhipster strategies, and comparing the success rates across those groups. Most companies won't go for that, of course, but the fact that evidence is hard to gather doesn't mean you should deceive yourself into thinking you already have it.

We can think of companies and product launches like investors and stock picks—some succeed and some fail. We commonly attribute the popularity of "one-hit wonders" to chance or luck, but even sustained success doesn't necessarily result from skill alone.

Let's assume that any investment has a 50 percent chance of counting as a success (say, by outperforming the average stock). If we start with 1,024 people who make a blind guess, on average, half (512) would be right the first time. Half of those people (256) would be right the second time. Half of those would be right the third time, and after the tenth pick, only one person would have been right every time—purely by luck. If we knew only about that person and had no information about the 1,023 others, we might unjustifiably conclude that we had discovered a brilliant investor. To be clear, we aren't saying that investors like Peter Lynch, Ray Dalio, and Jim Simons owe their success to luck alone—only that when thinking about success stories, we should keep in mind that most of what we hear is about people like them.[12]

Documenting the true causes of success requires more than a clever narrative. We have to think about the planes that never came back, the cards that weren't picked, and the other outcomes that a psychic performer could have accommodated. We have to focus on things we normally don't, like the shoes that didn't sell and the companies that didn't succeed.

TUNE IN, TURN ON, DROP OUT, AND GET RICH?

The trouble, of course, is that it's in our nature to be attracted to—and convinced by—a good story. Stories of marketing wizards and investment geniuses sell lots of books, but when we're drawn in by a good story, we don't think about what it leaves out. George Lifchits, Duncan Watts, and a team of researchers in psychology, sociology, and computer science made this point in a study published in 2021. They picked a common narrative from the business media that college dropouts are unusually likely to create startup companies that turn into "unicorns," which are privately owned firms valued at $1 billion or more.[13]

Bill Gates, Steve Jobs, and Mark Zuckerberg are famous examples, but they are the exceptions, not the rule. Chris, his collaborator Jonathan Wai, and their colleagues found that as of 2015, virtually all of the 253 unicorn founders and CEOs had graduated from college, and many had earned graduate degrees. By contrast, fewer than half of American adults ever earn a college degree.[14]

In the Lifchits study, each participant was told that there is disagreement about whether a startup company is more likely to reach unicorn status if it is founded by a college graduate or by a college dropout. They were asked to bet on which of two people, an unnamed graduate or an unnamed dropout, would be most likely to start a unicorn company. Before making their choice, though, the participants were shown either a list of five real unicorn companies whose founders had graduated from college, a list of five real unicorns started by dropouts, or no list of sample companies. Additionally, they were asked to confirm their understanding that the examples they saw had been selected to show only one kind of founder.

Of those who saw a list of successful dropouts, 68 percent bet on a dropout. But only 13 percent of those who heard about successful graduates bet on a dropout. That is, their bets were strongly influenced by the small set of selected anecdotes they had seen. Had they considered the relevance of the information they *weren't* shown, they might have chosen differently. Tellingly, almost everyone justified their choice by explaining why their chosen founder was more likely to succeed rather than why the rejected founder was more likely to fail. Either justification would be valid, but when we think about the positive examples, it's easier to think of reasons favoring them.

There was no deception in the conventional sense in this study. The researchers presented true anecdotes about real founders, but those anecdotes were not representative or typical of company founders. Similarly, disinformation campaigns can be successful—and evade conventional attempts to "fact-check" deception—without containing explicit lies or fake news as long as they choose real examples selectively enough.[15]

THE POSSIBILITY GRID

By now, it's clear that we tend to make decisions using only information about the planes we see and rarely even think of the ones that didn't come back. To be clear, drilling into what you can see is not dumb or irrational. Our ability to focus can be highly efficient and allows us to extract meaningful patterns, make inferences, and solve problems that we could not solve without the more intensive information processing that attention adds. Without focus, we could not even follow the action in a soccer game—we would see only a blur of bodies and a tiny round object ricocheting among them. But focus-based efficiency benefits us only when the object of our focus represents the full scope of the problem—when the planes that returned are just like the ones that didn't. If we watch a soccer game by focusing only on the side that possesses the ball, we have a chance of decoding that team's strategy, but we will learn little about what the defensive side is (or is not) doing to counter it.

This downside of focus creates one of the oldest and easiest ways for frauds, hucksters, and marketers to fool us into making bad choices. They don't have to hide critical information from us—they only need to omit it and count on us not to think about it ourselves.

To counter this problematic mental habit, we can ask, **"What's missing?"** Doing so before making a key decision reminds us to ask what information we actually need in order to evaluate the truth of what we're being told. A simple tool known as the *possibility grid* can help determine precisely what important information we do not have.

Imagine a two-by-two grid. For psychic predictions, the top row contains predictions that were made, and the bottom row includes predictions that were *not* made. The left column includes events that actually happened, and the right column shows events that did *not* happen. So the top-left box would include cases in which a psychic predicted an event and that event occurred. This part of the possibility grid is what makes psychics famous—it includes all of their success stories but none of their failures.

The top-right box is for psychic predictions that didn't come to pass: Sylvia Browne predicted that a missing child would be found dead in water, but she wasn't.

The bottom-left corner is for the many predictions that psychics should have made but didn't, like Sylvia Browne's failure to predict that the missing girl would be discovered alive (or that Browne herself would be convicted for securities fraud). Thinking about this box is challenging because we pay more attention to what people do than to what they don't do. A team led by Richard Saunders identified hundreds of consequential world events over a period of more than twenty years, none of which were predicted by prominent psychics. These included the explosion of the *Columbia* space shuttle, the 2004 Indian Ocean tsunami that killed more than 200,000 people, the devastating fire at Notre Dame cathedral, and the start of the Covid-19 pandemic.[16]

Finally, the bottom-right box contains events that no psychics predicted and that never happened (like our last book winning a Pulitzer Prize).

When we think of the full possibility grid, we see the success stories in the top-left box in the context of the other three boxes, which can leave us much less impressed by the handful of incidents or anecdotes that happen to wind up there.

In analyzing marketing success, the top row of the grid shows cases when a company tried a strategy, and the bottom row is for cases when it didn't. The left column is for products that succeeded, and the right column is for those that failed. So when we hear the vivid, compelling story of Hush Puppies, we're learning only about the upper-left box in which adoption by influencers was followed by increased sales. We should pause and think about companies that tried hipster marketing and failed, companies that didn't try it and succeeded anyhow, and companies that didn't try it and failed. Examining, estimating, or just imagining how many companies are in those other boxes, compared to the top left, will tell you whether you have any evidence that hipster marketing is linked to success.

Asking "What's missing?" is like thinking of the bullet-ridden airplane graphic to remind us that we might be looking only at survivors, not at everyone who started out with the same mission or goal. Once we bring those other three possibilities to mind and consider the information we don't have in front of us, it often becomes clear that instead of evidence, we have only coincidence.

Here's an everyday example of how the possibility grid helps. Marketing inherently focuses on success stories. While all reputable financial businesses acknowledge that past performance does not guarantee future success, they still point to past success as a way of attracting new customers. For years, the two of us regularly saw an ad in our social media feeds featuring a photo of a middle-aged White guy in an ill-fitting pink shirt with the headline "5 Years from Now, You'll Probably Wish You Grabbed These Stocks." In smaller print, the caption explained, "He recommended Amazon in 1997 and Tesla in 2011, and he's announcing his newest pick for the best stock to buy now." Leaving aside the typical marketing nonsense (was he really announcing a new pick "right now" every single time that ad popped up?), the copy implies that this guy must really know what he's talking about. After all, he was right about two of the biggest companies ever, so shouldn't he be right a third time?[17]

Taking him at his word, and being honest with ourselves about regretting not buying them years ago, we would put Amazon and Tesla in the top-left box of the possibility grid for Mr. Pink Shirt: stocks that he predicted would do well and then did well. But both those stocks belong in the bottom-left box for most of the rest of us: stocks that we didn't pick but that did well. To more accurately grapple with whether we should trust Mr. Pink Shirt for future stock picks, we have to look carefully at the rest of his grid.

No professional investor or stock-picker can survive by recommending only one stock every fourteen years. He must have picked others, but we have no idea whether those did well or poorly. It's quite possible that the list includes duds like Zynga, MySpace, and Pets.com ("Because pets can't drive!"). Stocks like those would fall in the upper-right cell: stocks he picked that were bombs. We wouldn't regret missing out on those picks! We also know he failed to pick some highly successful stocks, like Google, Facebook, and Mastercard, because if he had picked them, he would have bragged about them as much as he did about Amazon and Tesla. A lot of companies have increased hugely in value since the late 1990s, so there must be a lot of stocks in that lower-left box. Finally, in the bottom-right box go all the other stocks: the ones he never picked and that didn't do well.[18]

It doesn't matter exactly how many stocks are in each box—just thinking about the possible contents of the full grid tells you there is no reason to believe that Mr. Pink Shirt, a guy who made two good picks in fourteen years, is worth paying attention to now. The possibility grid is a universal weapon to draw attention to what is absent. Once you master its logic, you will start to notice so many uses for it that you will wonder how you got along without it for so long. A few more examples might help broaden your focus:

- Oprah Winfrey's magazine *O* celebrated "great moments in intuition" with examples like that of Ray Kroc, who went with his gut and against the advice of his lawyers when he borrowed $2.7 million (in 1961 dollars) to buy out his partners in McDonald's decades before it became the world's largest restaurant chain. No mention is made of the businesspeople who followed their lawyers' advice and succeeded, or any who ignored their lawyers and failed.[19]

- News reports about Ahmad Khan Rahami, who planted several bombs in the New York City area in 2016, noted that he had traveled between the United States and Pakistan and other Islamic countries several times in the preceding twelve years, but they did not mention the millions of people who traveled with similar itineraries equally often but were not terrorists, or any terrorists (or alleged terrorists) who did not go back and forth regularly to Islamic countries. [20]

- If we look for cases of people who died shortly after receiving a Covid-19 vaccine, we will find many—but we'll miss the hundreds of millions who did not die, plus those who died on the same dates and hadn't recently been vaccinated.

- The "law of attraction," often referred to as "manifesting," states that what you think about will happen. If you were thinking of your friend and they called you, it was because you were thinking of them; if you think of bills, you will get bills, but if you think of money, you will receive money; if you ruminate on your bad relationships, you will never have good relationships, but if you visualize the ideal partner, such a person will come into your life. Absent from our minds are the common but unmemorable times when we thought of someone and they didn't call and the times when we weren't thinking of someone and they called out of the blue, not to mention the times when we *weren't* thinking about someone and they *didn't* call us—which amounts to almost every moment of our lives.[21]

People seeking to deceive us will go on endlessly about what's in the top-left box while omitting the others. It's entirely reasonable to draw conclusions from a small amount of evidence in that top-left box as long as there's a plausible causal mechanism to explain why it's virtually certain that the examples in it didn't get there by chance. If someone lists examples of people who died after being shot, it's logical to infer that the bullets killed them since we know that guns can kill. That's why deceivers often appeal to secret, complex, or untestable causal mechanisms. When someone hands us a reason for success, even an invented one, it becomes even harder to think about what they're not telling us.

Proponents of the law of attraction attribute its power to the mysteries (for most of us) of quantum physics. John Edward claims to be a professional medium, as if the "profession" of "mediumship" entails an understanding of verifiable principles and certifiable mechanisms. When marketers refer to neuroscience (consumers literally love their iPhones because looking at them "activates the brain areas for love"), they're suggesting causal mechanisms that have little specificity to their products.[22]

The most recent and often egregious examples of focus-hacking in marketing come from startup companies whose products are based on AI. In 2018, a company called Nikola released a video that appeared to show one of its self-driving trucks tooling down a highway. When publicly revealing a prototype in 2016, founder and CEO Trevor Milton had said, "This thing fully functions and works, which is incredible." In 2020, the firm admitted that the prototype lacked a fuel cell and motors and that the video was created by rolling a truck down a shallow grade and tilting the camera to make the terrain seem flat. In their defense, they noted that the video caption merely claimed that the truck was "in motion," not that it was propelling and steering itself. Still, the purpose of the demo was *not* to convince investors and business partners that Nikola could build a truck with the self-driving capability of a pinewood derby car.[23]

Sometimes, we can't rely on reasoning alone to determine the contents of the other boxes of the possibility grid. But seeking more information can be uncomfortable. Imagine being the one person to stand up at a John Edward show and ask him for examples of his failed predictions or proclaim that you have an alternative explanation for what he claims to be doing. That is what happens in the *South Park* episode, and that's part of why it is so funny—it's not something that happens much of the time, even though in many situations, it should. That social discomfort might be why almost nobody asked the Theranos executives, "Did that machine right there actually carry out the assays you say it did?" But by politely not asking what was behind the curtain, investors and business partners cost themselves billions of dollars. Had they asked, they might not have gotten a straight answer, but a crooked answer could have been revealing too. It can pay to seek more information, even if we don't receive it, because the fact that the facts were hard or impossible to find is itself information.

Let's move from the sedate businesses of celebrity psychics, self-rolling trucks, and fraudulent biotech to the exhilarating industry of management consulting. Imagine a midsize retail chain wants to hire a consultant to improve retention of valuable employees, and the CEO suggests talking to Larry Taylor, who has a list of positive testimonials from executives at a dozen Fortune 500 firms. By now, we know that Taylor's list is just giving us the top-left box of the possibility grid, but what information would we need in order to make sure he's not the John Edward of consultants? We need to know his success *rate*, not just his successes. What proportion of his clients showed improved retention? Over what time window? How did retention change for comparable companies that didn't hire him? We should also ask how his results compare to those of other consultants.

In making this kind of decision, we should do whatever we can, within the bounds of reason and decorum, to gather the information we actually need to evaluate performance. Sales, like all types of persuasion, involves controlling which pieces of information are present—and which are absent. We should try to make a decision with the best evidence we can get, not just what we happen to be shown. In our experience, corporate decision-making can be so superficial that it's worth being a minor nuisance by asking for what's missing and explaining why it's important.[24]

WHEN ABSENCE IS EVIDENCE

The bottom-right box of the possibility grid can offer a wealth of insight, but it can be tricky to even determine what should go into it. When our actions prevent the occurrence of something bad, we rarely remember it. For example:

- We complain when a medication has side effects or doesn't resolve our symptoms right away, but we don't think about the possibility that we might have gotten much sicker without it.
- Successful precautions to prevent a catastrophic flood go unheralded, but a failed levee draws public ire.
- We respond with accusations when a bridge collapses, but we don't support the engineers who have documented the need for repairs for decades—much less give any thought to the engineers who have kept all the other bridges standing.
- Governments might move mountains to respond to an acute health crisis, but health departments responsible for preventing such crises in the first place are chronically underfunded.[25]

One of the most effective ways to use the possibility grid concept is to keep a "résumé of failure." We can track not only our successes, the upper-left-corner items that we would find on a résumé or business pitch, but also what didn't work. We tend to forget our failures because they rarely result in anything memorable: jobs we applied for and didn't receive, corporate rebranding exercises that were quickly abandoned, marketing campaigns that did not change sales, pickup lines that failed, and so on. A résumé of failure can also track things we got away with but probably shouldn't have, times when we should have succeeded but were unlucky, and even things we considered doing but passed on. Looking at this more realistic type of résumé helps us recall actions and events that we otherwise might forget or ignore but that are essential if we want to evaluate what does and doesn't matter for success.[26]

The venerable venture capital firm Bessemer Venture Partners takes the idea of a résumé of failure seriously by publishing an "anti-portfolio" that lists some of the companies they passed on but that became wildly successful—like Apple, eBay, and Airbnb. Bessemer has been around for over a century, and this list provides an institutional memory about decisions of which current partners have no firsthand knowledge (like why the firm passed on Intel in the 1960s and FedEx in the 1970s). It's not a complete possibility grid, but it acknowledges the existence of horrible investment misses in addition to the usual greatest hits. Many younger firms now follow Bessemer's example. We try to do the same humility check for our own investments. Chris will never forget that he advised his father not to buy Microsoft stock at its initial public offering in 1986 ("because MS-DOS sucked and Windows 1.0 was a joke," which he still believes but now realizes was not a sound basis for investment decisions), and Dan recalls enthusiastically investing in an environmental cleanup firm called American Eco that went bankrupt in 2000.[27]

In this chapter, we have examined both the power and the perils of focus—how we can be deceived by others who manipulate what we focus on but also how we can overlook the truth by not looking for what we might be missing. Unfortunately, it is not enough to just look in the right place, because what we find there and how we interpret it are subject to our expectations and predictions. When what we see is what we predicted or expected, we may not see any need to check more. The next chapter describes how bad actors deceive us by determining what we expect—and then giving us exactly that.

CHAPTER 2

PREDICTION—EXPECT TO BE SURPRISED

To make sense of our world, we rely on our experiences to predict what will happen next. When we are wrong, we revise our expectations accordingly. But when our experiences match our predictions, we tend not to question them, and we can be deceived by people who take care to make our predictions come true. Several strategies can help us realize when we are not thinking carefully enough about what we expected to happen.

IN LATE SEPTEMBER 2004, 60 *MINUTES* ANCHOR DAN RATHER IS- sued a rare public apology on behalf of CBS News: "We made a mistake in judgment, and for that I am sorry. It was an error made, however, in good faith and in the spirit of trying to carry on a CBS News tradition of investigative reporting without fear or favoritism."[1]

The story aired just two months before the presidential election. It reported that in 1972 and 1973, while he was in the Air National Guard, George W. Bush had skipped a compulsory physical and his superior officer had been pressured to report better performance than Bush merited. Reporters had long been investigating rumors that

Bush had shirked his required guard duties, but incontrovertible evidence had been hard to come by.

A retired national guardsman named Bill Burkett had provided CBS News producer Mary Mapes with a set of memos that purportedly came from the personal files of Bush's superior, Lt. Col. Jerry Killian, who had died in 1984. These contemporaneous memos documented what appeared to be then-guardsman Bush's criminal failure to follow orders and his requests to skip required drills because of a lack of time (he was working on a Senate campaign at the time). They also mentioned political pressure to "sugarcoat" Bush's poor performance.

To a reporter familiar with Bush's known history of drug and alcohol use in that era, the idea that Bush might skip a required physical exam met expectations. The idea that he would neglect his military duties and get away with it because of his political connections—his congressman father, future US president George H. W. Bush—similarly fit the narrative. Perhaps as a result, the CBS journalists didn't give Burkett's documents the critical scrutiny they should have, especially given that reporters at other news organizations considered Burkett an anti-Bush zealot who often made iffy claims.[2]

The CBS News reports said that the memos had been "authenticated," but almost immediately after the initial broadcast, their provenance came under fire from conservative bloggers and media outlets. Some argued that the proportional font in the documents resembled contemporary Times Roman, which was not used in typewriters of the early 1970s. Killian's son told Sean Hannity on Fox News that he doubted the documents' authenticity and noted that his father "had a high regard for [Bush]." When asked for the original documents, Burkett claimed to have burned them after faxing them to CBS.[3]

By September 20, the concerns had become too great to ignore. CBS admitted that it could not verify the authenticity of the documents and formed an independent review panel led by former US attorney general Dick Thornburgh to investigate what had gone wrong. Although the panel did not determine "with absolute certainty" that the documents were forged, its final report accused CBS of "a myopic zeal to be the first news organization to broadcast what was believed to be a new story" and of a "rigid and blind defense of the segment after it aired despite numerous indications of its shortcomings." Although the report noted that Dan Rather hadn't participated in vetting the segment and had not seen it before it aired, he stepped down from CBS and never returned to a prominent television news broadcasting role. Producers Mary Mapes and Josh Howard were both fired.[4]

What made this case exceptional is that reputable news outlets like CBS have processes in place to validate documents and verify sources. Sometimes fact-checking can be so extensive that it delays publication of an investigative report for months, as was the case in the *Wall Street Journal*'s discovery of the fraud at Theranos. Reporter John Carreyrou was ready to publish in the third week of July 2015, but the newspaper waited for ten weeks, until October 8, to do so and even had a final meeting with Theranos's lawyers a week before publication.[5]

Our expectations about the world are predictions and intuitions derived from our experiences. Just as the predictive text function on your phone uses a model of common word sequences in human language to guess what you're going to type next, we rely on a model of the world based on our cumulative experiences to better anticipate what's likely to happen in the near future. Prediction is so central to how we make sense of things that we often don't realize how much it influences our interpretation of the world. Even something as simple as perceiving a moving object depends on prediction. Our brain takes time to process the light that hits our eyes, so we perceive what's happening "now" with a delay of a few hundredths of a second. If we want to avoid being hit by a car, we need to know not where it was a moment ago but where it actually is right now and where it will be in a moment. But we won't have that visual information until it's too late, so our brain has to use the equivalent of autocomplete to anticipate where that car will be a short time in the future. Our extensive experience with moving objects, and the built-in knowledge that objects don't blink in and out of existence, helps us build an effective predictive model. The same principle holds for predictions about much richer behaviors, decisions, and actions at longer timescales.

When our predictions about motion are wrong, we can be hit. When our predictions about what might happen in the world are wrong, we're surprised. We naturally become skeptical when we are surprised, but we tend not to question experiences that are in line with our predictions. Just as we can't be skeptical of everything, we can't remain fully open-minded and still make sense of the world. We have to make predictions: We depend on experience-driven expectations to guide our interpretations, and they usually help us focus on the information that matters.

On occasion, though, looking for what we predicted and being satisfied to find it can amount to confirmation bias, which makes it easy for hucksters to tailor their "product" to match not only what we want but also what we expect. A good scammer knows the truth of Hannah Arendt's observation: "Lies are often much more plausible, more appealing to reason than reality, since the liar has the great advantage of knowing beforehand what the audience wishes or expects to hear."[6]

To avoid the type of mistake CBS made in its Bush reporting, we need to ask ourselves a somewhat paradoxical question: **"Did I predict this?"** If the answer is "Yes, this is exactly what I expected," that's a good sign that you need to check more, not less. One way to check is to pretend that you expected exactly the opposite outcome. If the CBS journalists had viewed Burkett's documents with the expectation that Bush would not shirk his responsibilities, they might have been more inclined to challenge the provenance of the memos. Evidence and arguments that support preexisting beliefs often crumble when subjected to this sort of scrutiny.

Pretending to believe something you don't can be hard, though. An alternative strategy, born in the military and intelligence worlds and recently adopted in the sciences, involves bringing in colleagues to serve as a "red team" whose goal is to spot errors in your thinking. Before advising President Obama to launch the 2011 raid that killed Osama Bin Laden, the CIA selected four intelligence analysts who had not been involved in the years-long hunt for the Al-Qaeda leader to challenge its conclusion that he was living in a compound in Abbottabad, Pakistan. The analysts evaluated the plausibility of three alternative hypotheses, each of which assumed that Bin Laden was not actually there. After trying to support those alternatives, they still concluded that there was a 40–60 percent chance that he was at the house. The ultimate decision was close, so if the red team had been any more skeptical, the operation might not have gone forward.[7]

IF THE MASK DOESN'T FIT, YOU MIGHT TRANSMIT

Being blinded by expectations happens to even the most capable and qualified thinkers. In fact, some evidence suggests that people who are better able to reason are *more* easily fooled when they are motivated to justify their beliefs.

In the midst of the Omicron variant surge in early 2022, the *Wall Street Journal* published an infographic showing the number of hours of protection against transmission of SARS-CoV-2, the virus that causes Covid-19, conferred by different types of masks. The graphic showed that an uninfected person wearing no mask would be safe for 2.5 hours if an infected person with whom they were speaking wore an imperfectly fitted N95 mask. If both people wore imperfectly fitted N95 masks, the uninfected person would be protected for twenty-five hours. But if neither wore a mask, they'd be safe from the virus for just fifteen minutes.[8]

Epidemiologists and infectious disease experts have long argued that better-quality masks help prevent the spread of airborne viruses. For people who were already trying to follow such guidance, the table provided justification for their cautiousness—it fit their expectation that N95 masks, especially well-fitted ones, provide much more protection than cloth masks or no masks at all. Among mask enthusiasts, the chart went viral (sorry).

There's little doubt that high-filtration masks, like the N95, provide excellent protection against airborne viruses. But whoever created this infographic simply multiplied the filtration levels of the masks by fifteen minutes (and divided the results by sixty) to obtain a nonsensical metric called "hours of protection." Where did that fifteen minutes come from? Most likely from the threshold used by the Centers for Disease Control, the UK National Health Service, and other authorities to define a "close contact" for the purpose of tracing to whom an infected person might have passed the virus. That criterion is not a biological fact or a law of virology. In fact, people can and do become infected with less than fifteen minutes of exposure. Fifteen minutes is an arbitrary but practical threshold for contact tracing, as people who test positive are likely to remember whom they were around for fifteen minutes or more and may be able to report their names. However, they're unlikely to remember the clerk who checked them out at a store or which coworkers they passed in a hallway.[9]

We can't calculate "hours of protection" by multiplying the filtration level by the cutoff used for contact tracing. In fact, we can tell that the numbers are nonsense based on other knowledge we already have. Many other factors contribute to transmission risk: whether we're outdoors or in an enclosed space, whether a room is ventilated, whether people are yelling at the top of their lungs or sitting quietly, whether the infected person is at peak infectiousness, and so on. We also need to know how many viral particles must get through in order to trigger an infection, which likely depends on factors like individual differences in immune responses and maybe even how much nose hair people have.[10]

If you wore a non-fit-tested N95 mask and stood face-to-face with a screaming, contagious person wearing a cloth mask, you almost certainly would not have 3.3 hours of protection (and even if you did, that protection wouldn't plunge from 100 percent at 3.29 hours to 0 percent at 3.31 hours). Yet several of our quantitatively sophisticated colleagues posted this chart to Facebook and Twitter as evidence in favor of using high-quality masks. We suspect they didn't think about it critically enough because its conclusions matched what they would have predicted.

Graphics like this one might succeed in encouraging people to use better masks, and masks with better filtration do offer more protection. But such graphics can also backfire. People who opposed the idea of requiring better masks—or any masks at all—could point to the silly numbers to undermine the credibility of an otherwise well-supported position. The virtuous end of persuading more people to use higher-quality masks to slow a global pandemic does not justify using erroneous means to reach it.[11]

EXPECTATION-BASED REASONING

It's common for business leaders to profess their faith in numbers with bromides like "We are a data-driven organization" or "Numbers don't lie." Paying attention to data is better than ignoring them, but we should remember that our preconceptions color our interpretations. In a 2017 study, Dan Kahan and his colleagues demonstrated exactly this. They first created a display of data about something unlikely to trigger strong opinions—whether a hypothetical new skin cream was effective in treating rashes. They showed a representative sample of 1,111 adults in the United States a two-by-two chart that tabulated the numbers of people whose rash did or did not improve grouped by whether they did or did not use the new cream.[12]

This structure might sound familiar because it matches the possibility grid described earlier. The top row showed people who used the skin cream, and the bottom row showed people who didn't. One column showed people who improved, and the other showed people who didn't. To determine whether there was more improvement with the cream than without, we have to compare the percentage of people who improved after using the cream (the top row) to the percentage who improved without the cream (the bottom row).

As we discussed earlier, people often focus only on what is in the top-left box of these two-by-two grids—here, people who used the cream and improved—and neglect the remaining boxes. In this type of research (and in this particular experiment), the numbers are usually chosen in such a way that if you look only at the top-left box, you will get the wrong answer. Not surprisingly, Kahan's team found that many participants made exactly this mistake. The key finding was that people with better numerical skills (as measured by a separate test administered in the same experiment) were better able to use the data correctly to correctly determine whether the cream was effective without being misled by focusing on the top-left box.

The critical part of this study kept the same design but replaced the expectation-neutral skin-cream labels with politically heated ones—increases or decreases in the crime rate as a function of whether a city had or had not enacted a ban on carrying concealed handguns. All participants saw the same numbers in the grid, but for half, the upper-left box showed cities where crime dropped after the handgun ban, and for the other half, it showed cities where crime increased.

In the United States, people who identify as politically conservative are more likely to oppose gun-control regulations, and those who identify as politically liberal are more likely to favor them. This study cleverly set up a conflict between the policy the data supported and the policy the participants could be expected to favor going in. Because the data were constructed so that relying solely on that top-left box would lead to the wrong answer half the time but the right answer the other half, the researchers could examine whether people thought more or less critically when the numbers in that box supported rather than contradicted their preexisting beliefs.

For the politically neutral skin-cream test, people who were good with numbers and logic generally interpreted the data correctly. When the topic was gun-control policy, liberals who scored higher on numeracy interpreted the data more accurately than conservatives when the correct interpretation linked gun control to less crime. Conservatives with greater numeracy were more accurate than liberals when the data showed that gun control led to more crime. Each group deployed critical thinking when the conclusion that resulted from relying on the top-left box violated their expectations; in contrast, they were uncritical when that conclusion matched their expectations.[13]

Liberals might be vigorous cross-examiners of dodgy evidence that undermines action against climate change but uncritical if the same numbers support increasing immigration—and vice versa for conservatives. Our tendency to favor expectation-consistent conclusions can lead us to focus only on the weak supporting evidence and not on the strong counterevidence. A *New York Post* opinion article published in January 2022, for example, relied on an August 2021 analysis to claim that the best-quality studies do not provide good evidence for the claim that masks "work" against respiratory viruses. However, all but one of these studies were done before the Covid-19 pandemic, and the piece failed to mention the best mask study ever performed, a sophisticated experiment on Covid-19 prevention involving six hundred villages and hundreds of thousands of residents in Bangladesh. That study, published in December 2021 in the journal *Science*, had received considerable publicity in the weeks before the *Post* article was published.[14]

Even our ability to apply basic principles of logic can be subverted by our expectations. Given the premise "If an animal is a dog, then it is a mammal" and the fact that Spot is a dog, we can easily conclude that Spot is a mammal (the logical principle known by the Latin name *modus ponens*). Thinking through these sorts of logical conclusions is easy as long as the premises and conclusions are consistent with our knowledge and beliefs. But try the premise "If an animal is a dog, then it is a reptile." If we now learn that Spot is a dog, logic compels us to conclude that Spot is a reptile. That's harder to do because we know that in reality, dogs are not reptiles.

Now, consider what happens for premises about contentious ideas for which we hold strong beliefs rather than about simple taxonomic facts. Does the conclusion below follow logically from the premises?

> All drugs that are dangerous should be illegal.
> Marijuana is a drug that is dangerous.
> ___
> Therefore, marijuana should be illegal.

Someone who believes that marijuana is a dangerous drug and that dangerous drugs should be outlawed would find the conclusion palatable. Someone who thinks marijuana is relatively low risk or that dangerous drugs should be legal would disagree.

The psychologist Anup Gampa and colleagues tested how well 924 online research volunteers evaluated logic problems whose conclusions either matched or contradicted their stated ideological views and beliefs. Overall, people did fairly well, solving 73 percent correctly. But conservatives were more likely to judge "liberal" conclusions as wrong and liberals were more likely to rate "conservative" ones as wrong. Both groups also tended to mistakenly treat incorrect conclusions as solid when the conclusions matched their beliefs.[15]

Take the following example:

> All Marxists believe the free market is unfair.
> Some of the president's advisers believe the free market is unfair.
> _____
> Therefore, some of the president's advisers are Marxists.

Whereas 94 percent of the liberal participants correctly said the conclusion didn't follow, only 79 percent of the conservatives did, presumably because it matched some of their expectations about the Obama administration, which was in power at the time. When the question bias was reversed, conservatives outperformed liberals, with roughly comparable overall performance for the two groups. Across three studies, including one with a nationally representative sample of 1,109 people, ideological match increased the chances of rating something as logical by at least 15 percent and sometimes more than doubled it.

The tendencies to apply greater scrutiny to outcomes we don't predict and to accept conclusions that match what we already believe contribute to a wide range of errors in science, business, and daily life. The economists Carmen Reinhart and Kenneth Rogoff learned this lesson the hard way. When analyzing historical data about the relationship between government debt and economic growth, they accidentally failed to "fill down" a formula to the bottom of a column in their Excel spreadsheet. As a result, they mistakenly concluded that once a country's debt reaches 90 percent of its gross domestic product (GDP), the growth prospects for its economy are fatally weakened. This finding supported their controversial policy recommendation that governments should be wary of spending too much and borrowing to pay for it—in short, they should practice austerity. Since Rogoff was the former chief economist of the International Monetary Fund, his advice was influential, and the book he and Reinhart wrote about debt crises, *This Time Is Different*, became a bestseller and a must-read text for policymakers.[16]

Many scientific errors are simple unintentional screwups like this one. Scientists, like everyone, are more likely to double- and triple-check their work if their results contradict their predictions, and they're unlikely to be as careful with results that match what they expected. Consequently, the errors that make it into the published scientific literature tend to cut in the direction of the researchers' preferred hypotheses. Therefore, it's not surprising that economists who disagreed with Reinhart and Rogoff caught their error. Had Reinhart and Rogoff teamed up with those skeptics in advance, the clash of expectations between the groups might have prevented the mistake from happening—or at least from being published. Inviting critics into your tent—a process known in science as adversarial collaboration—may not come naturally, but it can pay big dividends.[17]

SEEING WHAT WE EXPECT TO SEE

In American football, the center typically starts each play by "snapping" the ball between his legs to the quarterback, who then takes a couple of steps back before doing anything else. But there's no rule that a play has to start that way. In a 2010 game, a Texas middle school team had the center "hike" the ball by handing it to the quarterback over his shoulder. Rather than stepping back, the quarterback nonchalantly walked forward between the opposing linemen, who apparently did not realize the play had started. As soon as his path ahead was clear, the quarterback sprinted past the rest of the defense and scored a touchdown.[18]

In sports, "trick plays" like this one are a form of deception that exploits expectations. They aren't cheating—they don't break the rules of the game. But because they succeed by violating established patterns and norms, they reveal how powerfully our expectations influence how we interpret the actions of others.

The idea that our expectations affect what we see was a major theme of our first book, *The Invisible Gorilla*. To a surprising extent, we see what we expect to see, and we tend not to notice events, objects, or patterns in our lives if they are unexpected. Our original 1999 "gorilla experiment" showed that people who are busy counting how many times players are passing a basketball can miss a person in a gorilla suit walking through the middle of the scene. After a video from that experiment went viral, people knew to look for a gorilla whenever someone asked them to count passes. So Dan created a new video that he named *The Monkey Business Illusion*. You might want to watch it on YouTube before reading further.[19]

As with the original gorilla video, people are asked to count the passes made by the players wearing white. Also as in the earlier video, a person in a gorilla suit walks through the action, stops in the center, faces the camera, thumps their chest, and strolls off the other side. And just as for the original video, about half of the people who didn't expect a gorilla didn't notice it. People who had seen the earlier video knew to look for a gorilla, and they almost always noticed it. But knowing that a gorilla might appear did not inoculate them against missing other unexpected objects and events. If anything, people who knew to look for a gorilla were slightly *less* likely to notice other changes in the scene.

Our expectations and beliefs drive how we interpret what we see even when nothing surprising or unexpected happens. The Australian arm of the Japanese camera maker Canon demonstrated this with a video series showing how photographers create their art. They asked six professional photographers to make a portrait of the same middle-aged man, Michael, who came to each session dressed in black jeans and a partly unbuttoned blue dress shirt with a white T-shirt underneath. Each photographer received a description of Michael's history and accomplishments, but each description was different. One photographer was told that Michael was an ex-inmate, another that he had saved someone's life, and a third that he claimed to be psychic. The others were told that he was a self-made millionaire, a former alcoholic, or a commercial fisherman. Although the same person was photographed in the same studio for all six shoots, the results were radically different. The photographers attempted to capture an essence they saw in him—the expectations that they had been given influenced how they positioned their subject, how they lit the scene, what lenses and angles they used, and all the other decisions they made from first meeting Michael to producing their finished image.[20]

Con artists and impersonators deceive us by doing the same thing: mimicking what we would expect them to say and do if they were who they claimed to be. Ricardo Montalban's character Khan, the titular genetically engineered villain of the second *Star Trek* film, knew this principle well. To ambush the *Enterprise* and its crew, he took over the *Reliant*, another Federation starship, and approached the *Enterprise* in an unthreatening way. Even though the *Reliant* was acting strangely, Captain Kirk's inclination was to assume that it was having technical problems rather than plotting an attack. By the time he realized something was amiss, the trap had been sprung and the *Enterprise* was severely damaged. Matching expectations is a critical step in disarming a victim on the way to a successful fraud because when what we see is consistent with what we expect, we rarely pause to ask questions or dig deeper.[21]

FROM THE SCIENCE OF MESSES TO A SCIENTIFIC MESS

Science is the process of testing predictions with experiments and data, and scientists are known for being skeptical about poorly supported claims, so it may seem surprising that they can fall into the same expectations trap as the rest of us. Award-winning Dutch psychologist Diederik Stapel, a professor at Tilburg University in the Netherlands, gained international prominence by conducting experiments on how our surroundings subtly influence our thoughts and actions. One of his experiments, published in the journal *Science*, showed that merely passing through dirty train stations or walking along littered streets led people to have more racist thoughts. Stapel was one of many social psychologists reporting such examples of "metaphorical priming"—the claim that our perceptions and experiences activate concepts in our minds that are only metaphorically or tenuously related (e.g., physical filth and racism) and that those associations change our attitudes and even our behavior. Similar work has linked being physically outside a box to having more creative ideas, holding a hot cup of coffee to rating a person as having a warmer personality, thinking about the life of a professor to doing better at trivia tests, and smelling a fishy odor to being more suspicious of others.[22]

We mention Stapel's studies here because they differed from these other examples in one crucial respect: He didn't bother to do them. Instead, he simply fabricated the data. He duped his colleagues, students, and collaborators over a period of years by giving them what they expected to see.[23]

Although some scientific frauds involve radical new discoveries or breakthroughs, most fake findings are small, incremental variations on established and popular themes; to the relevant experts, they appear to be mainstream and typical rather than truly novel or unexpected. Upon first hearing of a result that later turned out to have been fabricated, most scientists in the same research area would likely nod and say, "Yeah, that makes sense," rather than shake their heads and say, "No way."

When prominent Cornell psychologist Daryl Bem published a series of studies purportedly demonstrating the existence of "precognition," a psychic ability to predict future events that were actually generated at random, the scientific community reacted with skepticism and incredulity. As with the premature reports of cold fusion in physics two decades earlier, most other scientists didn't predict Bem's results, so they questioned his methods and statistics thoroughly and largely found them lacking. There's no reason to believe Bem fabricated his data, as Stapel did, but his conclusions were too far "out there" to go unchallenged. Actual fraud often involves research that's novel enough to garner attention and accolades but not so shocking that it attracts skeptics inclined to take a closer look.

Scientists and nonscientists alike should be especially wary of results that fit our expectations when they rely on proprietary technology or require special access to resources unavailable to other researchers. Most such studies represent critical advances by careful researchers—collecting those data can require years of sustained work. But someone willing to cut corners may be even more tempted to do so if they know that nobody else could readily counter their claims by collecting data of their own. Diederik Stapel purportedly tested participants in an actual train station rather than having them look at pictures of train stations on a computer, making that study harder to replicate. The evolutionary biologist Marc Hauser tested the cognitive performance of cotton-top tamarins, a monkey species studied by only a few other researchers in the world. UCLA political science graduate student Michael LaCour supposedly deployed forty-one research assistants to conduct door-to-door interviews with 972 people to see whether interacting with a gay person would change their political views. All of these authors had papers retracted after investigations. In addition to disguising questionable (or nonexistent) data, descriptions of methodological heroics increase the appearance of both novelty and rigor, bringing accolades whether or not they are justified.[24]

In the late 1990s, our Harvard colleague Karen Ruggiero published a series of studies on the social psychology of stereotypes. Her work was influential and heavily cited, but just like Stapel's, it turned out to be fabricated. We observed the fallout and consequences of Ruggiero's fraud firsthand. Dan heard stories from colleagues who had struggled to publish their own legitimate work on similar topics because their results were not as definitive as Ruggiero's. Problematic as it is, editors and reviewers often treat the first published study on a topic as "correct" and ascribe weaker or contradictory results in later studies to methodological flaws or incompetence.[25]

After Ruggiero admitted to fraud, her coauthors, including some of her students, faced scrutiny as well. Most students pursue doctoral degrees to learn how to conduct research, and if their primary model of this skill is their mentor, they might never think to double-check data and analyses. It is usually only after our expectations have been shattered that we realize we should have looked more carefully. But even in hindsight, it can be difficult to recognize how powerfully our expectations may have blinded us.[26]

Like Ruggiero, Diederik Stapel eventually copped to his fraud; an astounding fifty-eight of his papers have now been retracted from scientific journals, placing him seventh on the all-time leaderboard of the independent group Retraction Watch. In a memoir of these events, he wrote, "What I made up was logical and not earthshaking." His fake studies nudged the boundaries of novelty just enough to garner attention but not skepticism. They were consistent with what everyone else expected, so nobody looked too closely.[27]

FAKING DATA ABOUT FAKING DATA

People don't all share the same expectations—and that's a good thing. What satisfies one person's expectations might trigger investigation by another. An instructive example comes from a fraudulent scientific study of fraud. In a paper published in 2012, a team of behavioral scientists from four leading business schools examined how to encourage people to report facts and information more honestly. Working with a US insurance company, they asked over thirteen thousand automobile policyholders to report their cars' odometer readings. A higher number could result in a higher premium since more driving increases the cumulative chance of an accident. So drivers had some incentive to cheat by underreporting how many miles they'd driven since their last report. Each driver was asked to sign their name under the statement "I promise that the information I am providing is true."[28]

This type of attestation is often used to counteract dishonesty. Before 2012, it most commonly appeared at the end of a document, as it does on US federal income tax forms ("Under penalties of perjury, I declare . . ."). In the odometer study, drivers were randomly assigned to receive one of two versions of the form: one with the traditional placement at the end and the other with the signed promise placed *before* the odometer mileage report. The idea was that signing first would emphasize the duty to behave ethically during the reporting process. Sure enough, drivers who signed the statement before the report gave odometer values that were about 10 percent higher.[29]

Ten percent might not seem like much, but when scaled to tens or hundreds of thousands of drivers, that small change in where people sign would generate a huge boost in insurance premiums for the company. After these results appeared in *Proceedings of the National Academy of Sciences*, government agencies and private organizations began adopting the sign-first trick to increase honest reporting. The only problem was that, unbeknownst to any of them, at least some of the automobile mileage data were made up.

The insurance company part of the study was led by Dan Ariely, a professor at Duke University and author of bestselling books on dishonesty, irrationality, and money. Nine years after the study was published, the behavioral scientists Joe Simmons, Leif Nelson, and Uri Simonsohn (along with a separate group of researchers who remained anonymous out of concern about reprisals) proved that the data couldn't be real. For example, most car owners drive 2,000–15,000 miles in a year, and far fewer drive much more than that. But in this dataset, people were just as likely to have reported driving 10,000 miles as 49,000 miles. After more digging, Simmons and colleagues discovered many duplicated rows in the dataset but with a random number between 0 and 1,000 added to disguise the similarity. Their intensive forensic investigation resulted in retraction of the article, and all five authors of the published paper agreed that their study had relied on fraudulent data. This case is unusual in that all the authors admit that the data were fraudulent while the identity of the person who actually perpetrated the fraud remains unclear.[30]

THAT'S FISHY

Are statistical anomalies enough to prove research fraud? In his own graduate course on research practices, Dan assigns an exercise based on one of Karen Ruggiero's retracted publications. He tells the students that the results are not genuine and asks them if they can find anything in the published article suggesting that something might be amiss. Astute students notice a few duplicated numbers that purportedly came from distinct data and that some measures of variability are more similar to each other than we should expect.

But there's a danger in combing through scientific data—or any other type of data—expecting to find evidence of fraud. Because virtually all real evidence is "noisy," we can almost always find sinister-looking patterns in legitimate data.

The political scientist Macartan Humphreys created a website called An Exact Fishy Test that cleverly demonstrates this principle. It invites you to type in ten random numbers between 1 and 100, and no matter what numbers you enter, it finds something about them that is statistically anomalous. For example, we entered the following randomly generated numbers: 71, 51, 90, 88, 65, 48, 87, 18, 57, and 35. The app reported that these numbers "show a fairly obvious pattern." The digit 8 appears five times in the sequence, whereas the expected number from a random process is just two. That would happen by chance less than 5 percent of the time. We tried again with the numbers 80, 11, 96, 40, 18, 29, 43, 29, 22, and 97. Again, our sequence was deemed unusual because it contained 5 prime numbers when, on average, you'd expect only 2.5 primes in a set of 10 random numbers between 1 and 100. Getting 5 prime numbers would happen less than 8 percent of the time. The site will also check for too many 2s or 3s or odd numbers or even numbers or numbers less than 50 or numbers less than 30 or numbers with one odd and one even digit, and so on. Sets of truly random numbers, especially if you have only ten of them, will have some anomalies if you look at them in enough ways.[31]

Just like the Fishy Test site, if you look at a real dataset with the expectation that something is odd, you'll find what you are looking for. It is a common trap for inexperienced data detectives to claim evidence of fraud from an unusual pattern alone, especially if they inspect the data first, notice the suspicious pattern next (rather than plan in advance to search for it specifically), and only then calculate exactly how unusual it is. The result can be superficially compelling but false allegations of fraud.[32]

Problematic numbers alone rarely suffice to confirm research fraud, especially because the published scientific literature inevitably includes many innocent mistakes. Still, in cases like the odometer study, the oddities and improbabilities can add up to leave no innocent explanation. Moreover, there are some known mathematical properties of real data that, when missing, provide compelling evidence of misdeeds, largely because they are so hard to fake.

ONE ISN'T THE LONELIEST NUMBER

If you ask people to generate a random number between 1 and 10, a disproportionate number will pick 7. When psychologist and magician Jay Olson and his colleagues Alym Amlani and Ron Rensink asked more than 650 people to name a playing card, more than half of them named one of four cards: the ace of spades or the ace, king, or queen of hearts. If you ask people to create random sequences of heads and tails, their sequences tend to alternate too often and don't have enough long runs. When people think about what counts as random, they instead produce patterns. But randomness can have its own sort of predictability.[33]

When numbers describe the results of natural growth processes, such as the accumulation of followers, likes, or views online, they tend to occur in patterns that follow a power law, with bigger stopping values happening less and less often (many more YouTube videos have 100–200 views than have 1–2 million, and many more parties have 5–10 guests than 500–1,000). A principle called Benford's law describes a regular pattern that results from randomness whenever a value can grow indefinitely and the range of possible values spans at least a few orders of magnitude. It holds true in domains ranging from the volume of lakes to sales revenues to follower counts on social media.

We can gain an intuitive appreciation for Benford's law this way: 1 is always the first digit we encounter when we get to a new order of magnitude. The single digits start with 1, so if we are counting things, we'll get to 1 first, and we'll get to 2 only if we've been at 1 previously. If we stop at some random point, we're more likely to have gotten to 1 than to any higher digit. If we make it past the single digits, the next ten numbers—10 to 19—will have a first digit of 1. So a leading 1 occurs eleven times in the first nineteen numbers, or 58 percent of the time. After 99, the next one hundred numbers (100–199) will start with a 1. If the increasing count is equally likely to stop at any point, and we have to go through first digit 1s before getting to any other digit, whatever number we stop at (e.g., whatever a Twitter follower count is at any particular point in time) is more likely to start with a 1 than any other digit.

Benford's law describes the precise proportions of each leading digit that we should expect to see in such data. Its signature is that the digit 1 occurs first about 30 percent of the time, with numbers starting with 2 to 9 decreasingly likely. When the data should follow Benford's law but don't, there's a fair chance that they are the product of fraud.

University of Maryland computer scientist Jennifer Golbeck is an expert on social networks. She monitors patterns in the underbelly of the Internet, including the spread of conspiracy theories and the operations of bot networks. When she examined the numbers of friends people have on a social network like Facebook or the number of followers they have on Twitter, she found that the counts follow Benford's law. Social media follower counts always start with one person, people accumulate followers over time, and more people have a few followers than a few thousand. Suppose you follow one thousand people on Twitter. If you examine each of those accounts and look at the number of people each of them follows, those follower counts will follow Benford's law as well.[34]

Bot networks, unlike human users, tend not to follow Benford's law because their follower counts are not generated by a natural growth process. Typically, bots follow a similar number of accounts, sometimes other accounts in the same bot network, and then tweet predesigned content or retweet other accounts. Golbeck successfully identified a bot network by looking at those second-order follower counts—the numbers of followers of the accounts that the bots themselves followed. Those did not conform to Benford's law. That red flag triggered a further exploration of that set of accounts, almost all of which appeared to be part of the same network run by the same people.[35]

Sometimes, when people first learn about Benford's law, they apply it overzealously to cases in which a Benford's pattern would be impossible. For example, some supporters of Donald Trump claimed to have found evidence of fraud in the 2020 presidential election by showing that Joe Biden's vote totals across precincts did not adhere to Benford's law. But the standard version of Benford's law should not apply in this type of setting. Precincts are deliberately designed to include similarly sized segments of the population—they can't continue growing in size indefinitely, so the distribution of precinct sizes won't follow a power law. Moreover, vote totals for Biden constrain the possible totals for Trump, and vice versa. Imagine a Chicago precinct with 1,000 voters in which Biden got 900 votes. If there were no third-party candidates, Trump would have received 100 votes. Across a number of such districts, Trump might have vote counts starting with 1 or 2 fairly often, giving a Benford's-like appearance. Biden's vote totals in those precincts would necessarily have a lot more initial 8s and 9s than would be expected under Benford's law. That's not evidence of fraud—it's a mathematical consequence of the fact that Biden and Trump split a fixed total number of votes.[36]

Even for data to which Benford's law does apply, sometimes a red flag is a false flag. For example, company revenue and expenses generally follow Benford's law. But if a company frequently purchases a product that costs $49.95, its expense reports will have a higher proportion of entries starting with 4 than the law predicts. A Benford analysis would show a potential problem, but that discrepancy can easily be resolved by verifying whether those expenses were legitimate. Sometimes investigating violations of Benford's law reveals innocent quirks of business data.

At other times, though, it reveals misconduct. In the United States, income taxes used to be calculated using a table with cutoffs in $50 increments. In the late 1970s, crossing a $50 cutoff increased the taxes owed by $7. In his book on applications of Benford's law to accounting, Mark Nigrini analyzed data from those tax returns and found an overabundance of reported incomes just under the cutoffs—numbers ending in 49 or 99—and a shortage of numbers just over the cutoffs (51 and 101). Collectively, people were willing to cheat on their taxes in a small way to save $7, and that cheating was visible as a departure from the expected distribution of digits.[37]

As Nigrini and others have shown, many cases of accounting fraud are detected in part because cooked books contain numbers that deviate from Benford's law. People making up sales or revenue figures probably realize they shouldn't concoct too many round numbers, but they might be unaware of subtler patterns that reveal their fakery; they won't ensure that the distribution of leading digits follows the expected pattern. And even if they are familiar with Benford's law, it is not easy to fake data in a way that is consistent with it. As it turns out, Benford's law applies regardless of the base of the number system being used. It applies in base 10, but it also applies in base 8. Even if you're a sophisticated fraudster, it's not easy to alter or fabricate data that still show the expected pattern of natural growth in all bases.

WHAT DRIVES EXPECTATIONS MOST

Expectations are often essential; we could not perceive or understand anything without them. Searching for something where we expect to find it (as opposed to searching randomly or arbitrarily) is a strategy that generally works; we remember the times it failed only because we left something in an odd place. Without expectations, we would never be surprised, and surprise triggers learning. In many circumstances, our minds automatically compare what we expected to what actually happened, leading us to revise our internal models of how the world works.

The chess grandmaster and professional gambler Jonathan Levitt argues that we should be even more explicit about our expectations by thinking ahead and then reflecting on what we failed to predict: "Chess has taught me to have a forward-looking mindset, to try to look ahead where you can. It is almost always better to be expecting something than just to do things without any idea of what might happen next. It has taught me a lot about the limitations of my own thinking." The best forecasters in the world engage in a constant cycle of writing down their predictions—their expectations of the future—and then comparing each of them to how events play out, in the process developing their own résumé of forecasting failure to keep themselves honest about their skills.[38]

We form expectations and make predictions based on our knowledge and experiences, which is why it's helpful to track when those predictions turn out to be wrong. But in many cases, our cumulative experiences can be so consistent that they turn into strong assumptions. To reason about the world and to act with common sense, we need to commit to some facts, but when we become overly committed, we stop rechecking whether our beliefs still hold true. People looking to fool us can tap into those unwise commitments and even strengthen them. The next chapter is about how failing to identify and examine our commitments can lead us down a path to being fooled.

CHAPTER 3

COMMITMENT—BE CAREFUL WHEN YOU ASSUME

When we commit to an assumption or belief, we rarely reconsider it later. Some unquestioned assumptions are critical for making sense of the world, but detecting and evading attempts at deception require a willingness to recognize and question our commitments—because they can lead us astray without our knowing it.

F ANS OF THE EUROPEAN ROCK SCENE IN THE 1970S AND EARLY 1980s may recall Lustfaust, a band based in West Berlin and known for its international membership and experimental bent. The guitarist hailed from Belgium, the bassist from Germany, the drummer from Japan, and the vocalist from California. According to *Lustfaust: A Folk Anthology 1976–1981*, a retrospective published in 2006, the band formed by accident when its members were scheduled as session players at a recording studio for a vocalist who didn't show up. They recorded their first album under the name "Mutter Theresa," adopting the moniker Lustfaust a year later when they began to tour German clubs.

Out of disdain for the norms of the music industry, Lustfaust distributed their music only on cassette tapes, left the inserts blank, and encouraged their fans to create their own album art. With their innovative sound and anticommercial attitude, Lustfaust was destined to be one of those bands whose fan base included a disproportionate number of other musicians. "Lustfaust were really a blueprint. . . . Without their presence and developments, our band would have never existed," recalled Blixa Bargeld, the lead singer of the later and much more successful band Einstürzende Neubauten. After a series of twists and turns, Lustfaust broke up in 1981, leaving behind only obscure tapes, concert posters, and memories.

It might come as a shock to anyone who remembers hearing Lustfaust in the 1970s to learn that the band didn't exist at that time. In fact, it didn't exist until the mid-2000s, when London conceptual artist Jamie Shovlin fabricated the band's origin story, members, discography, and touring schedules. He designed a series of beautiful flyers and posters for their imaginary 1970s gigs, created samples of the "fan-drawn cover art" for their cassettes, and made archives of photographs said to capture the band's performances and candid moments. He also created lustfaust.com, an extensive website for the band, complete with news of a reunion tour and accompanying blog. He set up a MySpace page and even managed to get a short Lustfaust entry into Wikipedia. To explain why recordings of their songs were not part of the exhibition, Shovlin created brief clips and ascribed the unavailability of full tracks to copyright disputes among the band members. When his exhibition of all this "memorabilia" opened in New York and London, with the tagline "curated by Jamie Shovlin from the archives of Mike Harte and Murray Ward" (two of the fictitious band members), many visitors didn't seem to realize it was a hoax. A few even told Shovlin that they recalled seeing the band perform live.[1]

The hoax was, of course, the point. By creating a simulacrum of all the physical and digital residue that a real German noise band from the 1970s would have left behind and then holding an event that encouraged people to believe that the band was real, Shovlin showed how easily we can be duped about the past. These sorts of memory errors have broader ramifications; authoritarian rulers and aspiring tyrants have long deployed misinformation to change beliefs about the past. Indeed, such memory tricks don't require a totalitarian regime or even a clever artist—we can play them on ourselves.

THE "MANDELA EFFECT"

The cliché says that those who do not remember history are condemned to repeat it, but what happens when different people remember entirely different histories? In 2009, a woman named Fiona Broome realized she had a memory of Nelson Mandela dying sometime in the 1980s in a South African prison, where he was serving a life sentence for conspiring to overthrow the country's White government. In reality, he was released from prison in 1990, negotiated the end of apartheid, served as president of his country from 1994 to 1999, and died in 2013 at the age of ninety-five. Even though Mandela was still alive in 2009, Broome vividly recalled having seen news coverage of his death, including riots in major world cities—and she discovered that other people had similar memories. But none could find corroboration for their version of events in history books, news coverage, or any other authoritative sources.[2]

How could a group of people remember a completely different version of history from the one contained in all official and credible records? Cognitive psychology had answered this question long before Broome had her revelation, and the answer is not that these people are mentally ill. All of us experience similar failures and distortions of ordinary memories. Do you recall Darth Vader saying, "Luke, I am your father," or Captain Kirk ordering, "Beam me up, Scotty"? Neither character ever uttered those famous lines. If you remember them, it's because you've heard those characters say similar things (Vader actually said, "No, I am your father," and Kirk said, "Scotty, beam us up") and you've heard other people utter the incorrect versions.[3]

Many people believe that memory works like a video recording or computer hard drive, storing perfect copies of events we deem important. The vividness of our recollections and the ease with which we can call them to mind leads us to feel that our memories are faithful. In reality, as 150 years of scientific studies have shown, memory is reconstructive as well as recollective. When we have the feeling of retrieving a memory, we sometimes are constructing a version of a past event that combines information from different sources. What seems to be a single coherent memory can be a mash-up of experiences that happened at different times and in different places.[4]

Our memories can even incorporate details we have heard from other people. Gaps are usually filled in by what we would expect or assume to have occurred. While writing this book, the two of us sometimes disagreed about whether and when we had previously written about certain topics. Each time our memories differed, we were able to resolve the discrepancy by looking at our published work. We didn't jump to the conclusion that we must be living in two different realities.

Fiona Broome did. She insisted that her memory of Mandela's death and all the accompanying detail about the worldwide response must have been true and was part of an alternate reality, or "forked timeline," in which Mandela really did die in the 1980s. In essence, she assumed that her memory could not be wrong, and by committing to the truth of that assumption, she closed off the correct explanation for her experience. Because she was committed to the accuracy of her memory, the door was open to any alternative explanation, no matter how outlandish, of why she and others had different experiences. The notion that reality was changing and fragmenting so that different people were truly experiencing different sequences of events (rather than misremembering the same sequence in various predictable ways) became known as the "Mandela Effect," and it is increasingly cited by people as a justification for holding on to vivid memories that depart from what is generally recognized as reality.

Most memory discrepancies attributed to the Mandela Effect involve the conflation of two or more similar memory traces into a single memory. For example, many people remember from their childhood a brand of peanut butter called Jiffy, but no such product ever actually existed—products called Skippy and Jif both did (and still do), and "jiffy" is a word in the English language. Likewise, some people recall a movie about a genie, called *Shazam*, starring the comedian Sinbad. Sinbad appeared in a genie-like outfit in another movie in the 1990s, basketball star Shaquille O'Neal starred as a genie in a movie named *Kazaam* around the same time, and an unrelated television show named *Shazam* ran in the 1970s. Nelson Mandela quite plausibly could have died in prison—his compatriot Stephen Biko died in police custody in 1977, an event memorialized in a popular song by Peter Gabriel—and there were riots in South Africa and demonstrations worldwide against apartheid throughout the 1980s. If you weren't paying much attention to South Africa in the 1990s, you could easily combine these facts into a belief that the most famous Black South African leader must have died in prison, which you learned about from television news, the most common way people consumed news in the 1980s.

Some Mandela Effect advocates argue that ordinary memory distortion can't explain why so many people independently share the same memories of the past, but that's not the case. The Mandela Effect examples are all based on well-known news events, leaders, products, movies, and celebrities, and the sorts of memory conflation they represent are predictable and common. If millions of children read the series of books about the "Berenstain Bears" then it is almost guaranteed that a large number will misremember them as the "Berenstein Bears." Names ending in "stein" are much more common than names ending in "stain," and many people probably misread or mispronounced the unusual "Berenstain" as "Berenstein" in the first place. We would be more shocked if everyone got this memory right than if a fraction got it wrong.

Moreover, our memories are rarely independent and exclusively personal. We talk about our experiences with our friends and family members, and because memories can change each time we retrieve them, these conversations can give rise to shared memory distortions. The Internet and social media accelerate this distortion process by making it possible to find other people who share virtually any belief you might have, no matter how implausible or how contrary it is to the laws of physics. (By the way, on *Star Trek*, Scotty really did say, "I can't change the laws of physics.") Remember, whenever you hear someone use quantum mechanics to explain human behavior, you should turn your bullshit detector all the way to 11.

It's not surprising that people's memories can morph and that people are overconfident in them—these facts have been known for decades. What is surprising is that people can become so deeply committed to the infallibility of their personal recollections that they will adopt outlandish belief systems—forked timelines, alternate realities, and worldwide conspiracies to alter every news story about Nelson Mandela and delete every Jiffy peanut-butter reference from the Internet—to justify their memories. Like mistaken memories of Lustfaust, the stakes here may appear low—it doesn't really matter whether Sinbad was in a genie movie or which vowel was in the title of a children's book. But it matters a lot that people reject well-supported scientific explanations of reality in favor of pseudoscience and conspiracy thinking. It matters when people believe that entire geographic areas don't exist or that entire centuries of history are fake. And it can be a life-and-death matter when people in power promote alternative versions of history to justify conquest and genocide.[5]

As best we can tell, the Mandela Effect phenomenon started and persists because people who were committed to the assumption that their memories are infallible were able to find other people who had the same incorrect yet confident memories. Treating the fact that memories are shared as a cue to their accuracy is rational in many circumstances. If most of the attendees at a meeting remember what happened the same way, the one or two people who remember it differently are more likely to be wrong. If two parents remember what their child did in the same way, but the child disagrees, you should bet on the parents being right. But when the accuracy of memory becomes a full commitment—an unalterable axiom in your reasoning that you're never going to give up—then it leads inexorably to absurd conclusions that can hurt you.[6]

ASSUMPTIONS VERSUS COMMITMENTS

A shared understanding of history is based on shared assumptions and beliefs. Assumptions are essential elements of thinking and reasoning, and we make them all the time. They become dangerous when we don't realize we are making them, when we don't realize the evidence no longer supports them (or never did in the first place), and especially when they cross the line into *commitments*—assumptions so deeply held that we no longer even think to question them. An anonymous commenter on the blog *Slate Star Codex* eloquently described the tenuous link between commitment and evidence:

> From the inside, all strongly held beliefs feel much the same, regardless of how they're supported or arrived at. That is, it's hard to internally distinguish between "I am highly confident in this belief based on examining all available evidence" and "I hold this belief for strong cultural, social, or personal reasons that have little to do with

the evidence." If you want proof of this, consider all the thinkers who were/are totally right in one area and horribly wrong in another, yet similarly forceful about both beliefs.[7]

When a commitment becomes so strong that we no longer feel the need to question it, we might resist learning anything more about its subject, and when presented with new evidence that contradicts our views, we might discount it or act as if we never got it. This is known as "willful blindness," and in many legal settings, being unaware of available evidence provides no defense for having "overseen" fraud or having unknowingly been involved in crimes.[8]

Even one strong commitment to an assumption can have knock-on effects for other assumptions about the world. If held strongly enough, it might logically require abandoning assumptions that are much better grounded—for instance, that we all live in the same reality and timeline. People who suffer from schizophrenia, for example, often come to hold bizarre or paranoid beliefs about the world. You might think a person's reasoning skills must be impaired if they believe their daily movements secretly encode a key to solving a deep mystery or that the CIA is tracking them via a device implanted in their brain. But people with schizophrenia are no worse at solving logical reasoning problems than people of equal intelligence who do not have schizophrenia.[9] Paranoid delusions seem to stem not from flawed reasoning but from incorrect perceptions or interpretations of daily experiences: Either the affected person hears or sees things that are not present (especially voices or people), or they believe that ordinary coincidences (like seeing the same people in the supermarket or hearing sounds in the house) are meaningfully related to them. Mental illness can make such experiences common, and if a person is committed to the belief that they are real and meaningful, then those delusional explanations become more rational.

Our commitments are most dangerous when we are unaware that we are making them. Such hidden commitments can distort our capacity for effective decision-making. Russia launched its war against Ukraine on February 24, 2022. It had been massing forces, conducting military maneuvers, and taking political steps that pointed toward an invasion, and the US government had been openly predicting for months that an invasion would happen. Yet people and governments around the world expressed shock at the news of the invasion. Even in Russia and Ukraine, most members of the general public did not think Vladimir Putin would give such an order. Virtually no one had fled Ukraine before February 24, but 6.5 million people did so over the next one hundred days. The fact that people could not at first believe what was happening suggests that they had unwittingly committed to the idea that Russia would rattle its sabers but never actually use them.[10]

When we experience surprise, it often signals that we committed prematurely to a belief when we should have remained uncertain. Buyers of the subprime mortgage–backed securities that were popular in the 2000s were committed to the idea that the housing market could never undergo a sustained downturn. But it did. Investors who visited Theranos's headquarters in the 2010s and watched its machines "test" their own blood assumed the results actually came from those machines. But they didn't. To guard against being deceived in these and similar ways, ask yourself, **"What am I assuming?"** before making big purchases, agreements, or investments and before drawing conclusions. Explicitly identifying relevant commitments and reframing them as tentative assumptions is the only way to systematically evaluate whether our decisions rest on shaky foundations.

MEASURING THE VALUE OF COMMITMENT

When we exercise rather than watch a movie, or save money rather than spend it, we sacrifice something now in order to receive future benefits, such as greater health or more wealth. Decisions between rewards available at different times are called "intertemporal choices." Would you rather receive $200 in one year or $100 right now? If you choose the $100, you are implicitly *discounting* the value of future money at a rate of 50 percent per year (since $100 is 50 percent of $200). In a series of studies, Chris found that young adults offered choices between various amounts of money now and later (at different delays of up to a year) exhibited discount rates of about 1 percent per day—much more than what they could earn from any legitimate investment.[11]

The economist Ned Augenblick and his colleagues used discount rates to explore how committed a group of cultists were to their belief system. A cult is a group of people who appear to share a common set of commitments that fall far outside the mainstream, such as adherents to a fringe religion, conspiracy theory, or charismatic leader. From the outside, cult beliefs can be hard to understand, and how committed the cult's members actually are is often not obvious. Harold Camping, a Christian pastor with a radio talk show, predicted that on May 21, 2011, the biblical "rapture" would occur: The faithful would ascend to heaven and everyone else would experience suffering equal to "hell on earth" for the next five months until all existence ended on October 21. Starting less than two weeks before the rapture date, Augenblick's team offered twenty-three of Camping's followers a series of choices between $5 right away and up to $500 four weeks later (which would be after the rapture). Consistent with the idea that earthly riches would be valueless in the afterlife, almost all of them preferred $5 before the rapture to $500 after. In contrast, a group of Seventh Day Adventists (Christians who did not believe the world was about to end) were all willing to wait for the $500.[12]

In 2010, over 40 percent of Americans surveyed by Pew Research expected that Jesus Christ would return to earth within the next forty years, sparking the rapture. According to the author Daniel Cohen, "it would be a mistake, however, to put down the modern catastrophist as a fraud, a fool or a madman. Usually he is honest, intelligent, and quite sane—he is simply devoted to an incorrect idea." In other words, the catastrophist has made a commitment to a belief that determines which conclusions will and will not follow, even if those follow-on conclusions (such as $5 today being worth more than $500 in four weeks) make no sense to someone who doesn't hold the same commitments. As it turned out, the world did not end in 2011, so Camping's followers lost out on some extra pocket money, and Augenblick preserved his research funds for future experiments.[13]

FRAGILE COMMITMENTS

Not all commitments have the strength of cult beliefs. Some commitments are far more tentative than we realize, and we can overcome them more easily than you might imagine. In fact, some experiments have shown that changing our commitments can work like magic.

In a 2005 paper in the journal *Science*, Petter Johansson, Lars Hall, Sverker Sikström, and Andreas Olsson reported showing 120 research participants printed photographs of two people and asking them to identify the one they found more attractive. The experimenters then handed the selected photo to the participant and asked them to explain their reasoning. People willingly gave reasons why they found that person more attractive than the other ("Their eyes," "I prefer brown hair," etc.). After doing this several times, the researchers then used sleight of hand to give the participants the rejected face rather than the one they said they preferred. Three-fourths of them not only missed the swap but even explained why they found the face they had rejected more attractive![14]

Such "choice blindness" studies show how malleable our commitments can be even when we think they are rational, unshakeable, and grounded in evidence. Choice blindness is an intriguing phenomenon because it reveals the contrast between how effectively we challenge the beliefs of others and how little we question our own.[15]

In another experiment, Hall, Johansson, and their colleagues Emmanuel Trouche and Hugo Mercier demonstrated how lazy we can be in evaluating our own assumptions and arguments. In the first phase, the participants viewed a set of five logic questions about shops on an imaginary street, each with two premises and a list of possible conclusions. For example, the premises might be

- The fourth fruit and vegetable shop carries, among other products, apples.
- None of the apples are organic.

Then, they were asked to select from the following list of what they could "say for sure about whether fruits are organic in this shop."

- All the fruits are organic.
- None of the fruits are organic.
- Some fruits are organic.
- Some fruits are not organic.
- We cannot tell anything for sure about whether fruits are organic in this shop.

They then explained their selection in a text box. (Incidentally, the correct answer is "some fruits are not organic.")

In the next phase, they were asked to evaluate the quality of other participants' choices and explanations in response to the same set of logic problems. At the top of each example, they saw what they themselves had chosen, and below that, they saw the other participant's choice and explanation. For each problem, they could decide whether the other participant's explanation was compelling enough to make them change their own answer.

What the participants didn't know was that one of the five examples they evaluated showed someone else's choice at the top of the page even though it was labeled as their own. And the answer and justification that were labeled as someone else's were actually the responses the participant had given when they did the problem. Just under 50 percent didn't realize that the "other person's" choice and explanation were actually their own! And over half of those participants chose to retain what they thought had been their own answer, rejecting the choice they had actually made and the explanation that they had written for it just a few minutes earlier. That is, they stuck with a different conclusion because they were led to believe it was the one they had reached before, even when presented with their own arguments for a different answer.[16]

We saw with the story of Reinhart and Rogoff's spreadsheet of debt and growth data that people are more likely to catch someone else's errors if they don't believe that person's claims. That principle applies more broadly: We are often critical when evaluating the logic and evidence for claims we disagree with but almost always acquiesce to claims that match our beliefs. The fruit-shop experiment shows that we'll even criticize our own arguments if we believe they came from someone else.

PAY NO ATTENTION TO THE ASSUMPTIONS INSIDE YOUR HEAD

Choice blindness studies rely on magical sleight of hand to reveal the fragility of some of our commitments and assumptions. Magicians make their living by upending our assumptions, and their insights into the nature of commitments are revealing.

In 2007, the Association for the Scientific Study of Consciousness held its annual meeting in Las Vegas. The big draw for Dan at that year's meeting was a special symposium on "the magic of consciousness," featuring some of the best-known magicians in the world: Teller, James Randi (aka the Amazing Randi), Mac King, Apollo Robbins, and Johnny Thompson (aka the Great Tomsoni). Professional magicians have long been interested in the psychology of consciousness, attention, and memory. As masters of misdirection, they have a keen understanding of how their audience members think and reason as well as a rich history in magic theory and practice that explores the nature of assumptions and commitments.[17]

Earlier, we discussed Harry Hardin's Princess Card Trick, in which the magician removes the card selected by an audience member. The success of that trick relies on the volunteer making an assumption. When the magician says that they will remove the selected card and then they do, the volunteer is committed to the idea that the magician did exactly what they said they would. They don't challenge or even consider the assumption that the other cards remain unchanged.

As part of the symposium, James Randi emphasized the importance of setting up an audience's expectations without explicitly stating what they should believe. As he put it, conjurers shouldn't tell their audience that a box is empty—they should show it. He said, "Allow people to make assumptions, and they will come away absolutely convinced that that assumption was correct and that it represents fact."

Johnny Thompson described how magicians lead the audience to make one assumption after another, guiding them to generate possible explanations for the trick. Then, over the course of the trick, they show how each guess was wrong. They say things like "You held the cards the whole time, you shuffled them as much as you wanted, you cut the deck, and you selected the card," and by doing so, they systematically rule out possible explanations. When all explanations are eliminated, we are left with nothing but "magic"—or at least a sense of amazement that we couldn't figure it out. (Perhaps because a switch was made before the audience member held the cards, a possibility nobody would consider.)

Mac King discussed how using different methods to perform the same effect—in his case, pulling a giant rock out of his shoe—can shut doors as well. If the first time he pulls a rock from his shoe, he drops it on the floor with a loud bang, you'll assume the next rock he pulls out is solid as well. If he shows his hands the whole time while pulling the second rock from his shoe, meaning that he couldn't have slipped it into the shoe, you'll assume he couldn't have done the trick the first time by slipping the rock into his shoe either. If the effect appears the same each time, people tend to assume that the same method was used each time.[18]

Magicians know their audience—both the commitments they start with and the types of assumptions they will make. That's true even when they are performing for other magicians. As you can see from watching the series *Penn and Teller Fool Us*, which awards an "FU" trophy to anyone who can do a trick that Penn and Teller cannot figure out, professional magicians know many methods for producing the same magical effect, so they too will make assumptions about how a trick was done. Their assumptions will be much better informed, but magicians can still be misled. An audience of magicians might assume, for example, that a magician performing for them would use a complex, elegant way of vanishing an object rather than a simple one that would work on laypeople.

TRUST AND CONFIDENCE

Just as committing to an idea can reshape our view of the world, committing to a person can shape the way we think. The concept of trust is often used to explain why people fall for frauds and scams. In our analysis of the factors that make us vulnerable to deception, trust is not a cognitive category of its own; we see it instead as a type of commitment. When we trust a person or organization, we assume that they tell the truth and we fail to scrutinize their claims or apply the amount of critical thinking we deploy against sources we don't trust—sources we do not assume are telling the truth. Trust is not a symptom of an inability to reason or a lack of intelligence; as the choice blindness studies and much other research show, we can identify flawed arguments when we believe they come from someone other than ourselves.

Strong interpersonal commitments help explain the longevity of some of the biggest frauds. Frank Casey, whose business partner tried to tip off the SEC about Bernie Madoff's Ponzi scheme, told a client's family members that they were taking too great a risk by investing all of their money with Madoff. When Madoff's scheme collapsed a couple of months later, the client told Casey that his father-in-law had reacted to Casey's warning by saying, "They're probably well intentioned, but they do not understand. Bernie would never screw us." That sort of commitment is what helped Madoff keep his scheme going for so long.[19]

Trust is more likely and can grow stronger the more familiar the trusters are with the trustee. By most accounts, Madoff did not turn to fraud until he was already a well-established leader in the New York financial industry. Many of his investors were members of his family, friends, and acquaintances. Others were connected to those people. In essence, he used familiarity to grow his network of trusting investors. A few years after Madoff's arrest, a former SEC lawyer told us that while Madoff's crime was vast, at its core it was an "affinity fraud" perpetrated by a sociopathic insider against the Jewish community.

EVERYDAY COMMITMENTS

Our ability to make assumptions about how the world works and to act without questioning them is a feature, not a bug. More often than not, those assumptions will be right. Consider something as simple as how we recognize a common object. When we teach classes on visual perception, we sometimes draw a circle on the whiteboard, add a line bisecting it, and ask our students what object we've drawn. Some say it's a globe with an equator line, others a Poké Ball, still others a flathead screw. But nobody says it is a bucket with its handle up when viewed from directly overhead. From virtually any vantage point other than directly overhead, it would be easy to tell you're looking at a bucket. That overhead view is a strange accident of alignment, a "degenerate view" that shows too little distinctive information. Most of the time, when we see an object, we assume that we're seeing a typical view, not a degenerate one. And we're almost always right.[20]

We don't know of any cases of fraudsters using degenerate views of objects to steal millions, but there are other categories of commitments that we unwittingly make every day that increase our vulnerability to deception. In this chapter, our advice has been to ask yourself, "What am I assuming?" more often. Here are a few commitments we need to watch for in our own thinking.

Everyone else knows what I'm talking about.

When we toss around jargon, use acronyms, and drop names, we implicitly assume that others know what we mean. That assumption, called the curse of knowledge, reflects the difficulty in imagining and keeping track of what other people don't understand. People are usually reluctant to interrupt a speaker (especially a higher-status one) to ask for clarification for fear of revealing their own ignorance. Without that feedback, we rarely notice our curse of knowledge, and we can fool ourselves into thinking we have conveyed information that we haven't.

Natural products are better than artificial ones.

You might believe that natural or organic foods or medicines are inherently superior to artificial or genetically modified ones. You might be right in some cases, but many so-called natural products are inferior in both quality and cost. Some genetically modified foods, for example, are easier to grow, require fewer pesticides, and can feed more people per unit of money spent on them. An excessive commitment to the natural can lead us to pay premium prices for risky products like unpasteurized milk, unregulated medicines, and even what's marketed as "raw water"—unfiltered and untreated spring water, replete with pesticides and potentially harmful bacteria. To be fair, it is also possible to be excessively committed to technological solutions. The key is to check the facts behind our preferences so we can allow ourselves leeway to make what really are the best choices.[21]

Peer-reviewed articles convey scientific truth.

Peer review is a process through which new discoveries and results are examined and critiqued by experts before they are published in a scientific journal (or in some fields even before they can be presented at a conference). Whether an article has been peer-reviewed is often treated as a bright line that divides the preliminary and dubious from the reliable and true. Vetting scientific findings before they are made public is valuable but fallible.

Paolo Macchiarini was a surgeon on a mission to develop an artificial trachea—a custom-molded plastic windpipe, coated in stem cells, that could be transplanted into patients to restore their ability to breathe normally. In 2012, the third time he performed this operation at the Karolinska Hospital in Stockholm, the patient did not recover as quickly as the medical team had expected. Macchiarini's published reports on his first two cases, which had appeared in top medical journals, suggested that the third patient should have been doing much better. Bosse Lindquist, who followed Macchiarini for over a year while making a film about him, told us that after months of following the procedures outlined in those peer-reviewed articles, one of Macchiarini's colleagues looked at the hospital's official medical records for the first two patients. The serious discrepancies he found between those records and the published reports led to a whistleblower complaint within the hospital, several investigations, and ultimately Macchiarini's conviction for the crime of causing bodily harm to a patient. His third patient never left the hospital, and after having approximately two hundred additional surgeries, she died—as did nearly all of Macchiarini's twenty trachea transplant patients.[22]

The "bullshit asymmetry principle" states that the amount of energy needed to refute a heap of nonsense is an order of magnitude greater than that required to produce it. A similar rule applies to incorrect scientific claims. Once a result is accepted into the peer-reviewed literature, ten times as much evidence (or more) can be required to get a contrary finding published. In 2007, social psychologist Adam Alter and his colleagues conducted a study with forty Princeton University students as participants and reported that they solved tricky mathematical puzzles more accurately when the puzzles were printed in a hard-to-read typeface. The decision scientist Andrew Meyer and a team of other researchers were skeptical of Alter's finding because it violated their own expectations. So they attempted to rerun the study. Collectively, they tested 7,367 participants—gathering not one but two orders of magnitude more evidence—and found no difference in how many puzzles people solved in difficult-to-read and normal typefaces.[23]

Unfortunately, the publication of Meyer's paper in 2015 did not prevent researchers from continuing to give Alter's initial, counterintuitive, positive finding greater weight. In their book *The Smarter Screen*, Shlomo Benartzi and Jonah Lehrer first described the Alter study in detail, then mentioned that "not every study" has found the same results, and finally concluded, "Clearly, more research is needed." When we read this in their book, we wanted to yell back at the page, "More research has already been done, and it shows that the original study was wrong!"

The statistician Andrew Gelman has suggested a useful antidote for the tendency to accept the truth of whatever came first: Use the "time-reversal heuristic." Imagine what you would think if the information had reached you in the opposite order. If you heard that a study of seven thousand people found no effect and then a later, identical study of just forty people found an effect, you would not give the smaller study much credence.[24]

The information comes from proper data collection and analysis.
We call this assumption the "dashboard fallacy." Businesses and other organizations increasingly rely on software-generated tables and graphs to provide real-time summaries of the organization's activities and indicators of its financial state. While instruments on a car's dashboard—the speedometer, temperature gauge, and fuel gauge— are fairly precise indicators, the information on a corporate dashboard has a more tenuous link to reality. It typically is produced via a more complex and error-prone process than the one linking a fuel tank to a fuel gauge; it is subject to human choices and interventions that can add bias; and the longer it is in use, the more likely it will become detached from what it was meant to reflect. For example, a company might build a new facility or make a change to a software system, but if the existing analytics pipelines aren't updated accordingly, the dashboard will provide outdated or inaccurate information. In our experience, everyday users of dashboards often fail to question the source or quality of the data they display—they trust the numbers they see nearly as much as they trust their car's speedometer.

The results have not been gamed to convey a particular impression.
We tend to assume that the information we're given has been generated by an objective, neutral process that honestly reflects what it claims to, like a thermometer or a clock, rather than a process that has been tweaked or distorted to give a particular impression. During the bull market of the late 1990s, a group of high-flying companies, including Enron and Coca-Cola, managed to impress investors quarter after quarter by reporting profits just above the estimates published by Wall Street analysts, thereby "beating expectations" and causing those analysts to boost their forecasts of future earnings growth.

Later investigation revealed that some firms manipulated how and when they booked sales around the end of each quarter in order to ensure that earnings appeared to be at least one cent per share better than expected.[25]

Consider for a moment the *U.S. News and World Report* rankings of colleges and graduate schools. To assign the rankings, *U.S. News* collects data from colleges and universities and applies a secret weighting formula. Schools pay inordinate attention to these rankings, using them to attract students and donors. They even hire consulting firms to reverse engineer the formula and advise them about how to move up the list. If we assume that all schools report their data accurately, we might neglect the possibility that institutions engage in creative counting or tweak their data to earn a higher rank. In 2022, mathematics professor Michael Thaddeus published an essay analyzing the surprising rise of his own institution, Columbia University, from eighteenth in 1988 to a tie for second with Harvard and MIT in 2021. His investigation revealed that the university had supplied many dubious figures to *U.S. News*. For example, it had included $1.2 billion spent on hospital patient care in the category of "instructional spending." In response, *U.S. News* temporarily suspended Columbia from its list and dropped it from second to eighteenth when the next rankings came out.

Even well-intentioned changes can make ratings unreliable. For example, by making standardized test scores optional for admission, colleges such as Union College, where Chris was a professor for ten years, were able to report higher average standardized test scores—because the applicants who had good scores tended to submit them, and those with lower scores chose not to.[26]

The authorities wouldn't allow fraud to happen.

When an activity is regulated by government agencies, it's easy to assume that it must be legitimate. Many of Bernie Madoff's victims admitted that they believed the SEC had checked him out and was keeping such a close watch over the financial markets that fraud could not occur. Madoff himself stated publicly that chronic rule-breakers would not last long on Wall Street. But as Jim Campbell notes in his book *Madoff Talks*, "The SEC is not a cop on the beat." Regulators are not constantly surveilling the entities they regulate, and they are also fallible human beings who can themselves be compromised or exploited by others. Most regulated financial and medical products probably are safer than unregulated ones, but none are guaranteed to be risk-free.

A system is secure and tamperproof.

When a business or government operation depends on keeping information or physical property secure, we can underestimate the chances that it has been hacked. The Stones Casino in California decided to broadcast one of its regular poker games live online, using the same technology as the World Series of Poker, which lets viewers see all the players' cards—and thereby kibitz on the quality of players' decisions in real time. To make sure viewers couldn't inform players at the table about their opponents' cards, the broadcast ran on a thirty-minute delay. One player, however, performed so consistently well whenever the game was broadcast that some of his opponents grew suspicious. The casino insisted that the broadcast system was secure against hacking, radio-frequency monitoring, and other technological attacks. It might well have been, but based on all the circumstantial evidence, most informed observers concluded that the player in question must have been getting information from someone inside the casino organization who had access to the live, undelayed video.[27]

In the 1990s, the FBI uncovered a similar case of insider fraud with the McDonald's restaurant Monopoly promotion. A person responsible for ensuring the security of game pieces that were meant to be inserted randomly into customers' food packages was skimming the most valuable ones and selling them to acquaintances, who then pretended to have gotten them at their local restaurants. Often our strongest assumption about security is that the people responsible for it won't exploit it, but this possibility can never be entirely ruled out.[28]

I am not dealing with a known criminal or cheater.

As Taylor Swift noted, "Fakers gonna fake fake fake fake fake." The most useful thing to check before dealing with an individual or organization may be whether they have previously been convicted, found liable, or professionally sanctioned for fraud or other unethical behavior. We have reviewed many stories of fraud while researching this book, and we have been surprised at how often the perpetrators were people who had previously been caught and even convicted of misconduct. The Fyre Festival scam—a bogus music festival on a Bahamian island that promised ticket buyers luxury villas and fancy meals but provided them with refugee-grade tents and boxed lunches—was so audacious that it spawned two separate documentary films. The man behind it, Billy McFarland, was convicted of two more felonies for another scam that he ran while he awaited sentencing for the Fyre Festival fraud. Amazingly, he carried out those additional frauds using the lists of customers he had built up while promoting Fyre. Indeed, many science fraudsters fake data over and over; criminologists suggest that a high percentage of uncovered frauds are committed by repeat offenders; and compliance experts report that the vast majority of internal fraud comes from a small percentage of workers who repeatedly steal from their employers. Even if we generally believe in the principle of second chances, giving a convicted fraudster another shot in life doesn't mean we have to be suckers.[29]

In 2022, the Orlando Museum of Art in Florida opened an exhibition titled *Heroes & Monsters: Jean-Michel Basquiat, the Thaddeus Mumford, Jr. Venice Collection.* It consisted of twenty-five previously unknown paintings by the celebrated American contemporary artist, all said to have been painted in Los Angeles in 1982 and sold in a single lot to Mumford, an award-winning screenwriter. Mumford purportedly had put them into storage for thirty years, but when he failed to pay the rent on his storage unit, a pair of entrepreneurs bought the paintings at auction and enlisted a third partner as an investor. The trio planned to exhibit the paintings and then sell them for $100 million.

While following this news story, we observed several telltale signs that things might not be right: Experts offered praise for the works but not definitive authentication; some disputed the owners' story about the paintings' provenance (the complete history of their ownership, from the artist to the present); and key people who could have verified the story had died. Finally, forensic evidence showed that at least one of the paintings could not have been made before the 1990s, after Basquiat's death. In June 2022, the FBI seized all twenty-five paintings and the museum fired its director. We learned only well into the second *New York Times* article about the case that the three men behind the find had previously been convicted of a total of at least seven crimes, including drug trafficking, campaign finance violations, securities fraud, and consumer fraud. The museum director likely regrets not examining that publicly available information about his new business partners.[30]

In the early 2000s, we were each contacted by a fellow "cognitive scientist" who wanted to work with us on research. It wasn't clear whether he knew that we knew each other, and the projects he proposed to each of us were distinct. He dropped the names of respected researchers we both knew, he had some interesting ideas, and he was unfailingly polite. Neither project got off the ground, however, and that turned out to be fortunate, as he had been involved in dozens of legal cases involving fraud or misrepresentation. By most indications, our "colleague" appears to have had a side hustle as a fraudster, pretending to have credentials he didn't and bilking people out of a few thousand dollars here and there.

If we relied less on "gut instincts" and checked credentials more thoroughly, we would less often become victims of fraud. Someone who is entirely trustworthy and credible will come across that way when you talk to them—but so will a con artist.

Sometimes we can rely on others to do the checking for us. Schoolteachers, bus drivers, and other workers who take care of children undergo formal background checks, so parents typically don't need to do that research. Unfortunately, some of these background checks are fallible, and we can't check everyone's background all the time. Even so, we should do more checking whenever it is feasible. Hiring a contractor? Check their ratings and references to see if they've done shoddy work or bilked their customers. Switching to a new doctor? Make sure they have a degree from a good medical school and that they haven't repeatedly been sued for malpractice (but don't be swayed by the small and biased samples of patient reviews displayed on their websites). Starting a new business partnership? Make sure your partner hasn't embezzled from their last employer. Unromantic as it sounds, you might even want to do a little discreet online sleuthing before getting married, getting engaged, or even going on your first Tinder date.[31]

We are all vulnerable to being fooled when we accept information, including purported facts, without checking more deeply. The next chapter describes how our habit of efficiency—doing the minimum necessary cognitive work to accomplish our goals—can lead to complacency when everything superficially seems okay. Those looking to fool us capitalize on that efficiency, but we can learn when we need to slow down and ask more questions.

CHAPTER 4

EFFICIENCY—ASK MORE QUESTIONS

When making decisions, we tend to economize on information seeking, preferring to act efficiently rather than to investigate exhaustively. When faced with the most consequential decisions, we must overcome this natural habit—and doing so can be as simple as asking just one more good question.

EVERY JULY, OVER ONE THOUSAND CHESS PLAYERS GATHER AT A Philadelphia hotel for the World Open—nine rounds of serious, face-to-face competition. Games can last five hours or more, and first prize in the top section is $20,000. With such large amounts at stake (for the relatively impoverished world of tournament chess), occasional incidents of cheating have occurred. For example, in 1982 a well-known professional player was caught in the chess book sales room looking for hints about the opening of the game he was playing. But no one was expecting what happened in 1993.[1]

It began with a minor sensation. In the second round, when the top seeds are normally still mowing down weaker opponents on their way to eventually playing against one another, grandmaster Helgi Ólafsson of Iceland was held to a draw. His opponent, a player from California named John von Neumann, was unrated and playing in his first official tournament—or so he said when he registered for the event and joined the US Chess Federation.[2]

It wasn't unheard of for players to make the World Open their first US tournament. The large prize fund attracted many players from the former Soviet Union who had not stood out in their home country, where chess was practically a national sport, but who were good enough to compete for prizes in the United States. Von Neumann, however, was not Russian. As a young Black man sporting dreadlocks and a US Navy Seals baseball cap, he stood out in the mostly White chess scene. A chess master from the Boston area, David Vigorito, was one of the first to notice something odd about von Neumann's games: He wasn't playing chess the way everyone else was.

For one thing, his movements were off. Serious players have held and moved chess pieces thousands of times, so their movements are fluid, even graceful. They don't grab and plunk down pieces or bang the clock like actors in movie chess scenes. They also tend to stare intently at the board for minutes at a time, eyes darting back and forth to different squares. Von Neumann moved his pieces awkwardly and seemed uninterested in the game whenever it was his opponent's move—and sometimes even when it was his own turn to play. In round three, he ran out of time and lost in a good position against a strong player. He also occasionally took a very long time to make moves that were obvious and necessary. Early in one game, he had the choice of capturing a piece, losing his own queen, or moving his king toward the middle of the board (the least safe place for the piece you are trying to protect from your opponent's forces). The capture would have been automatic for any player who was not a pure beginner, but von Neumann inexplicably delayed making it for forty minutes.

After drawing Ólafsson in the second round, von Neumann lost his next three games but he then won three of his last four games, his final loss coming when he again ran out of time. His total score of 4½ out of 9 possible points qualified him for a special prize reserved for unrated players. By this time, however, Vigorito had shared his suspicions with several other players and some of the tournament directors, and von Neumann's bizarre combination of amateurish movements, puzzling behavior, and remarkably strong play was the talk of the tournament. The two main theories were that his games were being observed by a strong player somewhere else in the room, who then sent him moves via an earpiece concealed under his hair, or that he was surreptitiously transmitting his opponents' moves to a distant confederate who entered them into a computer program and sent back the machine's recommended replies.

Either strategy could have enabled a novice to win the top unrated prize, since the chess software of thirty years ago was already stronger than many human grandmasters. Most expert observers concluded that von Neumann was getting his moves from a computer and buggy transmission explained his bizarre pattern of time use. A noisy signal could also explain why he made some nonsensical moves, such as moving a bishop to the f5 square and losing it for nothing rather than moving a pawn to the same square, which would have kept the game even.[3]

Interrupted transmission would also account for sightings of a mystery man who occasionally appeared near von Neumann's game, wrote something down, and then disappeared. That might have been the confederate emerging from base camp to correct a discrepancy between what was on the board and what his computer thought was going on.

After the final round of the tournament, this "accomplice" (who wasn't playing in the tournament himself) accompanied von Neumann to the room where the prize checks were being handed out. Chief tournament director and organizer Bill Goichberg was aware of the questions Vigorito and others had raised and of the circumstantial evidence suggesting that von Neumann had cheated. Goichberg did not want to award a prize to a cheater and thereby deny the money to an honest player who deserved it. But he had no direct proof. Von Neumann offered to decline the prize if he could get his entry fee refunded. Goichberg was amenable, but he still didn't want to reward cheating, so he asked von Neumann to solve a simple chess puzzle: a checkmate in two moves with just a handful of pieces on the board.

Goichberg knew that anyone capable of drawing a grandmaster and beating a master could solve the chess problem in one second. But when asked to prove himself, von Neumann refused to even try. He left the playing area in a huff and never received a prize or a refund. Indeed, he never entered another rated chess tournament—at least not under the name of John von Neumann—and neither he nor his accomplice has been seen in the chess world again. The case of John von Neumann remains one of the great unsolved mysteries of chess.[4]

Since 1993, there have been many similar incidents of computer-assisted cheating, a form of "intellectual doping," in chess tournaments. Now that the processing power of a smartphone is sufficient to outplay the human world champion, it has become easier than ever to gain an unfair advantage. And although von Neumann appeared to be a total beginner who barely knew how the pieces moved, many of the cheaters who followed him were already strong players. Most notably, in 2019 the Latvian grandmaster Igors Rausis was caught using his phone in the bathroom during a tournament in Strasbourg. As with von Neumann, people were already suspicious of his performance, but with Rausis, the reason was not his erratic behavior but his meteoric rise. In his fifties, he suddenly started gaining rating points in every tournament he played, becoming one of the top one hundred players in the world. He was on course to crack the top fifty had he not been caught. Chess players can improve in middle age, but to reach the top fifty for the first time at that point would have been unprecedented.[5]

Ronald Reagan famously explained his willingness to negotiate with the Soviet Union by quoting a Russian proverb: "Trust, but verify" ("Doveryai, no proveryai"). The first part comes to us easily—often too easily—but the second part requires effort. When something seems improbable, that should prompt you to investigate by *asking more questions*. These can be literal questions, such as Goichberg's "Can you solve this chess puzzle for me right now, please?" Or they can be asked implicitly, such as by following a suspicious player to see what they do when they walk away from the game they're playing.

Finding the answer to such questions sometimes requires a little digging. Chris once had a student who asked to take a final exam one day later than the rest of the class because he had two other finals on the scheduled day. Chris agreed and proctored the test himself. Halfway through the two-hour session, the student asked to go to the bathroom. A few minutes later, Chris visited the bathroom himself. After washing his hands, he threw away a paper towel and noticed an unusual object at the bottom of the waste bin. He reached into the garbage and pulled out a yellow pad that turned out to contain the course notes taken by the best student in the class. A quick email confirmed that the top student had already taken the exam and had lent her notes to the guy who was taking the exam late—but she hadn't asked him to throw the notes away.[6]

If asking more questions can be so helpful, why don't we do it more often? When we have enough information to make *a* decision, we tend to make it quickly based on the information we have, so we don't spend time and effort asking for more. But this tendency toward *efficiency* means that we often fail to check out information that might prove critical. Sometimes that additional information is deliberately concealed from us, but sometimes it's readily available.

SHROUDED ATTRIBUTES

Everyday life is filled with factors that affect our decisions without our even knowing it. To give a relatively simple example, desktop printers used to be expensive, but they are now so cheap that it seems manufacturers almost give them away. Yet today's prices are not such bargains if we account for the total cost of the toner or ink consumed over the life of the printer. For a color laser printer, a complete set of four new toner cartridges (black, cyan, yellow, and magenta) can cost twice as much as the printer itself and may last for as few as two thousand pages. The companies that sell printers know the total cost of ownership, but they choose not to highlight it. The long-run cost of ink and toner is what the economists Xavier Gabaix and David Laibson call a "shrouded attribute"—a critical input to the purchase decision that is in effect concealed from consumers.[7]

Some shrouded attributes, like extra fees for "handling" or "service," are easy to reveal—yet consumers still spend more when those charges are not made transparent. In other cases, uncovering shrouded attributes to reveal a product's true cost can be difficult. A retail salesperson likely won't know the cost per page or the total amount a customer will spend over the lifetime of the printer. The same is true for fees charged by banks and mutual funds. Their disclosure is government mandated, but the companies' customer service representatives sometimes don't understand their fee structures well enough to explain them to customers.[8]

In some cases, such information asymmetries can undergird the profitability of entire business sectors. For example, the penny-auction industry, represented by websites like DealDash and Quibids, is entirely built on shrouding the source of its profits. Company advertisements feature video testimonials in which auction winners claim to have paid absurdly low prices for expensive merchandise—an iPad for $23.13, a mountain bike for $11, a Samsung TV for $7.48. "Auctions start at zero, and each bid raises the price by just one cent," says the Quibids announcer. "And even if you don't win, you'll never pay more than retail." What Quibids leaves out, and DealDash mentions only in tiny print at the bottom of the screen, is that customers pay a fee each time they make a bid, regardless of whether they win the item in the end. These shrouded fees are as much as twenty times the standardized bidding increment, so when an iPad sells for $23.13 on DealDash, the company receives 2,313 bidding fees for running the transaction. At 20 cents per bid, their revenue is $462.60, and they make a tidy profit.[9]

How tidy? Ned Augenblick, the same Berkeley economist who studied whether members of Harold Camping's doomsday cult would put money behind their commitments, examined data from auctions at Swoopo, a German company that operated the leading online penny-auction site in 2010. Most of its auctions used 15-cent bidding increments and charged 75 cents per bid. From 2005 to 2009, Swoopo made an average of $160 per auction, a gross profit margin of 51 percent, with about fifty-two losers for every winner. In other words, Swoopo made $3 per auction from every single bidder. Swoopo even auctioned cash payouts, and so many people bid so many times that the company collected an average of more than twice the value of the payout.[10]

This process resembles casino gambling or a government-sponsored lottery more than a traditional auction. At each point, there are only two options: drop out, or press "bid" and cross your fingers. The auction ends whenever a set period, often ten seconds, passes with no new bids, so bidders can't wait long if they want to try again. Moreover, participants must purchase bids up front, which means that they don't pay additional money each time they make a bid—rather, one abstract unit is deducted from their supply. As the saying goes, whoever invented gambling was smart, but whoever invented chips was a genius; money flows more freely if the experience doesn't look and feel like cash leaving your pocket.

Augenblick offered a mechanism to explain why people participate in these seemingly irrational auctions. Imagine you spent $100 on a concert ticket, but when the day arrives, you're feeling lousy and would prefer not to go. If you go to the concert even though you'd rather not, you've succumbed to the sunk-cost fallacy. The cost of the ticket is "sunk" because you won't get the money back whether you attend the concert or not. In poker, whatever money you have put into the pot no longer belongs to you—it belongs to the winner of the hand, so it too is a sunk cost. But if you believe that money is still in some sense yours, you may take excessive risks, betting too much with too little chance of winning, in the hopes of retrieving it.

The bidding fee in a penny auction is a purely sunk cost, as neither the winner nor the dozens of losing bidders will get their fees back. But bidders keep bidding because they've already sunk money into the auction (this is not true of traditional auctions, where losing out leaves you in the same financial position that you were in before the bidding started). These sunk costs are the shrouded source of the auction site's profits.

Identifying hidden costs is essential to avoid being taken in. In some cases, the needed information may be readily available but hard to understand intuitively, like the total cost of owning a home. Homes, like printers, are listed by the asking price, leaving the buyer to figure out and account for the closing costs, mortgage, taxes, maintenance, and insurance costs. We have to make the effort to work through the implications of shrouded attributes ourselves—but that's better than pretending they don't exist. Unfortunately, people with lower income, education, financial literacy, and mathematical ability tend to be the most vulnerable to shrouding and other exploitative marketing efforts. Fortunately, they can also benefit the most from well-intentioned efforts that provide "boosts" and "nudges" at the time they need to make decisions, such as a preselected default choice that is most likely to be financially correct. Many people, however, don't realize that they need such help. In one study, 65 percent of people predicted that they would make the right decision if they were given good advice. Yet almost the same number—64 percent—thought they would make the right choice if given bad advice.[11]

THE QUESTION NO SALESPERSON WANTS YOU TO ASK

Physical products like printers and financial products like penny auctions lend themselves to shrouding, as do bank accounts, credit cards, mortgages, and heavily marketed investment products that commonly include hidden fees and penalties. But every expenditure has one attribute the seller doesn't want you to consider: the *opportunity cost*.

Economists define the opportunity cost of a purchase as the next-best use for the money spent—in other words, the most valuable opportunity passed up by the decision to make a purchase. The concept also applies to limited resources besides money, most notably time. People who choose to attend college for four years, for example, are choosing not to spend those years doing other things, such as earning a salary. In standard economics, consumers are assumed to be fully aware of their opportunity costs, and the fact that they choose to spend their money on item A over equally priced item B reveals that they prefer A to B. Someone might choose to attend college because they value the education more than the salary and experiences otherwise available during those four years or with the expectation of earning more in the long run. In standard economics, we make that choice by weighing the relative costs and benefits according to our own way of valuing them and by selecting the option that provides the greatest return.

The decision scientist Shane Frederick and his colleagues showed, however, that actual consumers often fail to consider opportunity costs. In one of a series of studies, they asked college students to imagine that they had just won $1,000 from a scratch-off lottery ticket and were shopping for a new stereo system. They had narrowed their options to a $700 system and a similar $1,000 system with a better amplifier and CD changer. Some participants were randomly assigned to receive one extra piece of information: a statement reminding them of the simple fact that if they bought the cheaper system, they would have $300 left over. Eighty-six percent of the participants who were

105

reminded of this fact selected the cheaper stereo, but only 70 percent of those who weren't reminded chose it. Thus, about half of those who selected the expensive stereo absent the reminder had not sufficiently considered the opportunity costs.[12]

ABSTRACT DECEPTIONISM

Thinking about shrouded attributes and opportunity costs means evaluating the financial wisdom of a transaction. But a great bargain becomes a bad deal if the goods themselves are fake. Nowhere is that problem more central than in the market for one-of-a-kind collectibles, such as fine art.

Art fraud is surprisingly common. The Musée Terrus in Elne, France, has admitted publicly that over half of the artworks on its walls are fakes. Some experts estimate that 20–50 percent of all the paintings in museums are forgeries and many of the works auctioned every year are inauthentic. One art historian determined that at least twenty (and possibly all twenty-one) of the paintings in the 2017 Ducal Palace exhibit in Italy were not what their labels said they were. The works of a single forger, Mark Landis, turned up in the collections of forty-six different US museums.[13]

Located on the upper east side of Manhattan, the Knoedler art gallery was one of the oldest in the United States. For over a century, it had specialized in selling Old Masters to wealthy Americans. By the 1970s, it had moved into modern and contemporary art. Yet in the mid-1990s, it found itself at the center of one of the most spectacular art forgery scams ever, and in 2011, it went out of business.

Under the ownership of Michael Hammer, grandson of the industrialist Armand Hammer and father of the actor Armie Hammer, Knoedler began to offer a series of newly discovered works by famed abstract expressionists of the mid-twentieth century, such as Jackson Pollock and Mark Rothko. The paintings had been brought to the gallery's director, Ann Freedman, by an obscure art dealer named

Glafira Rosales. Over a period of fifteen years, Freedman bought forty paintings from Rosales and sold them for a total of $80 million—an amount that accounted for the entirety of the gallery's profits during that time. But questions began to arise over their legitimacy.[14]

All of the paintings were previously unknown and undocumented—none could be found in the catalogues raisonnés of the artists, no documentation existed of prior gallery sales or exhibition displays, and there was not even a single photograph showing any of them in the background of an artist's studio. Rosales and Freedman told various stories about the provenance of the paintings, many involving a wealthy foreign collector who had bought them all directly from the artists in the 1950s, taken them to a foreign country, and then willed them to his son, who was now "deaccessioning them" piecemeal rather than in a single blockbuster auction. Crucially, there was no direct evidence to back up any of this.

To "authenticate" the paintings, Freedman invited experts to see what she had on hand in the gallery and made note of their comments. If they said something positive like "This is a beautiful canvas" or "This looks pristine," she would add their impressive names and credentials to a document that went to prospective buyers. These documents were artfully worded to give an impression of authentication without explicitly asserting it. One read, "The painting has been viewed by the following individuals with special expertise in the work of Mark Rothko," and the first name listed was that of Rothko's own son. Experts who had expressed doubts were not mentioned.

By now, you won't be surprised to learn that none of the forty works was painted by the artists to whom Rosales and Freedman attributed them. Chemical analysis of several showed that they contained "anachronistic pigments"—types of paint that did not exist at the time the paintings purportedly were created. One of the paintings attributed to Jackson Pollock was signed "Jackson Pollok." Freedman kept that one for herself but interpreted the misspelling as evidence *for* authenticity, reasoning that world-class forgers would never make such an error.

In fact, all of the paintings were created by a Chinese artist named Pei-Shen Qian at his house in Queens, only a few miles away from Knoedler. Rosales, her Spanish boyfriend José Carlos Bergantiños Díaz, and his brother paid Qian a few thousand dollars per canvas and split the profits from selling them to Knoedler. Rosales eventually pleaded guilty to fraud charges; her foreign coconspirators were indicted but never extradited to the United States.[15]

A buyer who is offered a newly discovered midcentury masterpiece for millions of dollars should be prepared to ask tough questions. But if they want to believe that a painting is genuine, they may not stop to wonder whether it could look "beautiful and pristine" without being authentic. In order to benefit from asking questions, you have to listen carefully to the answers (Did he actually say "authentic" or "true"?) and take care not to interpret vague, ambiguous, or evasive information as confirmatory (for example, assuming that because experts are listed by the gallery, they must have accepted the painting as legitimate).

Some buyers did ask astute questions, but too late. After buying a different purported Pollock (one of five that were part of the scam), the collector Jack Levy retained the International Foundation for Art Research (IFAR) to assess its authenticity. IFAR's experts didn't accept the Rosales-Freedman origin story. According to *New York Times* reporter Patricia Cohen, who covered the case for several years, "IFAR said there were just too many questions raised about the supposed provenance—it just didn't add up."

Art forgeries fool not only amateurs but also experts, precisely because, intuitively, they look correct. An effective forgery meets expert expectations of the look, feel, and composition of a piece by a particular artist at a particular point in their career. Frauds most often come to light not because they look wrong but because their creators used materials that didn't exist at the time. Fakery is revealed only when the right questions are asked—through deliberate, effortful scientific analysis of physical composition or documentary analysis of provenance. Unfortunately, both types of analysis are challenging and expensive, and the tendency to rely solely on intuition is powerful. The South Korean star artist Lee Ufan claimed that thirteen suspected forgeries of his own work were, in fact, genuine, even after an art dealer publicly admitted that they were counterfeits. Ufan said, "An artist can recognize his own piece at a glance."[16]

What if the documented provenance of a suspect artwork checks out? Is the possibility of forgery then eliminated? Unfortunately not. In the 1980s, a struggling British artist named John Myatt ran a small business producing what he openly advertised as "genuine fakes" on commission. Someone calling himself John Drewe started ordering reproductions of works by Matisse, Gleizes, and Klee, which he then passed off as genuine and sold for thousands of pounds each. Drewe and Myatt became collaborators in the scheme, which grew to include "original" works by Chagall, Giacometti, and other modern artists.[17]

Drewe (whose real name was John Crockett) had a harder time passing off works with no provenance than did Ann Freedman and the Knoedler Gallery, so he forged documentation of the history of many of these paintings and sneaked it into archives at the Victoria and Albert Museum, the Tate Gallery, and other authoritative London art institutions that auction houses and dealers would check to make sure the paintings were legitimate. In some cases, Drewe modified old catalogs and books by inserting photographs he had taken of Myatt's work. In the end, the pair sold about two hundred paintings for over two million pounds before they were caught. Both went to jail, but an estimated 120 of the forgeries were never recovered.

Many of Myatt and Drewe's buyers did some homework. They checked seemingly independent sources to verify that the artist had painted the work on offer, but they stopped there. Given how common and sophisticated art fraud has become and the high potential cost of buying a fake attributed to a major artist, it is often worth doing more checking than our instincts initially suggest. Imagine suddenly finding yourself standing in the middle of what appears to be a town in the nineteenth-century American West. You look around and see cowboys, horses, hitching posts, a general store, a sheriff's office, and a saloon. If you walk through the saloon door, you might see tables, stools, a bar with glasses and liquor bottles, and a door to the back office. When you open that door, however, instead of four walls and a desk, you see nothing but sand, cactuses, and mountains. It turns out you were on a movie set all along, but you had to open more than one door to figure that out.

We said earlier that elaborate cons requiring theatrical levels of deception—like the fake betting parlor in the climactic scene of *The Sting* or the fake town at the center of *The Truman Show*—are far outside the norm of everyday cheating. But when the stakes are high, as in finance and fine art, forging one or two additional layers of supporting documentation is hardly unheard of. Drewe did it to back up Myatt's forged paintings, Bernie Madoff's staff did it to back up their boss's phony investment returns, and Diederik Stapel did it to back up the fake scientific discoveries that he wanted his students to make for him. When people create additional layers of complexity in their scams, it's harder to find the right doors, but in every case, there eventually is a door that opens to nothing—a question that yields no satisfactory answer.

THE FAKE ORCHESTRA THAT WASN'T

Of course it's easier to keep asking questions when something seems amiss from the start. While researching examples of fraud and deception for this book, we came across a remarkable 2020 article in the *Guardian* entitled "'Milli Violini': I Was a Fake Violinist in a World-Class Miming Orchestra." The article featured Jessica

Chiccehitto Hindman, a creative writing professor whose 2019 memoir detailed her experiences as an amateur violinist who became a professional fake violinist.[18]

The story is amazing. Hindman traveled the country as part of a nationwide tour led by "the Composer," an unnamed but famous leader of their ensemble. They contributed to PBS specials narrated by George Clooney and were even invited to tour China. All the while, she and the rest of the musicians pretended to play in front of dead microphones; audiences heard the sounds of a CD blasted over speakers, not the performers.

We made a note of the story as an entertaining example of fakery and deception, but as we thought more about it, we became suspicious of something else. Is it really plausible that an entire "world-class" orchestra could mime playing without anyone noticing? Is it possible that a composer leading an orchestra would fail to recognize Beethoven's Fifth Symphony, as the memoir claimed? As we read more coverage of Hindman's story and her memoir, we wondered whether Hindman was an unreliable narrator. Perhaps her story was a deceptive blend of biography and fiction?

Our skepticism grew when we read a piece in *Vulture* that unmasked Hindman's "Composer" as Tim Janis. The article, entitled "Scam Season Comes for the Orchestra," quotes music critic Justin Davidson's reaction to the story: "WTF? How could audiences not see nobody was really playing? If you crash cymbals together at the wrong time it shows! I mean, if fake musicians were trained well enough to make it look real why not hire real musicians?"[19]

We had the same reaction as Davidson. Performances aren't exactly the same every time, and synchronized fakery by everyone both within a section—strings, winds, brass—and across sections would be next to impossible. Musicians readily notice when actors pretend to play instruments. Surely audiences at fake orchestral performances would include enough musicians that some would be suspicious. If nothing else, they'd notice that the sound was coming from loud-speakers rather than from the instruments. It didn't add up.

Was the memoir the real hoax? We bought Hindman's book and read it carefully, focusing on each performance she described. We scoured YouTube for videos of the PBS tour. We searched for information about the author to see if the public record matched her story. We read articles about Janis and his ensemble, and we interviewed Katie Rothstein, the author of the *Vulture* article. The more we read, the more we realized we had been fooled. But not by Hindman.[20]

The deception instead came from the news headlines—the ones that had led us, and presumably many others, to believe that we were reading a story about a classical composer leading a fake orchestra. A "world-class orchestra" implies an elite group of dozens of musicians performing symphonies at a famous hall—the Los Angeles Philharmonic, the Royal Concertgebouw Orchestra in Amsterdam, the London Symphony. It does not imply a trio of journeyman violin, keyboard, and penny-whistle players hawking bland new-age CDs in open public spaces.

Except for one performance at a craft market held on the outdoor concrete plaza at Lincoln Center, almost all of the performances Hindman described took place far from famous venues. They were held outdoors at county fairs or in shopping malls, where the "orchestra" (trio) mimed their music while selling Janis's CDs. It was more like new-age busking than orchestral performance, and it took place in settings where faking either wouldn't be noticed or where nobody would care. In fact, at one point in the early 2000s, there were eight to ten clones of the "Tim Janis Ensemble" traveling around the country selling CDs and faking in sync with them.[21]

There was no orchestra, at least not as musicians generally define the term. The Tim Janis Ensemble was indeed famous; Janis has sold millions of CDs, and his ensemble has appeared on PBS specials and fundraisers. The PBS concert broadcasts consist of a large screen showing nature videos coupled with occasional shots of musicians on-stage (mostly of the flute or penny-whistle performer or of Janis grinning while appearing to play a keyboard).

Nowhere in Hindman's book does she claim that she was part of a fake *orchestra*, let alone a world-class one. In fact, she relates conversations with a friend who does perform in an orchestra to draw a contrast with what she was doing. Nor does she claim that the Composer wrote classical music. In fact, the book makes it quite clear that he didn't. The memoir refers to the ensemble as an orchestra only once—in a story about how they were mistakenly introduced in China as the orchestra that performed the music in *Titanic*.

What we don't know is why so many articles called it an "orchestra" and implied concert-hall performances. In one of the first national media interviews about the book, NPR correspondent Scott Simon interviewed Hindman and repeatedly used the word "orchestra" to describe the ensemble. Hindman then said the word herself several times. It's possible that that initial interview, with a transcript titled "A Fake Orchestra Performance in 'Sounds Like Titanic,'" led other journalists and headline writers to misunderstand the scale of the fakery.[22]

Readers might not realize that journalists often don't get to title their own stories. Writers of newspaper essays and opinion pieces seldom write their own titles, and even book authors rarely have final say over their own book titles. Headline writing is a bit like the children's game of Telephone. A publicist distills the author's book and summarizes it for a general audience. A harried journalist reads those press materials, interviews a few people, and writes a story for the public. The headline writer then reads the journalist's story and adds the most attention-grabbing title they can.[23]

It's entirely possible that misleading headlines were written without the intention to deceive. The body of the *Guardian* article under the "world-class orchestra" headline never described the ensemble as an orchestra, but if the headline writers got the mistaken impression that the story was about classical concerts, they might have described it as an orchestra without realizing their error. When they read that the composer was famous, they might have added "world-class." After all, the goal of headlines is to hook readers—and this one worked on us. In the end, a three-person group faking new-age music at malls morphed into a world-class touring orchestra.

The same transmogrification happens regularly when scientific research progresses from peer-reviewed publications to university press releases to viral stories for the public. The Twitter account @justsaysinmice has gained over seventy thousand followers by doing nothing more than reposting news headlines like "Vaping with Nicotine Causes Heart Problems in Teenage Boys" or "New Therapy Cures Cancer with Just One Injection" and tagging them with "IN MICE" to make clear that the underlying research involved no humans. Had the headline writers read or even skimmed the scientific article, they'd have realized it wasn't about people, and they might not have written a headline about the health habits of "teenage boy" laboratory rodents.

The misleading headline about the fake orchestra made us both interested in and skeptical about this story—it was incredible both in the sense of "amazing" and in the sense of "not credible." But we had to read most of Hindman's book to find the disconnect between what she had written and how the media framed her story. Only after asking questions did we understand that our skepticism was justified but misplaced.

SHOW ME THE RECEIPTS

Usually, when we read a story or book, asking critical questions is not our default mode—it's something we have to decide to do. But when scientists review a paper submitted to a journal, they are expected to scrutinize it carefully, asking questions about the provenance of the results rather than accepting the author's claims at face value. Even scientists can still be deceived by their peers.

Take the case of Dirk Smeesters, who was an up-and-coming psychology professor in the Netherlands—until an independent commission found him guilty of scientific misconduct and he lost his faculty position. One of the ways Smeesters slipped up began with the task that he gave participants in one of his studies. He showed them a picture of a T-shirt with an abstract graphic design and asked how much they would pay for it. Not surprisingly, he received a range of responses. Some people said the equivalent of $9, others said $11, with an average right around $10. To try a similar example, imagine you got an unexpected tax refund and wanted to spend it on a nice pair of noise-canceling wireless headphones. How much would you be willing to pay for the top-of-the-line Bose QuietComfort 45? Come up with an answer before reading on.[24]

At the time of this writing, Amazon.com sold these headphones for $329.00. We doubt most readers would pay full price, so let's assume the average answer was $249. Many people might offer something close to that, but not exactly $249. Some people would bid $274, others $221, a few much higher (say, $351), and others much lower (perhaps $156). A graph of these offers might look like a bell-shaped curve, with the peak centered near $249 and increasingly large or small bids becoming less and less common. But as reasonable as that pattern of bids might sound, it actually would provide compelling evidence that the data are faked. A bell-shaped pattern seems plausible only if you don't ask how people would actually respond to a question like this.[25]

We've discussed how magicians capitalize on common tendencies in what people think and choose—such as what playing cards they're likely to select. Think about the amount you were willing to pay. Hold it in your mind. We're pretty sure it was a multiple of $10. No? Then it must have been a multiple of $5. Right? For "willingness to pay" judgments like this one, only a few people give answers as precise as $221 or $249. Most people round to values like $220 or $250. The more expensive the product, the higher the proportion of bids that are multiples of $5 or $10 (or even larger increments like $100 or $1,000). But even for a T-shirt, far fewer people would say $9 or $16 than would say $10 or $15.[26]

In 2013, the behavioral scientist Uri Simonsohn explained how he discovered the implausible data patterns in Smeesters's work. He looked at the willingness-to-pay numbers in a spreadsheet of the study data and saw that they didn't show the usual surfeit of bids that were multiples of $5. Instead, bids of $5 were no more likely than bids of $6 or $9. In fact, the pattern of data matched what you'd expect if people were equally likely to pick any number—$1, $4, $5, $19, etc.— across the whole range, a pattern known as a uniform distribution. With all responses equally likely, you'll find answers that are multiples of 5 only one-fifth of the time, which was precisely what Smeesters reported.[27]

Simonsohn then ran the Smeesters study himself and found that more than 50 percent of his participants bid a multiple of $5. Simonsohn also examined many other published willingness-to-pay studies with similar goods, and in all of them, at least 50 percent of the bids ended in a multiple of 5. For somewhat more expensive items, nearly 90 percent did. The responses in Smeesters's study were inconsistent with the pattern we should expect, which suggested that the data had been manipulated. Before publishing his own findings, Simonsohn supplied them to Smeesters's employer, Erasmus University Rotterdam, which conducted a thorough investigation that resulted in accusations of scientific misconduct (and to the retraction of the relevant papers).[28]

How did Smeesters's bogus findings get into the scientific literature in the first place? We previously observed how Diederik Stapel's fraudulent research received too little scrutiny because his results fit what researchers expected. We don't know whether the peer reviewers and editors of Smeesters's manuscripts noticed their anomalies, but Simonsohn was the first to ask the obvious follow-up questions: Can

I have the underlying data? What do they look like? Do their patterns match those of similar studies? With each new question, he got closer to a true understanding of what Smeesters had really done.

An irony in this case is that "examine your raw data" is one of the first rules scientists are taught when they learn how to do original research. (Dan preaches the importance of plotting data in his introductory statistics class.) Before computing the statistics that will say whether an experiment "worked," we are supposed to look at how the numbers are distributed, how noisy or smooth the lines are, and whether there are observations that point to potential flaws in our methods.

Before computers existed, researchers wrote down all their data in laboratory notebooks and did all their calculations by hand, so they necessarily had a degree of intimacy with their numbers. Today, software collects the data and computes the statistics, eliminating many transcription errors and mental mistakes. But because we are more removed from the details of the data underlying our studies, noticing anomalies and asking questions is even more important. That process ought to be the collective responsibility of everyone who views, approves, and acts on such data, whether in science, government, or business.

DOING THE WORK

Uri Simonsohn went so far as to program computer simulations of Dirk Smeesters's studies and replicate the experiments himself to verify that the multiples-of-$5 pattern was robust enough to treat its absence as an indicator of misconduct. He engaged in a tremendous amount of work despite having little at stake. The broader scientific field and general public benefit from this kind of work, but the individual investigator often does not. As Simonsohn himself noted in an interview with Ed Yong, "Everybody likes the fact that whistle-blowers exist, but nobody likes them."[29]

Simonsohn's energetic detective work is in marked contrast to the insufficient effort many people make, even when much more is at stake. A compelling illustration comes from the world of money management. Guy Spier is a disciple of Warren Buffett and his philosophy of finding underpriced assets that should reach their proper value in the long run. Early in his investing career, Spier thought he had found an uncut gem in a company called Farmer Mac, which bought farm mortgages from banks. Farmer Mac was a US government–backed company like Freddie Mac and Fannie Mae, which buy home mortgages. Buffett and other savvy investors owned Freddie and Fannie shares. Spier bought shares in Farmer and excitedly told some of his hedge-fund friends about his discovery, hoping they would "go long" on the stock as he had.[30]

A few weeks later, he heard from one of them. Bill Ackman, the founder of Pershing Square Capital Management, invited Spier to his office to discuss the Farmer Mac idea. Upon arriving, Spier saw that Ackman had a shelf filled with annual reports and other documents from Farmer, annotated with sticky notes and highlighter. Ackman had asked far more questions than Spier, and the answers had led Ackman to the opposite conclusion: Farmer Mac was in deep trouble and likely to fail spectacularly. Unlike Freddie and Fannie, which dealt with huge numbers of standard residential mortgages, Farmer dealt with far fewer and more idiosyncratic farm mortgages, which made its performance harder to predict. Rather than taking a long position or staying out of the stock, Ackman shorted Farmer—in effect, he put money on a prediction that its shares would fall.[31]

This experience chastened Spier, who said, "It was absolutely clear to me that I didn't understand nearly enough about Farmer Mac to justify owning it." He sold his shares at a small profit. He later met with Farmer's management and came away unimpressed, confirming Ackman's impression for himself. Ackman had done the necessary work to form an opinion robust enough to bet his clients'—and his own—money. Ultimately, Farmer Mac lost almost all of its value during the 2008 market crash.[32]

A surprising number of highly touted, publicly traded companies lack clear business models or simply do not do what they claim to do, yet investors buy their stock without asking the right questions. In 2010, Orient Paper Ltd. was a publicly traded company valued at $150 million. A team of American investors went to China, visited its paper-making factory, and counted the number of trucks going in and out to see whether the activity was commensurate with the amount of business the company claimed to have been doing—an excellent way of testing abstract claims against concrete reality. They also examined Chinese government records and Chinese media reports on the firm. After concluding that Orient was overstating its revenues by at least a factor of ten, they shorted the stock and went public with their findings. Twelve years later, the company (renamed IT Tech Packaging, Inc.) had lost 90 percent of its value.[33]

This story is repeated over and over in the world of finance. As documented in Michael Lewis's book *The Big Short*, while banks and most large financial institutions lost fortunes during the 2008 US housing market collapse, a few savvy investors made a killing. Why? They paid attention to stories of underqualified buyers getting massive loans to buy second homes, stalled high-rise projects watched over by motionless cranes, and new developments where almost no one lived. While the banks traded on shaky investments derived from high-risk loans, these contrarians asked whether all of this new housing was being occupied by real people or just traded by speculators trying to capitalize on what turned out to be a housing bubble. A handful of people did what the Orient Paper skeptics had done. They left their offices and flew to once hot markets, drove to newly sprouted exurban towns, and viewed the rows of empty houses firsthand. Armed with the truth underlying the Potemkin mortgage-lending industry, they found ways to establish short positions in the housing market, waited for the crash to start, and took the fortunes that more incurious investors lost.

Complacent investors sometimes fail to check whether the fine print in an offering matches the much shorter executive summary. In 2014, the financial journalist Matt Levine related the story of how Caesars Entertainment Operating Company, a subsidiary of the Caesars casino gambling conglomerate (which has the confusingly similar name "Caesars Entertainment Corporation"), enticed bond investors with the claim that "the notes are irrevocably and unconditionally guaranteed by Caesars Entertainment Corporation." This wording suggested that the parent company would pay its subsidiary's debts no matter what. Any investor who had not read all the way to page 106 would not have known that the document listed a few specific events that would vitiate the guarantee—and thereby slash the value of the bonds.

Asking more questions is akin to actually reading the fine print. When the stakes are low, it's often okay to be efficient and skip that step. But when making large decisions or big investments, it's worth the effort.[34]

QUESTIONS AND EVASIONS

Once you appreciate the potential downside of being too "efficient" in your decision-making and you begin seeing opportunities to ask questions, you might still wonder what questions to ask. The most useful questions are those that are specific to the situation and open a door revealing more previously hidden doors. We'll finish this part of our book by describing some questions that can be useful in almost any circumstance. It is said that a lawyer shouldn't ask a witness a question to which they don't already know the answer, so let's first consider the types of answers we might get.

Beware of the tendency to accept a nonanswer as a real one. Politicians are masters at answering a different question than the one they were asked, and they rely on listeners to either accept that answer or to misinterpret it as if it did answer the question. According to studies by psychologists Todd Rogers and Michael Norton, people often don't notice when politicians answer a different question than the one they were asked. Provided that the dodge is artful and the answer is at least loosely related to the topic of the original question, people can fail to realize they've been duped.[35]

Some nonanswers provide "placebic information"—responses that make us feel that our concerns have been addressed when they actually haven't. For example, Bill Clinton's "I did not have sexual relations with that woman" felt like an answer, but it left open what he meant by "sexual relations" so that he did not explicitly deny a specific activity. Norms of politeness and efficient communication imply that whatever a person says in response to a question should be a complete answer, so we sometimes treat an evasive or empty response as a meaningful one. Journalists are, of course, acutely aware of this and sometimes call it out with counter-responses like "That's a nondenial denial."[36]

We can learn to spot common nonresponses—"stock" answers people use to cut off further inquiry. These answers aren't always deliberately deceptive, but we should regard them as signals to press for more information. Here are a few that make us cringe.

"We did our due diligence."

This sounds good—and it's more persuasive than "We didn't look into that at all." But what does it really tell us? Most fields have no standards for how much diligence is due, let alone what qualifies as diligence in the first place. Even in finance, where due diligence can be legally or contractually required, it often has no specific meaning—as Guy Spier realized when he saw how Bill Ackman's version compared to his own. Experienced venture capitalists also get carried away and invest heavily in trendy industries without sufficient investigation beforehand. Absent a clear definition of what someone means by due diligence, we should interpret this response as meaning "We believe this," and we should follow up by asking exactly what evidence led to their conclusions.

"It's been validated."

In science, "validation" means that a tool, scale, test, or other method has been carefully studied to ensure that it actually measures what it purports to. A validated scale for measuring clinical depression is preferable to one that has not been validated. But most users of this phrase don't know what it truly means to validate something. If they did, they would tell you about the validation process rather than simply assert that it has occurred. Often something is called "validated" solely because it has been used before, often not even in the same form. We should follow up by asking, "What's the evidence that it's valid?"

"It's been vetted or authenticated."

There are even fewer standards for vetting and authentication than for conducting due diligence. "Vetting" a person could mean as little as asking for a couple of informal references or doing a Google search or as much as conducting a full background check for a security clearance. (Be especially wary if anyone refers to "extreme vetting," which is not a thing.) As we saw in the case of CBS's story about George W. Bush, it's easy to claim authentication, but the value of that claim depends on the proof provided. We need to ask for specifics of what procedures were used and what information was collected.

"Here's a list of stuff that supports our claim."

People and companies promoting questionable products like to list prestigious organizations, experts, or scientific publications that supposedly back their claims, but closer scrutiny often reveals that the impressive list is itself untrustworthy. Ann Freedman provided a list of experts who had "viewed" each of the forged paintings she sold for the Knoedler Gallery, but one of them (Mark Rothko expert David Anfam) later said that he had actually seen only a picture of the item that was for sale. Theranos, the dodgy blood-testing startup, falsely claimed that large pharmaceutical companies had "comprehensively validated" (hmm . . .) its technology, going so far as to stamp these companies' logos on its own reports without their permission. And a network of attractively produced websites lists dozens of studies purporting to show the efficacy of the drug ivermectin for treating Covid-19, but most of the listed studies were poorly designed, poorly run, or otherwise suspicious. Before being impressed by the length of such a list, we should wonder whether the people, companies, or studies on it truly support what they are said to.[37]

"The originals have been lost."

Many of the frauds that we have studied involved a mysterious, untimely, or convenient disappearance of evidence. Such an occurrence should lead us to question more. For example, why would Burkett have burned the original documentation that George W. Bush was lying about his military service right after he faxed it to a single news organization? Do scientists suspected of fabricating results lose their hard drives or throw away old data at the same rate as honest researchers? Before accepting an excuse for lost data or poor record keeping, we ought to ask why we should trust someone to tell the truth any more than we would trust them to keep their files intact. Asking for copies of key documents is a simple thing to do, and being told that they no longer exist can be an informative response. The Orlando museum's Basquiats, for example, were validated via a letter from the collector who purportedly purchased them, but he had passed away by the time of the exhibition, making it impossible to verify that he had written it.

"We have multiple sources."

Getting the same information from multiple independent sources can be valuable. But if one source got their information from the others or if several sources come from the same firm, discipline, or viewpoint, those multiple sources might be worth no more than just one. People who argue that aliens routinely abduct human beings cite the similarity of accounts that "abductees" give, especially in their descriptions of the aliens as humanoids with thin limbs and large heads and eyes. Careful investigations have shown that there were no accounts of people being abducted by aliens until 1962—the exact year when alien abduction, complete with sexual interaction, medical experimentation, and memory erasure, became a plot element on television and in films. So it's perhaps unsurprising that seemingly independent claims of meeting aliens have many features in common. That there are multiple sources for a claim does not by itself make the claim reliable. We need to consider checking who the sources are, whether they are interconnected in any way, and what their incentives and biases might be before relying on them.[38]

"Rigorous, robust, transparent . . ."

We could compile a long list of words and phrases that can be deployed to signal quality without providing evidence of it. If someone says that "a rigorous process is in place," we should ask for a description of that process and assume that it is not rigorous until proven otherwise. When someone says, "We are being transparent," we ought to wonder why they are bragging about it instead of pulling back the curtain.

"[Crickets]"

Sometimes questions are answered with bullshit or evasion, but surprisingly often they are simply ignored. A candidate for the US Senate in Pennsylvania in 2022 refused to answer questions like "When did you move to Pennsylvania?" "Did you graduate from Troy State University?" and "What is your hometown?" (She still finished only a few percentage points behind the top two candidates in the Republican primary.) When we get no answers or sense too much evasion, we should summon the courage to walk away. Investors who couldn't get Theranos to answer their detailed queries simply gave up on the deal, as did some who tried to question Bernie Madoff and decided that he was being too secretive about his operation.[39]

OPENING DOORS

Now that we've discussed some ways that people might dodge questions, how can we get them to start opening doors? Chris once participated in a chess training camp led by Jacob Aagaard, a grandmaster who specializes in coaching other players. Aagaard tells students to open doors by asking themselves three questions: What is the worst-placed piece on the board? Where are the weaknesses? What is my opponent planning? This checklist almost always leads to an idea for a good move to play. When the stakes are high, we suggest preparing a list of relevant questions that need answers and leaving placeholders for possible follow-ups.[40]

If you think you might be missing something but aren't sure what, or if you want to press for more information but don't have specific concerns in mind, consider falling back on a generic question, such as one of the following.

"What else can you tell me?"

A simple request for more can turn up surprisingly useful information. It can also be useful to start with a friendly question like this one before getting to more difficult or confrontational questions. One of our colleagues occasionally deploys the simple prompt "Say more," and we've never seen him not get more in response.[41]

"What information would get you to change your mind?"

If someone is trying to persuade you and seems absolutely committed to their position, it's possible that they haven't thought much about that commitment or considered whether any evidence could shake their belief. Asking this question might reveal weaknesses in their arguments. Two related questions are "Why might someone disagree with your position?" or "Are there any experts who disagree with you?" Had customers asked Ann Freedman whether any experts had looked at her rediscovered abstract expressionist paintings and *not* accepted their authenticity, they might not have bought one.[42]

"Can you do any better?"

This standard haggling question is useful in many other contexts. A friend once told us that whenever he and his wife are assigned a room at a hotel, they tell the clerk at reception that if they go up to the room and don't like it, they will come down and ask for a change, so everyone will save time and effort if the clerk gives them a better room now. This approach can work whenever the norm is to present one option at a time. Asking "What better options do you have?" or "What are your two best options?" might work better than asking "Are there any other options?" which invites a "No" response.

AND ONE MORE THING...

Once we start asking questions, we must take care not to fall in love with the new information we get in response. Ask questions, but don't automatically give the answers you get more weight than you would if you'd had that information from the outset. Donald Redelmeier and his colleagues asked 574 academic physicians to imagine that they were the only doctor on a flight where a passenger experienced chest pain, and they had to decide whether to recommend continuing the flight or diverting it to the nearest airport. The researchers randomly assigned these doctors to one of two groups. Either the doctors were given the patient's heart rate and blood pressure or they were given the heart rate and asked if they also wanted to know the blood pressure.[43]

Most of those in the second group requested the blood pressure, and those who did were given the same number as the doctors in the first group: systolic pressure of 120 (right at the upper limit of "normal" for an adult). But simply asking for this information changed their recommendation. Of those doctors who were given both vital signs up front, 89 percent recommended landing immediately. Of those who had to (and did) request the blood pressure information, only 15 percent recommended landing. Whether the plane should continue or land is a judgment call, but the massive difference in judgment between the two groups had nothing to do with the information they received, which was identical.

FROM HABITS TO HOOKS

In the first part of this book, we've described four habits of thought, judgment, and reasoning that serve us well most of the time but that can be used against us if we fail to check more. These habits allow us to work productively and efficiently and to make good decisions with confidence most of the time. But because they are essentially shortcuts, they occasionally lead to dead ends or to places that feel right but are wrong. When we focus too much on what's immediately available to us, we risk missing out on information that would make a difference. When we rely on past experience to make predictions about what should happen, we enable others to entice us with exactly what we expected. When we act on our beliefs and commitments, we open ourselves up to being deceived by someone who knows what they are or is skilled at manipulating them. And when we try to operate as efficiently as possible, we sometimes decide before asking critical questions.

In the simplest cases of deception, a scammer might capitalize on just one of these habits of thought. But more complex and long-running frauds rely on all of them. They work because we could not function without taking a lot of shortcuts and making an assumption of honesty and truthfulness in our interactions. If we spent time double-checking everything around us, we would become paralyzed by skepticism. The challenge in avoiding being fooled is knowing when it's okay to accept something and when we should investigate it further.

We will revisit this challenge at the conclusion of the book, but first we will examine four hooks that scammers use to trick us into accepting untruths. We are attracted to people and systems that behave consistently, things that seem familiar, ideas expressed precisely and concretely, and treatments and policies that appear to have potency.

Hooks are like candy for the mind—they are enticing, rewarding, and sometimes sticky but not necessarily healthy and filling. Most acts of deception involve at least one of these hooks, so while it's not irrational to pay extra attention to information and opportunities that we find appealing, it's unwise to act on them without reflecting first.

PART 2

HOOKS

CHAPTER 5

CONSISTENCY—APPRECIATE THE VALUE OF NOISE

We often interpret consistency as a sign of quality and genuineness, but authentic data almost always include some variability, or "noise." Looking for a realistic level of randomness and change can help us avoid getting fooled.

IN FEBRUARY 2022, THE US GOVERNMENT CHARGED SATISH KUM-bhani with five counts of criminal fraud, carrying a maximum sentence of seventy years. He was thought to be living in India at the time. A month later, he disappeared.[1]

Kumbhani was the founder of BitConnect, an organization that offered a way for people to participate in the market for cryptocurrencies, or "crypto"—digital assets whose values are not tied to any particular government's policies or actions. Bitcoin, the original and most famous cryptocurrency, was invented in 2008 by one or more people using the pseudonym "Satoshi Nakamoto." Bitcoin has a finite supply, and its value is connected to that scarcity. In that way, it is less like a regular currency than like gold or oil; you can "mine" more Bitcoin, metaphorically, by spending computational resources (literally, computer processing time and the energy required to power it) to solve complicated mathematical problems. The ingenious code behind Bitcoin ensures that no more than about twenty-one million bitcoins can ever be mined, so in a way, it is an even more stable commodity than gold.[2]

Like gold and traditional currencies, Bitcoin can be bought and sold online with no mining or technical skills required, and its value can rise or fall greatly from day to day. Smoothing out that price volatility was the promise of BitConnect. By late 2017, its proprietary BitConnect Coin was one of the top twenty cryptocurrencies in the world, even though it could be used only for transactions on the BitConnect platform. Under what it called a "lending program," BitConnect accepted Bitcoin deposits and gave customers its own in exchange. BitConnect then invested the Bitcoin deposits using its "BitConnect Trading Bot" and "Volatility Software" to return steady profits to its customers, buffering them from up-and-down swings in the value of the underlying Bitcoin assets.[3]

According to Kumbhani's indictment, although the program ultimately took in $2.4 billion in Bitcoin from investors, it never invested any of it. BitConnect disguised its fraudulent nature with a variety of phony transfers and other complex transactions to make it look like its customers' BitConnect investments were increasing in value. But when customers wanted to extract those profits, they were paid from deposits made by other investors. In other words, BitConnect was a classic Ponzi scheme dressed up in modern digital currency clothes.

Ponzi schemes are named after Charles Ponzi, an Italian immigrant living in Boston who, in 1919, thought he had found a way to make money by buying and selling international postal coupons in different countries. Suppose such a coupon was being sold for the equivalent of $1 at post offices in Italy but for $2 in the United States. Ponzi could send money to people in Italy, have them buy the coupons and send them to him, and then sell them to his local post office at a nice profit.

This simplistic arbitrage scheme turned out to be unworkable at scale and broke international rules, but by the time Ponzi realized this, he had already started advertising for investors. He offered them such guarantees as a consistent 10 percent *monthly* return, about forty-six times what banks were offering on savings accounts, and he attracted over thirty thousand customers within a year. He had no legitimate way to fulfill his promises (the coupon strategy became just a cover story for anyone who asked how he made money), so he began to pay his earlier customers from the growing balance of new deposits. With the absurd rates of return he promised, he soon fell behind on payments. Rumors of his bankruptcy triggered a rush to withdraw, a criminal investigation, and Ponzi's conviction for fraud.[4]

A Ponzi scheme is now defined as a business structure in which early participants profit at the direct expense of later ones. Commonly, victims think their money is being used to trade real assets. In reality, some is being stolen by the operators, some is paid to other investors as "profits," and the rest is held in reserve to pay for future withdrawals so the scam can continue. Most Ponzi schemes follow the same script. The scammer promises an unusually high and consistent monthly or quarterly return and describes the investment principal as completely safe from loss. Eventually, all such schemes—from multilevel marketing organizations to gifting clubs to phony investment funds—run out of new investors/victims, and those who join last lose all their money.[5]

Variants of the scheme named after Ponzi have since been perpetrated over and over throughout the world. It should go without saying that no investment pays a guaranteed, consistent return remotely approaching 5 percent per month (which works out to almost 80 percent per year), nor is any investment completely safe from losses. The closest to "safe" that investments get is US Treasury notes; the standard ten-year note currently pays about 3.5 percent per year, and the highest it ever reached was about 16 percent in 1981. If you are ever offered a guaranteed return higher than that or promised that you can't lose, be wary. Don't be like the investors who gave their money to Celsius, another cryptocurrency startup, which used the slogan "Banks are not your friends." Celsius offered 18.9 percent interest per year on Bitcoin deposits but stopped allowing withdrawals during the market downturn early in 2022 and filed for bankruptcy later that year.[6]

SMOOTH LIKE BUTTER

The phony "hedge fund" operated by Bernard L. Madoff was perhaps the largest and longest-running Ponzi scheme on record. Madoff started managing money for people in the early 1960s, but his Ponzi scheme began later (perhaps as early as the 1970s and definitely by 1993). From that point until 2008, when the fraud was exposed and the fund shut down, Madoff made no real trades for his customers. Investors deposited about $20 billion with Madoff over the years, and according to their account statements, there should have been about $65 billion in the fund when it closed. Instead, there was just $222 million.[7]

Although Madoff's fraud has been documented widely, there are many misconceptions about how it worked and what lessons we should take from it. What Madoff operated has been called the mother of all Ponzi schemes, but it differed radically from Ponzi's original in several respects. Madoff did not promise investors an outlandish rate of return, nor did he guarantee against losses. Most of his investors were too sophisticated to fall for a flamboyant Ponzi offer. What Madoff offered instead was something more desirable than a fast buck: steady growth with no losing years and little volatility.

The *consistency* of a smooth upward trend was the Madoff scheme's unique "value proposition." He returned 7–14 percent each year, even though the overall market fluctuated from annual gains as high as 37 percent to losses as great as 25 percent during the years of the scheme. Consistency removes the discomfort of uncertainty and eliminates fear of risky negative outcomes. People often prefer to avoid risking losses, even if accepting a level of variability that includes occasional losses should yield better cumulative results in the long run.[8] In fact, if someone invested money with Madoff from 1991 through 2007, his last full year of operation, their (phony) average annual return of 10.35 percent would have underperformed the 11.29 percent return of the S&P 500 stock index (the standard benchmark for large US company shares). Madoff did report occasional down months, but those were barely perceptible jitters in a performance graph that went smoothly up and up over time. Madoff's investors sought the safety and stability of Treasury bills, but with returns more like the stock market's.

People avoid risky bets, even ones with extremely high expected returns, partly because losses feel more painful than equivalent gains feel pleasurable. Imagine a coin-flip bet that somewhat resembles the stock market. If the coin lands heads, you will receive $10, but if it lands tails, you will lose some amount. How much would that amount have to be for you to be willing to play? If you are rich, and you can play for a long time, even a loss of $9.99 for tails would be acceptable because over time, you would gain an average of one penny on every flip. Most people, however, answer closer to $5, and many say $0— that is, if there is any possibility of a loss, they will not play.[9]

The risk of loss is an inherent feature of any legitimate investment. People who are averse to this risk might flock to what Madoff offered: a narrow band of annual returns, all positive, with nary a losing year. Just as new viruses can overcome existing immunity, Madoff schemes can plague investors who know enough to avoid schemes with outlandish guarantees (like BitConnect and Celsius) but who still believe that consistent positive returns are plausible. According to financial journalist Diana Henriques, who wrote *The Wizard of Lies*, the most complete account of the Madoff fraud, Madoff schemes are the up-and-coming form of Ponzi fraud. She told us that many of the professional investors who had money with Madoff "thought it was their God-given right to earn at least 8 percent per year, risk-free," and that whenever Madoff tried to make his returns more realistic, meaning they would occasionally dip below that value, those customers were not happy.[10]

The proliferation of Madoff schemes likely results from another aspect of our preference for consistency beyond risk aversion and loss aversion: our poor understanding and unjustified dislike of consistency's opposite, "noise." In this context, noise refers to the essentially random aspects of any complex process. The temperature doesn't go up by 1 degree every day as winter turns to spring; baseball teams don't score the same number of runs in every game; and stock market prices can fluctuate wildly from day to day, week to week, and even decade to decade. The average company's highest and lowest values during a single trading day differ by nearly 2 percent. In short, real data from the real world are noisy. But even experts often find the absence of noise plausible and appealing.[11]

One of our colleagues recently conducted an exercise with teams of investment managers. He showed them a graph that depicted Madoff's performance over the years prior to his scheme's collapse compared to that of three other hedge funds and the market as a whole—but all four funds were given fake names. He asked them which fund they would put their institution's money in. Naturally, the Madoff line was much smoother than the others, yet even these professionals preferred it—not a single one dissented. Consistency was a powerful hook for them, even though Madoff's impossible returns had been a major topic in their own industry just a few years earlier.[12]

It's not irrational to regard inconsistency as a warning sign. A suspect who can't keep their story straight from one interrogation to the next is more likely to be lying. A business mogul who tells the government his assets are not worth much when it's time to pay taxes on them but tells the banks they are many times more valuable when he wants a loan at favorable interest rates must be telling an untruth to someone. And politicians who change their positions depending on the audience they are addressing might be more interested in winning public office than enacting good public policy. But there are limits. Too often we think that strong leaders should never change their beliefs, and their opponents will describe policy shifts as "flip-flopping" or "playing politics." Great leaders are willing to change their minds when the facts change; updating beliefs in response to new evidence is, in fact, the rational thing to do.[13]

It is unfortunate that noise gets a bad rap because we should expect to see it, and we should notice its absence. In any complex system, where many factors contribute and interact, performance in the short term should vary a lot; we shouldn't expect to see long-run averages reflected perfectly in short-term returns. Asking **"Where is the noise?"** can trigger us to investigate suspiciously smooth performances. We can consider all of the factors that might contribute to an outcome and evaluate how noisy they are individually and in combination. From an idealized robotic assembly line with perfect quality control, every product will be the same. But if assembly depends on imperfect people, materials, or tools, the interactions among them will undermine consistency and produce some lemons. The more sources of noise in the generating process, the less consistency we should expect in the outcome. We should be especially careful not to be misled by short runs of consistency—any random process can produce the same results a few times in a row just by chance.

WHEN TIME CATCHES UP WITH YOU

Human behavior is complex and therefore noisy enough that unexplained consistency should make us skeptical—as we've learned from recent experience. We are both tournament chess players, but Chris is more serious about the game than Dan. He learned to play at age five, achieved the master title at nineteen, and still plays in tournaments. One evening in 2020, Chris was playing some casual games on Chess.com when he was paired with someone from the Philippines who went by the screen name "lazzir." By rating, they were about evenly matched. Chris felt that he was playing well but grew frustrated as lazzir parried every one of his threats. Eventually, lazzir cornered Chris's king, used a subtle pawn move to cut off its escape, and delivered checkmate with his queen.

Chess.com provides a useful summary of each game as soon as it ends as well as detailed data on each move. It showed that lazzir's moves were almost 94 percent accurate, meaning they were among the best possible moves according to a computer analysis. Chris has played a few 94 percent (or higher) games himself, and grandmasters play them often, but in this game, he reached only 85 percent. When you play less accurately, you almost always lose. What caught Chris's attention more than the accuracy difference, though, was the difference in how he and lazzir had used their available time. For the entire game, lazzir had never made a move in fewer than five seconds or more than twelve seconds. Chris, on the other hand, made his opening moves in just one or two seconds each but took over thirty seconds on several moves and almost two full minutes on one of them.

Recall that odd timing between moves was one of the tells that revealed John von Neumann's chess cheating. Master-level players often rely on memory for the initial moves in a game, which tend to follow well-established plans. Later parts of the game require more thought and decision-making, and at some point, taking extra time to find the best move—or at least avoid a losing one—can be critical. Chris's more variable pattern is typical of competent players, but what about lazzir's? It was unlikely that he had a preternatural talent for making accurate decisions with the same efficiency no matter how challenging the situation in the game. It was more likely that he had cheated.

Because today's smartphone chess programs are better at the game than the human world champion, it is easy to play chess online even better than a world champion could—simply enter your opponent's move into your phone's chess app and play whatever response it recommends. Since computer analysis is nearly instantaneous, doing so would take about the same time for each move.

Other aspects of lazzir's Chess.com account were curious. The platform calculates separate ratings for games played under different time limits. For regular games, in which each player has ten or more minutes in total for all their moves, lazzir's rating had gained 1,442 rating points in eleven days—after having been almost unchanged for the previous five years. According to the statistical model underpinning the rating system, that 1,442-point gain meant that the lazzir who beat Chris would have been over a 1,000-to-1 favorite to beat the lazzir of just two weeks earlier. No one in chess gets better so consistently over such a short time window; even the fictional Beth Harmon from *The Queen's Gambit* had more setbacks in her meteoric rise to the top.

Not all consistency is unexpected. Just as some professional tennis players play better on clay courts and others excel on grass, chess players have their best speeds of play. But across tennis surfaces and chess speeds, there is more consistency than variation. Rafael Nadal crushes everyone on clay, but he beats almost everyone on hard courts too. By contrast, lazzir appeared to be a professional at ten-minute chess but a pushover at any faster speed (or at other chess tasks like solving puzzles). There is only one logical explanation. The lazzir who played ten-minute chess was a different lazzir from the others.

The fundamental pattern in lazzir's chess playing was similar to the one in Madoff's stock market returns. In the face of a devilishly complex challenge—winning at one of the most difficult games ever devised or profiting in a financial market with millions of competitors—their performances were too consistent. Just as Madoff didn't have the highest returns on Wall Street, lazzir didn't have the highest rating on Chess.com. But his rise was too smooth, his performance lacked variability, and no human could have legitimately achieved what he did. Chris tries not to take it hard when he loses, but his suspicions of cheating were too strong to ignore. He reported lazzir and their game to the Chess.com administrators. Mysteriously, lazzir stopped playing on the site a couple of days later, and within months, his account was permanently closed for violating Chess.com's "fair play" policy. The lazzir case is not an isolated one: Chess.com closes about eight hundred accounts every day for cheating, often because their behavior too closely matches statistical models of what a nonhuman entity would produce. An absence of noise, of the human tendency to make occasional blunders in complex situations, is a critical signal.[14]

COME ON, FEEL THE NOISE

Most people and organizations think of noise in human behavior as a problem to eliminate. That's the meaning of noise popularized by Daniel Kahneman, Olivier Sibony, and Cass Sunstein in their book *Noise*: problematic, unpredictable, or unjustified variability in performance between decisionmakers. But if we're trying to avoid being cheated, noise is our friend. There is no simple, universal rule of thumb for how much noise to expect. But we suggest three principles to help us evaluate whether someone's results are too noiseless to be true.[15]

First, *real human performance is usually noisier than we expect it to be*. In 2016, Leicester City overcame 5,000-to-1 preseason odds to win English soccer's Premier League, but they were not and are not one of the elite clubs. They had finished fourteenth of twenty teams the season before and sank back to their more typical twelfth place the season after. Their performance from one season to the next varies around their long-term average, just as an 80 percent basketball free-throw shooter doesn't hit exactly 80 percent in every game and a .250 hitter in baseball doesn't go one for four in every game.[16]

What's true in sports performance also holds in financial markets— no investment will perform consistently all the time. Bruno Iksil, the trader who came to be known as the "London Whale," lost billions of dollars in 2012 for JPMorgan Chase because he put his firm's money on a prediction that the value of certain bonds would not exhibit much volatility. If that prediction were wrong, the price swings would drive down the value of his position. As it turned out, what Iksil thought was low volatility was yet another illusion caused by a simple spread-sheet error—using the wrong formula to combine two numbers— perhaps the most costly Excel mistake in history.[17]

Second, *we have to pay attention to consistency to even notice it.* Many nonprofessional investors don't compare their investment returns from one year to the next, let alone plot them over time and look at the fluctuations (or lack thereof). Madoff's clients didn't get state-ments with pretty charts and graphs or the instantaneous online ac-cess provided by all mainstream financial firms today. Their account balance appeared on the final page of a thick stack of confirmation slips ("confirming" the fake trades that were supposedly being made in their accounts). Some of them may not even have noticed the re-markable absence of negative months. Likewise, when he was losing at chess to lazzir, Chris sensed that his opponent was playing quickly and well—but not that his timing was inhumanly consistent. To see the consistency, he needed to look at the time lazzir took for each one of his moves. Sometimes we need to deliberately search for the ab-sence of short-term noise to see the presence of excessive consistency.

Third, *see if the suspected performance is more consistent than the per-formance of other people* who purportedly are doing the same thing. For example, when Uri Simonsohn wanted to see if Dirk Smeesters reported too many multiples of $5 in how much people were willing to pay for a cool T-shirt, he compared the distribution of bids to his own replication of the Smeesters study as well as to the patterns in many other "willingness to pay" studies. Likewise, in the aftermath of the Madoff scandal, an accountant named Michael De Vita, hired by several of the victims, tried to benchmark Madoff's reported annual returns. He gathered data from sixteen established mutual funds from four leading companies (Fidelity, Janus, American, and Vanguard) and observed that their average annual returns were comparable to, if not better than, Madoff's. From that, he concluded that "the returns reported by Madoff were in line with those that an investor might reasonably expect by investing in the market for the long term." That much is true, but De Vita missed an opportunity to compare the *consistency* of Madoff's returns to those of the other funds. It's an axiom of finance—a version of "There's no such thing as a free lunch"—that getting higher returns requires taking on greater risk. We checked De Vita's data ourselves and found that the funds with returns comparable to Madoff's averaged more than six times his volatility—and not a single one had lower volatility.[18]

TIP OF THE TONGUE

In the denouement of the classic poker movie *Rounders*, Matt Damon's character, Mike McDermott, confronts his nemesis, Teddy KGB (played by John Malkovich), an unsavory poker expert with a dubious Russian accent who runs an underground club in New York City. Mike has to win enough money to pay off his gambling debts in this final heads-up game, or the Mafia will extract repayment in its own way. Over the course of a grueling match, he notices KGB doing something unusual with the Oreo cookies he's eating. When KGB has the best possible hand, he breaks a cookie in half before eating it. Mike notices this "tell," folds his own strong hand, and then taunts KGB by telling him exactly what cards he must have had, leading KGB to go on tilt and lose all the money Mike needs to win.

Poker tells are patterns of behavior that unintentionally reveal something to your opponents about the cards you hold. They're not as critical to high-level poker skill as the movies make them out to be, but any detectable, consistent link between what we do publicly and what we know privately can provide an advantage to our opponents.

Just as a consistent tell reveals more than its maker would like, exploiting someone else's tell might reveal that you know it exists. In a 2017 interview, given years after he retired from competitive tennis, Andre Agassi revealed why he had been so good at returning the powerful serve of his rival Boris Becker. After losing the first three times he played Becker, he won nine of the next eleven matches. Agassi told Unscriptd that he had spotted a tell:

> Well, I watched tape after tape of him and stood across a net from him three different times. And I started to realize he had this weird tic with his tongue. I'm not kidding. He would go into his rocking motion, his same routine, and just as he was about to toss the ball, he would stick his tongue out and it would either be right in the middle of his lip or it would be to the left corner of his lip. So if he's serving in the deuce court and he put his tongue in the middle of his lip, he was either serving up the middle or to the body. But if he put it to the side, he was going to serve out wide.

But Agassi couldn't capitalize on the tell on every serve, and he knew why. Nobody can guess where a player will serve with that much consistency. "I didn't have a problem breaking his serve. I had a problem hiding the fact that I could break his serve at will because I just didn't want him to keep that tongue in his mouth. I wanted it to keep coming out." He realized he needed to use that information only on critical points so that Becker would never realize he had a tell. Years later, Agassi asked Becker whether he knew about his tell, and Becker apparently "about fell off the chair." Becker told him that he used to go home and tell his wife, "It's like he reads my mind."[19]

Although much of the poker literature is devoted to explaining how to detect and interpret an opponent's tells, minimizing your own tells can be equally valuable. After all, your tells are visible to all of your opponents. The advice to focus first on your own tells applies to any adversarial situation with incomplete information, such as sales, negotiation, law, politics, and journalism, where you can gain from keeping the other party guessing about what you do (and don't) already know.[20]

In most competitions, having a consistent tell is a competitive disadvantage. In the game of bridge, though, tells are a form of cheating. Bridge is similar in some ways to card games like hearts or pinochle except that it's played in pairs. In competitive bridge, each player sits across from a partner with whom they can communicate only via a system of "bid" cards with predefined, conventional meanings. For example, a bid of "one spade" implies that a player holds a lot of spades and some valuable face cards. Partners agree on their conventions in advance, but they have to make those agreements public. According to the American Contract Bridge League, "All information available to your partnership must be made available to your opponents." That means partners can't talk during the game, and they can't do anything that might hint at what cards they hold. Any unjustifiable departure from those public bidding conventions or any variation in how players communicate their choices could provide illicit information to a partner.[21]

Unlike in chess, *inconsistency* in the time taken to make a bridge bid provides illegal information to a partner. Suppose a player typically bids in about five seconds. If, on a particular hand, they instead take ten seconds, that tells their partner that they are struggling to decide between bids, which means that the bid isn't obvious, which implies certain things about the cards they hold.

Tournament organizers at elite levels of bridge go to extraordinary lengths to prevent pairs from communicating outside their bids. When leading players were caught signaling each other about how many hearts they held in their hand by holding their cards with different numbers of fingers visible, tournament organizers erected opaque screens to prevent players from seeing their partners. That led to players getting caught for signaling by playing footsie, which in turn led to dividers under the table. Tournament directors are in a constant race with players to discover and counteract new signaling methods, but no detection method can be perfect.

In 2015, the top pair of players in the world, Fulvio Fantoni and Claudio Nunes, were accused of cheating by orienting the card they were playing differently to signal what other cards they held. The American Contract Bridge League banned them, but similar actions by other bridge organizations were overturned because the statistical evidence wasn't conclusive enough. Even so, other players suspected the pair of cheating, and when Italy included Fantoni on its European championship team in 2021, every other team boycotted their games against the Italian team. In 2016, one of the top Israeli bridge duos, Lotan Fisher and Ron Schwartz, were expelled from the American Contract Bridge League for signaling by placing the "board" that holds all the cards at the start of each hand in different places.[22]

In both cases, observers suspected cheating because the pairs consistently performed too well relative to their peers. They made excellent bids that no other top pairs did, as well as unorthodox decisions about what card to play. Those choices worked out surprisingly often, implying that they were based on extracurricular information. These patterns are signs of an illegal tell, the bridge equivalent of Boris Becker's tongue. Unlike Becker, though, bridge cheaters must know their own tells because effective cheating requires them to collude with a partner.

HAVEN'T I SEEN YOU SOMEWHERE BEFORE?

As in chess and investments, too much consistency can be a symptom of misconduct in science. In some cases, consistency is so extreme that there's no variability at all and no explanation other than outright duplication of data or graphical images. In 2000, Jan Hendrik Schön, a physicist at the storied research institute Bell Labs in New Jersey, published five papers in the top American journal *Science* and three in its British rival *Nature*. The next year, he published another four papers in each, for a total of sixteen over two years—a rate of breakthroughs that rivals that of an entire physics department at a leading university. Schön's papers concerned superconductivity—a property of a substance that has no electrical resistance—which was a hot scientific topic at the turn of the millennium. He reported discoveries with enormous practical implications, and the graphs of his results left no doubt about his conclusions. Most impressive of all, the thirty-one-year-old Schön had done all of this revolutionary work by himself. Or had he?[23]

The scientific charts, diagrams, and graphs that appear in journal articles and conference presentations are designed to convey information and make ideas easier to understand. In contrast, fine art is made to evoke emotion and aesthetic appreciation. Yet both types of images can persuade and influence. Both can inspire awe and insight. Both can leave us with an impression of clarity, elegance, and perfection. And both can fool us.

Consider the case of Ely Sakhai and his gallery, Exclusive Art Ltd., described in detail by Anthony Amore in his book *The Art of the Con*. Sakhai purchased original but minor works by a variety of twentieth-century artists, such as Marc Chagall and Amedeo Modigliani. He then hired—and occasionally even sponsored for immigration to the United States—talented Chinese artists who had trained by copying masterworks. Sakhai set them up in a studio and bought aged canvases upon which they could forge copies of the paintings he legitimately owned.[24]

Why forge stuff you already own? First, it is easier to make perfect copies if the original is right in front of you; all the detail can be seen, down to the shape of each brushstroke and the markings on the back of the canvas. Second, your documented acquisition of the originals means that nobody will have reason to question the provenance of the copies you put on the market. Sakhai sold hundreds of paintings in this way while keeping the originals for himself. He was finally undone when he sold some of the same works twice, first the copy and then the original version. His original of Paul Gauguin's *Vase de Fleurs (Lilas)* appeared in a Sotheby's catalog in the same season that his ersatz *Vase* was offered for resale by its purchaser via Christie's. Another collector bought a Paul Klee painting and later saw the same one for sale by Sotheby's. The FBI found more such cases, and Sakhai was involved in all of them.[25]

The sometimes murky world of art provenance makes it possible to explain away a lot of contradictions, but as Bugsy Siegel is said to have learned after he convinced several individual investors to buy what added up to more than 100 percent of his Flamingo casino, it's hard to talk your way out of the fraud of selling the same thing more than once. Ely Sakhai was hardly the only unscrupulous dealer to do this; he was unusual only for attempting the scheme with high-end paintings and relatively sophisticated clients.

Like Sakhai, the physicist Schön managed to fool the experts for a while. He was caught only when his colleagues could not replicate some of his supposedly groundbreaking experiments (and, in wasting their time and effort, became victims themselves). According to one report, a hundred labs collectively spent tens of millions of dollars trying, and failing, to build upon Schön's findings. Then they started to pore over his papers and his stunning results. In 2002, an independent investigation commissioned by Schön's employer found that he had repeatedly "sold" the same work. He fabricated data for some of his papers and then repurposed the results figures for other papers by changing the scales and labels or by multiplying or dividing all the values by a constant factor. The resulting graph looked elegant and compelling when examined in isolation, but when placed side by side with its siblings, it was plainly a copy.[26]

Except for Jan Hendrik Schön himself, everyone in physics, including his coauthors, now accepts that his results were fraudulent. As of September 2022, thirty-two of Schön's papers had been retracted from the scientific journals that published them, and it has taken years to correct the record.[27]

Twenty years ago, when Schön was recycling his black-and-white line graphs, scientific image manipulation was thought to be rare, and the idea of deliberately searching for it would have seemed as productive as looking for needles in haystacks. With the proliferation of scientific journals, increasing pressure on researchers to produce breakthroughs and high-impact publications, and slipping standards of review in many scientific outlets, this is no longer the case.

In the late 1990s, cognitive scientist Ron Rensink conducted some of the first and most important studies of the phenomenon known as "change blindness," in which people fail to notice the one thing about an image that changes as long as the change occurs during a brief disruption, such as an eye blink or a screen flash. In one demonstration, Rensink alternated an original photograph of an airplane with an edited version in which the plane was missing one of its engines. When the two versions were separated by a brief blank screen, people often missed the change repeatedly, even though it was obvious once they knew where to look. Spotting changes is hard, but Rensink also showed that finding a lone unchanging thing in a sea of changing things is even harder. Imagine trying to spot one shape that's staying the same color when a dozen other shapes change color every time.[28]

The difficulty of this task makes what Elisabeth Bik does extremely impressive. Bik, a Dutch microbiologist who became an independent fraud investigator, is a grandmaster at spotting "sameness" across images that are supposed to be entirely different. She relies on exceptional pattern recognition skills to spot duplicated parts of scientific images, even when the copied bits have been tweaked to make them look different—for example, by enlarging, shrinking, rotating, or adding random visual noise to them. Bik has exposed thousands of cases of duplication in published articles and was primarily responsible for exposing at least one "paper mill"—a single source of apparently fabricated data that went into four hundred different scientific articles. In her audit of the journal *Molecular and Cellular Biology*, she found that fifty-nine papers—about 6 percent—had evidence of altered or duplicated images. Because of her efforts, five papers have been retracted and another forty-one have been corrected.[29]

Sometimes data duplication is so obvious that finding it doesn't require exceptional pattern recognition skills—it only requires noticing the mysterious recurrence of the same numbers in different papers. Data sleuth Nick Brown observed a suspicious level of consistency in the numbers of people responding to surveys by nutrition researcher Brian Wansink, even when the recruiting procedures for the studies differed. One received 770 responses after 1,002 surveys were mailed to a randomly selected national sample of adults. Another also had 770 responses, but from 1,600 mailings. A third again got 770 responses, but from 2,000 mailings. As Mr. Spock would tell Captain Kirk on the original *Star Trek* series, "The odds of three separate studies each receiving exactly 770 responses are approximately [insert astronomically large number here] to one."[30]

Wansink was one of the best-known researchers in the nutrition sciences. He appeared regularly on television and helped develop school nutrition guidelines for the US government. Brown and others were inspired to investigate his work after Wansink wrote a blog post in 2016 entitled "The Grad Student Who Never Said 'No'" that promoted cherry-picking, flexible analyses, and reanalyzing data in a quest for significant results. When we first read his post, we mistakenly assumed that it was a satirical take on the perverse incentives that lead to shoddy science. It wasn't. It was a how-to manual for publishing misleading, headline-generating "findings."

When Nick Brown and others investigated Wansink's oeuvre, they discovered not only excessive consistency but also text reuse and other problems. In response to these accusations, Cornell University investigated Wansink and concluded that he had "committed academic misconduct in his research and scholarship, including misreporting of research data," among other things. Wansink was stripped of his research and teaching obligations and resigned from Cornell.[31]

THE CRITICAL DIFFERENCE BETWEEN "ON AVERAGE" AND "EVERY TIME"

Duplicated data are clear evidence of scientific malpractice, whether due to sloppiness or to deliberate misconduct. But even when results aren't literally copied from one study to another, excessive consistency should raise suspicions. Consider the case of a 2012 article by Jens Förster and Markus Denzler that was published in the journal *Social Psychology and Personality Science*. The article reported twelve separate experiments on the impact of global and local sensory processes on creativity and deliberate thinking—the hypothesis being that thinking about an object as a "whole" (that is, globally) rather than focusing on its details (thinking locally) would lead people to respond more creatively or to think more broadly when completing other cognitive tasks shortly afterward. A control group that isn't primed to think either globally or locally should fall in between the two primed groups. In each of the twelve experiments, Förster predicted and found a linear trend—a straight line connecting the average of the participants primed to think "globally" and those primed to think "locally." And, in each case, the unprimed control group that was expected to have middling scores did. So middling, in fact, that a line connecting the three groups would have been nearly straight in every study, making his results and his predictions line up perfectly. Too perfectly.[32]

On average, across many studies of thousands of participants, the middle group might fall right between the others. But we shouldn't expect that for each of the small studies going into the average. Just by chance, we'd expect the middle group to vary around the center point between the other two groups and sometimes to fall far from that midpoint. Occasionally, the "middle" group might even score higher or lower than the other groups. Having the middle group fall right between the other two groups every time is unlikely. It's a bit like flipping a coin one hundred times and having it come up with exactly fifty heads, something that we expect to happen just under 8 percent of the time. Now imagine repeating that coin-toss "study" a dozen times and coming up with exactly fifty heads every time. That would happen less than once every fourteen trillion times.

After the Dutch National Board for Scientific Integrity investigated several of Förster's papers, this twelve-for-twelve study of creativity was retracted. The report stated, "The diversity found in the scores of the control group is so improbably small that this cannot be explained by sloppy science or questionable research practices." In other words, the results were too consistent to have come from bad record-keeping, analyzing the data in biased ways, or excluding data that didn't show the pattern. At the time, Förster had been awarded a €5 million research grant and was on the verge of tenure at Ruhr University Bochum in Germany, but he left academia and started a private practice of "positive psychology" instead.[33]

OFF BALANCE

An excessive level of consistency has triggered misconduct investigations for studies with much higher stakes than the subtle effects of perceptual processes on creativity. For instance, the Japanese biomedical researcher Yoshihiro Sato fabricated data for dozens of clinical trials on bone fractures. He consistently reported large benefits from nearly every treatment he tried. But it was another form of consistency that provided the most compelling evidence of problems with Sato's work.

While reviewing papers for an article she was writing, the nutrition scientist Alison Avenell noticed something odd about two of Sato's papers: The groups assigned to the treatment and control conditions had nearly identical average scores on many measurements collected *before* the trials began. Clinical trials like those Sato had purportedly conducted randomly assign people to a treatment group or a control group. That random assignment is intended to ensure that the people in one group are comparable to those in the other group in all aspects that aren't directly manipulated in the study. Or, more precisely, random assignment ensures that there is no systematic *bias* in who ends up in which group.[34]

Imagine we're picking teams for a basketball game; let's call them the Reds and the Blues. It would be unfair to assign all the jocks to the Red team and all the nerds to Blue—that would be a systematic bias. If instead we flipped a coin to assign each person to a team, then each nerd and each jock would be equally likely to end up on each team. One team might still be better, but that advantage would be due to chance, not bias. A coin toss doesn't systematically favor one team over the other. If we used coin tosses to form Red and Blue teams every time we picked teams, the average Red team and the average Blue team would be expected to have equal proportions of nerds and jocks. The process would be completely fair, but for any particular game, the Reds might end up with several more jocks than the Blues (or vice versa).

Random assignment in clinical trials works the same way. Each person is equally likely to be in the treatment or control group, so individual differences in factors like education or age, or, more importantly, disease severity, health behaviors, and other predictors of how well a person might respond to a treatment (including ones that were not or could not be measured), will be evenly distributed *on average*. That is, there won't be a systematic bias favoring the treatment group or the control group. But in any given study, random assignment won't guarantee that the treatment and control groups will look exactly the same in every respect. In fact, it ensures that they shouldn't. If you measure enough things in a study, the treatment and control groups are bound to differ on some of them *before* anyone starts receiving a drug, a placebo, or anything else. If it's a small study, some of those baseline differences might be big. For example, if most of the participants in a small study happened to be in their thirties but one was in their sixties, whichever group happened to include that older participant would have a higher average age. If you repeated the study an infinite number of times, the over-sixty person would be equally likely to be assigned to the treatment group or the control group, so the average ages of the two groups would be equal. But in the short run, randomization doesn't "even things out."[35]

Ironically, researchers still prefer not to find baseline differences because they can complicate the interpretation of any effects of the intervention in *that* study. For example, the treatment might not have gotten a fair test if the group that received it started out sicker than the group that didn't. That's why unscrupulous researchers looking to confect convincing results sometimes go too far in trying to eliminate baseline differences. But when groups are too similar on all measures, that's a warning sign that something is amiss. And it revealed Sato's misconduct; in many of his studies, too many of the baseline differences were too close to zero.

Avenell teamed up with Mark Bolland, Greg Gamble, and Andrew Grey to gather 513 variables from 32 clinical trials published by Sato and various colleagues. Had Sato randomly assigned people to conditions, we should expect a range of differences between the treatment and control groups. But just as Madoff's year-to-year differences in returns were too consistently small, too many of Sato's baseline differences were implausibly close to zero to be explained by chance.[36]

This approach—comparing the pattern of baseline differences observed in a study or set of studies to what should happen if there were true random assignment—was originally developed by a British anesthetist named John Carlisle. He applied it to over 5,000 randomized controlled trials on anesthesia, 72 of which had already been retracted due to known data manipulation or fraud. Of those retracted papers, 43, or 60 percent, had the same problem that Sato's did: too many consistently small baseline differences. Another 15 percent of the papers that were still part of the scientific literature failed Carlisle's test as well, suggesting both that baseline consistency was a reliable sign of trouble and that more trouble still lurked in the field. Carlisle's work contributed to the retraction of 183 journal articles by a single researcher, Japanese anesthesiologist Yoshitaka Fujii, who currently holds the record for the most papers removed from the scientific literature.[37]

Exploiting consistency is not just a tool of cheaters. Many legitimate organizations know how much we prize consistency, and they go out of their way to ensure that customers have a reliable experience with their products and services. Having a "brand" means that customers can count on getting the quality they expect every time, no matter where or when they encounter that brand.

The expectation of consistency is one reason why companies seek and protect trademarks on their products. A renegade hamburger joint giving customers a poor experience with its own version of "McDonald's" not only takes a bite of revenue from nearby real McDonald's locations but also eats away at customers' overall experience of McDonald's, which hurts the larger organization. Your products, like McDonald's burgers, might not be the best of their kind in the world, but if they are the same every time, customers will trade a chance at upside quality—the chance that another restaurant's burger will be much better—for the downside protection of consistency (a much lower chance of getting a really bad burger).[38]

Consistency over repeated experiences creates a sense of familiarity, and familiarity can provide useful information above and beyond consistency. A feeling of familiarity with something is usually a fair signal that we've encountered it before, that it's not dangerous, and that it is trustworthy. But familiarity can also be weaponized. Cheaters can mimic what we know, build phony brands, or reap the benefits of associating with well-known names, at least until they are caught. Chapter 6 is about how the hook of familiarity lowers our shield of skepticism and raises our risk of being deceived.

CHAPTER 6

FAMILIARITY—DISCOUNT WHAT YOU THINK YOU KNOW

We rely on a sense of familiarity as a rough-and-ready indicator of truthfulness and legitimacy. When something rings a bell but we don't know why, we should consider the possibility that it is merely similar to the real thing and that someone might be deceiving us.

IN MARCH 2021, FRANK ARTILES, A FORMER REPUBLICAN STATE senator in Florida, was arrested for campaign finance fraud and charged with propping up a fake third-party candidate in the previous year's state senate election.[1]

Artiles allegedly paid someone named Alex Rodriguez more than $40,000 to switch his voter registration from Republican to Independent and provided the paperwork to file for his candidacy. Rodriguez no longer lived in the district he was running to represent, so he used a driver's license that showed his previous address. He neither campaigned for the seat nor spoke publicly during the run-up to the election, but he still received thousands of votes. The Democratic incumbent, José Javier Rodríguez, ended up losing by fewer than forty votes. In addition to charging Artiles, prosecutors charged Alex Rodriguez with violating election laws. Rodriguez pleaded guilty to placing his name on the ballot with no intention of running. Following his arrest, he claimed that he had been scammed by Artiles and offered to cooperate with authorities.[2]

Running what's known as a ghost candidate is not illegal per se, even if it is antithetical to basic democratic principles. Investigations by the *Orlando Sentinel* found evidence that undisclosed sources had funded nearly identical mailers supporting little-known, third-party ghost candidates in three races. Heading into the election, Republicans held 23 seats in the state senate and Democrats controlled 17, with 20 seats up for grabs. In all three races, the "ghosts" likely siphoned votes from Democratic candidates, helping Republican candidates to win and transforming what might have been a fragile 21–19 edge into a solid 24–16 majority.[3]

The case of the two Rodriguezes illustrates how we can be fooled by familiarity. Running a spoiler candidate with a name identical or similar to your opponent's is perhaps the most blatant example of such political deception, but candidates have long gained an advantage from familiar-sounding names. In 1986, two relatively unknown followers of the extremist politician Lyndon LaRouche managed to upset established Democratic candidates in the primary elections for Illinois lieutenant governor and secretary of state. By some accounts, the familiarity of their more common names (Janice Hart, Mark Fairchild) to relatively low-information American voters might have contributed to their victories over candidates with less common names (Aurelia Pucinski, George Sangmeister).[4]

In a 1988 study inspired by the Illinois primary results, a team of researchers led by Chris O'Sullivan asked college students whom they would vote for given only the names of the candidates: Fairchild or

Sangmeister. Thirty percent of the students chose "neither"—a reasonable choice given that they knew nothing about either candidate. Of those who entered a vote, though, two-thirds (31 out of 46) preferred Fairchild. In the absence of substantive information about the candidates' positions on the issues, the more "typical" name was preferred.[5]

When a member of the Kennedy dynasty wins an election, it could be due in part to superior political skill, voters' greater knowledge of the candidate and their positions, higher campaign spending, or other factors, not just name recognition or mere familiarity. But it could also be that simply encountering a name more frequently leads to a preference for people with that name; perhaps the ghost candidate Alex Rodriguez would not have received as many votes if there were no baseball superstar named Alex Rodriguez.

FAME, FAME, FAME, FAME, FAME

In Oscar Wilde's *The Picture of Dorian Gray*, Lord Henry quips, "There is only one thing in the world worse than being talked about, and that is not being talked about." Wilde was onto something. All publicity boosts familiarity, and if we forget that the familiarity we feel originated in negative information, we tend to treat it as a positive signal—hence the adage that all publicity is good publicity.

Have you heard of Sebastian Weisdorf, Valerie Marsh, and Adrian Marr? A 1989 study made them famous overnight and by doing so provided some evidence for Wilde's conjecture. The cognitive psychologists Larry Jacoby, Colleen Kelley, Judith Brown, and Jennifer Jasechko asked college students to read a list of nonfamous but distinctive names, like Sebastian Weisdorf. Later, they created a longer list of names that included some of the made-up names alongside the names of actual famous people, like Roger Bannister, Minnie Pearl, and Christopher Wren. The same students were asked to judge whether each name belonged to a famous person. When they made their judgments right after reading the original list, they knew that Weisdorf wasn't famous. But when there was a twenty-four-hour delay between reading the list and making the fame judgment, they were a bit more likely to think Weisdorf was famous. His name was familiar, but because the students were no longer sure why, they were more likely to interpret their familiarity with it as a sign that he was famous. In general, we are more likely to be familiar with the names of well-known people than with obscure ones, so it's sensible to infer that a familiar name of someone we don't know personally belongs to someone famous.[6]

In fact, merely increasing the familiarity of a name can increase preferences for it. The political scientists Cindy Kam and Elizabeth Zechmeister compared voters' relative preferences for two fictitious candidates, one named Mike Williams and one named Ben Griffin. Williams is a more common last name, and it was the answer option listed first under the question "For which candidate would you vote?" Two-thirds of the participants chose Williams when given no additional information, a result consistent with research showing that familiar names and names appearing first on a ballot have an advantage.[7]

However, Kam and Zechmeister were able to counter these advantages by repeatedly flashing Griffin's name on a screen too briefly for viewers to be confident they had seen it. Under these conditions, voter preference for Williams dropped by 13 percent so that instead of winning by a two-to-one margin, he prevailed in a squeaker. Repeatedly exposing people to Griffin's name increased the number of people saying they'd vote for him.

Whereas unknown candidates in down-ballot races might benefit more from increased familiarity, in real elections, we should not expect shifts of 13 percent in voting preferences from something as subtle as briefly flashing a name. Any effect of something that subtle would likely be swamped by advertising, phone banking, public events, media coverage, unexpected news, and all the other influences on real-life voting, especially in a high-profile race. But this study provides a demonstration of how familiarity might contribute to our decisions in ways we don't fully realize.

Research like this also helps explain why yard signs and banners proliferate before American elections. They mostly signal preferences and affiliation, and they might help make an unpopular candidate seem more mainstream. But they can also boost support for a candidate via increasing familiarity. Field experiments in which yard signs are placed at random have shown that they do have a small causal influence, shifting vote share by about 1.7 percentage points on average.[8]

The same principle applies in other areas of our lives. A persuasive, credible message from a questionable source has little influence at first—people discount it because of the questionable source. But the message can become more persuasive over time because of its familiarity. Even more potent are deceptive messages delivered by a trusted source or presented in a trusted format.[9]

Marketers regularly rely on familiarity to instill a sense of recognition and trust. That might be why companies like Ralph Lauren and IKEA apply proper names to their products (such as the "Hampton" shirt or the "Billy" bookcase) and why new companies name themselves to evoke familiar icons (like the self-driving truck firm Nikola using Nikola Tesla's first name, thereby linking itself to both an iconic inventor and the most famous company in its industry). In New York City, there were once dozens of "Ray's Famous Original Pizza" restaurants, none of them related to one another. Companies also adopt familiar color schemes, typefaces, and other elements of "trade dress" for their products to catch the attention of consumers looking for what they already know. In central Pennsylvania, where Chris lives, the local and regional brands of ridged potato chips come in bags that look quite a bit like packages of Ruffles, the leading national brand they compete with.[10]

Familiarity and similarity usually are such reliable cues that they greatly influence our decisions. That's why companies invest heavily in advertising designed solely to raise public awareness of their brands. In the 1980s, the new Japanese automobile brand Infiniti famously ran a series of TV commercials in which not a single car was shown, purely to increase the familiarity of its name in advance of introducing actual products. Likewise, 84 Lumber, a relatively obscure building supply firm, spent over $10 million on a 2017 Super Bowl commercial that did not feature any of its products or services. Instead, it attempted to draw attention to its brand by telling a positive story about immigration. Shortly after that, Chris started noticing their locations when he passed them, and he even considered stopping to check one out.[11]

According to the cognitive psychologist Gerd Gigerenzer, the *recognition heuristic* is a rule we instinctively use to evaluate which of two options we should prefer—regardless of the context. The rule simply says, "When in doubt, pick what you recognize." In his course on judgment and decision-making, Chris used a version of one of Gigerenzer's studies to demonstrate the power of this heuristic. He showed the students a list of all the teams in La Liga, the top division of professional soccer in Spain, and asked them which teams were leading the league on the day of the lecture. Being Americans, most of his students knew little about soccer and not much about Spain. The majority still guessed that Real Madrid, Atlético Madrid, and FC Barcelona were the best teams. In this case, as in many others, it was a good bet, because on any given date, the teams from the two best-known cities in Spain are likely to be among the top teams in the league. The recognition heuristic codifies our bias for familiarity into a normative decision rule that is surprisingly effective in a wide variety of situations.

Familiarity can also be weaponized for dark purposes. In his essential analysis of business fraud, *Lying for Money*, Dan Davies describes the "same-name scam" as a long-standing type of con that was used by the New England Mafia in the mid-twentieth century. They established credit for fraudulent firms by naming them similarly to legitimate ones. Or consider the example of Jho Low, a Malaysian businessman who allegedly plundered billions of dollars via the 1Malaysia Development Berhad sovereign wealth fund he helped to establish. Like the perpetrators of most complex and lengthy frauds, Low at one point or another tapped virtually all the psychological habits and hooks that we describe in this book. He adopted a variant of the same-name scam by creating entities with names similar to those of famous or established companies. In 2012, for example, he established "Blackstone Asia Real Estate Partners," a shell firm that had nothing to do with Blackstone Inc., the New York–based financial colossus. Most bankers would have been suspicious of a huge international transfer to a personal bank account, but they didn't ask enough questions when permitting a transfer to Low's fake "Blackstone." In 2014, Low had an associate open a bank account in Singapore in the name of "Aabar," not coincidentally part of the name of Abu Dhabi sovereign wealth fund Aabar Investments, for the purpose of stealing over $100 million.[12]

Chris and some college friends tried a sort of familiarity gambit when they attempted to start a technology business in the mid-1980s. In the era before Silicon Valley startups founded by teenagers routinely went on to billion-dollar valuations, a company run by a bunch of nineteen-year-olds lacked credibility. So they chose a name that created the illusion of being a well-established firm: "Consolidated Electronics." After all, a company that was "consolidated" must have been formed from several preexisting companies, like the energy company Consolidated Edison. (Unfortunately, Consolidated Electronics never raised enough money to launch, so we'll never know how its familiar-sounding name would have played with consumers.)

Instilling a false sense of familiarity is a tactic usable by anyone trying to make products or solicitations seem trustworthy. Even book authors can take advantage of familiarity, for example by adopting the title of a famous novel and award-winning film for their nonfiction book.

FAKE OPINIONS ON THE REAL NEWS

Sinclair Broadcast Group, a right-leaning media company, exploited familiarity in 2018 when it required all of the television stations it owned to have a local news anchor read an editorial about the dangers of one-sided news presentations and fake news. Aaron Weiss, a former news director for a Sinclair station, told journalist Nicole Lafond that such "must-run" promotions were commonplace at his station. Sinclair gave stations preproduced video segments and scripts that the anchors had to read verbatim. Anchors had to pretend the words were their own, could not disclose the true source, and had to show the segments during time slots with high viewership—they felt that they had to choose between violating professional ethics and losing their jobs.[13]

In a *Huffington Post* commentary, Weiss wrote, "Sinclair knows its strongest asset is the credibility of its local anchors . . . they have often been on the air for decades before Sinclair purchased their stations." Sinclair executives knew that a message from a local anchor, one familiar to the station's audience, would be more persuasive than one from an unknown, remote executive. Media watchdogs flagged this egregious example of propaganda masquerading as local news by creating a video montage of news anchors around the country reading the same material.[14]

On June 4, 2021, *USA Today*, the leading US newspaper by paid circulation, wrapped its weekend edition in a four-page advertisement for Netflix's upcoming fantasy series *Sweet Tooth*. The design was strikingly different from that of advertising circulars for car dealerships and department stores normally found inside and occasionally around newspapers. The Netflix ad mimicked a normal *USA Today* front page, complete with almost believable headlines, and gave no indication it was not the real thing except for the single word ADVERTISEMENT in small print at the very top. We both were momentarily fooled by it when we first saw it in the supermarket.

So-called advertorial content is not a new phenomenon. As early as the 1970s, Mobil Corporation was paying the *New York Times* to run essays on the op-ed page that communicated the company's views on energy policy and other issues. These pieces were printed in a different typeface, enclosed in a box, and adorned with the Mobil logo, but they inherited some of the authority of their surroundings, being placed next to the words of the newspaper's regular, respected columnists like William Safire and Russell Baker.[15]

The gradual transmutation of familiarity into trust is a curious phenomenon. Top television news hosts are paid millions of dollars per year because their personal "brands" attract reliable audiences who prefer to receive fairly generic information (the day's headlines) from one particular individual over others. When those voices are hijacked to read someone else's words, people can be misled, as the Sinclair case shows.

But there is a more subtle form of this effect. Before his hedge fund transformed into a full-on scam in the early 1990s, Bernie Madoff was respected for his legitimate activities, including his service as chairman of the Nasdaq stock exchange, which helps explain why so many people entrusted him with their money. Similarly, Donald Trump gained national fame as a celebrity who played "Donald Trump," a dramatization of a decisive, no-nonsense, fabulously wealthy business leader on the 2000s reality show *The Apprentice*. People familiar with that Trump—a more appealing version than the tabloid-dwelling operator of bankrupt casinos in the 1990s—were likely more receptive to the idea of him as a serious presidential candidate.[16]

MANUFACTURING TRUTH

In *Brave New World*, Aldous Huxley wrote, "Sixty-two thousand four hundred repetitions make one truth." He was off by 62,399. Much as reading a name once can make us more likely to think it's famous when we read it later, hearing or reading a statement once can make us more likely to believe it's true when we encounter it again, regardless of its actual accuracy. Unlike the "false fame" effect, which requires the passage of time for the source of the name to be forgotten, this "illusory truth" effect occurs quickly.

In a study conducted by Emma Henderson along with Dan and their colleague Dale Barr, a sample of 567 adults from the United Kingdom read 64 statements about obscure facts, half true and half false. They then read other lists of such statements immediately, a day later, a week later, and a month later. Each of the other lists included 16 statements repeated from the original list and 16 statements that the participants had not seen before. The participants were asked to rate the veracity of the statements on a 7-point scale that ranged from definitely false (1) to definitely true (7). When tested immediately, the new items averaged about 4.12. A value right in the middle isn't surprising because the items were selected so that most people wouldn't actually know whether each one was true. Items repeated right away were rated 0.68 points higher than the new items (4.80). That is, simply reading the same statement once earlier shifted the participants' later belief in it. The effect lasted for a month, although by then, the judged truth was only 0.14 points higher for repeated items than for new items. To repeat, simply having previously read a statement made people think it was more likely to be true.[17]

In Michael Ritchie's 1972 political drama *The Candidate*, Robert Redford plays a young activist who yearns to be a more authentic leader than his estranged father, a former governor of California. But after party operatives talk him into running for a US Senate seat, he discovers that his campaign gains traction with the public only when he accepts the advice of his handlers and starts giving the same formulaic speech over and over again. The effect of repetition on illusory truth was first documented scientifically just five years later.

Perhaps not surprisingly, research on illusory truth has grown rapidly during the past decade. Although the vast majority of studies have focused on trivia statements and have tested groups of college students over fairly short time periods, some studies have shown effects of repetition in news headlines, marketing claims, and even statements about health and medicine. As Huxley appreciated, when we hear something frequently enough, we start to believe it.[18]

THE TRAPPINGS OF TRUSTWORTHINESS

Just as we associate familiar statements with truth and familiar names with credibility, we often conflate the superficial traits associated with honest actors with the honesty of their actions. Pharmaceutical companies, for example, tend to have convincing websites with links to scientific publications. But anyone can mimic those websites to promote untrustworthy products.

Groups like America's Frontline Doctors, Front Line COVID-19 Critical Care Alliance, and World Council for Health all have names that resemble those of reputable medical groups (the latter sounds a lot like "World Health Organization"), but all touted questionable treatment and prevention measures during the pandemic, including the antiparasitic drug ivermectin, which was never shown to be effective against the coronavirus. These official-sounding "medical" groups have fancy websites that provide the trimmings of an established organization without any of the meat. For example, ivmeta.com provided an attractively designed page offering impressive-sounding "real-time meta-analysis" of ivermectin studies (a term that has no established meaning outside a network of pro-ivermectin websites). Evaluating the quality and quantity of evidence for a claim requires time and expertise. In this case, the old adage of garbage in, garbage out seems to apply.[19]

Unfortunately, consumers deciding whether to trust an organization, product, or information source often lack the resources to assess its credibility, so we tend to rely on whether it looks similar to whatever we already happen to use. We trust a veneer of authority when it can be a risk factor.

That might be why Theranos stocked its board of directors with retired military leaders, cabinet secretaries, and politicians. The presence of well-known people comforted investors of the type Theranos sought—wealthy individuals and family funds—but it actually turned off professional investors and those who specialized in the biotech and healthcare sectors that Theranos operated in. We once heard a hedge fund manager tell an investing conference, "The more generals on a company's board, the more you should think about shorting their stock." He reasoned that any company that so badly needs to impress investors with famous names and military associations must have something to hide—perhaps even fraud. His instincts might be right. A study of board composition and financial performance of public companies between 2000 and 2017 found that those with retired military personnel on their boards did worse, and those with retired generals and admirals did worse than those with lower-ranking officers. Of course, given what Theranos was up to, keeping the industry-expert foxes away from their henhouse was a strategic choice, not a staffing error.[20]

Publishers also use the hook of familiarity to attract readers. Most books bear endorsements from authors of similar books, and some famous authors endorse dozens of books a year. How do they find so much time to read all of those books while writing their own? In our view, the credibility of an endorsement is inversely proportional to the number of such things produced by its author. At the extreme, a superblurber must either endorse everything they read (so they lack a discriminating palate) or endorse books without reading them first (so their recommendations are uninformed). Readers should discount endorsements from people who seem to endorse a ton of books. Really, we might as well ignore blurbs altogether. Even if all book endorsements were genuine and the blurbers truly believed everything they wrote, we have no idea how many people were asked to endorse the book and declined. As we noted in our discussion of the principle of focus, rapturous blurbs—and job references and letters of recommendation—tell us nothing about the neutral, negative, or unwritten reactions we weren't shown.[21]

When a marketing campaign relies almost exclusively on testimonials—which is what book blurbs are—it's easy to mistake them for actual evidence that the product is good. Unless we personally know the people offering their support or have other ways to determine that their claims are true (for example, by checking whether their reviews of other products we know match our own opinions), they are likely to be more misleading than helpful. Testimonials are the equivalent of brief and vacuous five-star reviews: We often can learn more about a product by reading four-star and two-star reviews than five-star and one-star ones. And if there are few or no negative reviews and a ton of positive ones, you should take the positive ones less seriously.[22]

Even evaluations by well-known, independent, and credible organizations may not be particularly meaningful. Individual investors often rely on Morningstar ratings to select mutual funds. Morningstar acknowledges that its ratings are based on past performance, but fund managers promote its star ratings to attract new investors. According to an analysis in the *Wall Street Journal* of the performance of thousands of mutual funds over a period of decades, only a small percentage of funds receiving Morningstar's highly touted five-star rating performed well enough to still have that rating five years later. In fact, about the same number of five-star funds became bottom-ranked one-star funds! Past performance never guarantees future returns, but in this case, it barely even predicted them.[23]

That high-flying, high-star funds tend to return to earth over time exemplifies the phenomenon called "regression toward the mean." The best-performing stocks, salespeople, bands, teams, athletes, and anything else during any defined time window will, on average, do worse over the next period. That's because high-flying status can result not from intrinsic, enduring qualities (management, talent, skill) but also from relatively random factors that won't benefit them as much, if at all, in the future. Popularity, celebrity, and public awareness can result in large part from being in the right place at the right time, so whatever we find familiar is probably not as inherently good, valuable, or worth emulating as it might seem. The flip side, of course, is that many worthwhile things are presently unpopular only because of randomness, and examining them closely can reveal uncut gems.

Just as ratings can be unreliable, sources that are highly credible for some purposes can be misleading for others. The US FDA is a familiar and trusted source of validation for medical treatments—so familiar, in fact, that many people don't realize that there are critical nuances and distinctions in what "FDA approval" really means. Medications, including vaccines, undergo multiple stages of rigorous clinical trials that assess whether they have harmful side effects and whether they show medical benefit when compared to placebo treatments.

But for software or devices with therapeutic applications, FDA approval might mean only that the product does little harm and could potentially help. A product can thus get a form of FDA approval even if there's little compelling evidence that it provides real, practical benefits. A computerized brain-training game, for example, could gain FDA approval as a therapy, and the game's maker naturally would say "FDA approved" in its marketing. Its customers and investors might mistakenly assume that the game underwent the level of scrutiny required for drugs and vaccines and that it achieved the same level of proven real-world benefit.[24]

GOING PHISHING

In this era of constant connectedness and information overload, it's easier than ever for scammers to take advantage of our reliance on familiarity. On March 19, 2016, Hillary Clinton's presidential campaign chair, John Podesta, received an ominous email. Under a red banner stating, "Someone has your password," a short note beginning "Hi John" warned him that someone in Ukraine had hacked his Google password, and it urged him to click on a blue "CHANGE PASSWORD" box. According to an AP News report, Podesta's chief of staff forwarded the message to the campaign's tech support personnel, who replied that the email was legitimate, provided a proper link to reset Podesta's password, and advised him to enable two-factor authentication (so that he would have to enter a onetime code, in addition to his password, each time he wanted to log in). Although the "Hi John" email bore some indicia of an authentic email, it came not from Google but from "myaccount.google.com-securitysettingpage.tk." The .tk at the end of the address meant it came from a territory of New Zealand. It was a phishing attempt designed to steal Podesta's password by making him enter his current password in an attempt to set up a new one.[25]

Starting a fake address with a real .com address is a common tactic because many people don't realize that it might be from a different domain if the link doesn't end properly. We also might not recognize a fake address if we don't read and process all the letters and punctuation marks carefully enough to notice anomalies. It's not clear whether Podesta clicked on the link and gave the hackers his password, although the "It's legit" response from the help desk might have led him to do so. Regardless of whether this phishing attempt succeeded in hooking Podesta, his emails were accessed and posted on WikiLeaks just weeks before the 2016 election. The leak, which most investigations linked to Russian state-sponsored hackers, redirected attention from Donald Trump's travails to the controversies over Clinton's email and her use of a private server, and it could have influenced the outcome of the election in critical states.

The term "phishing" refers to sending messages intended to lure people into providing personal information such as passwords and account numbers. As with regular old hook-and-line fishing, the idea is that enough people in the sea of users will take the bait to make it worthwhile to cast out a line and wait. The origins of this form of social hacking can be traced to the early days of widespread email use in the mid-1990s. In that era, hackers used phishing and other techniques to steal America Online account information. Podesta's was likely a case of "spear phishing," which refers to a phishing attack pointed at a specific target.[26]

Phishing may be the most common form of social engineering fraud, in part because it's relatively easy to mimic the style and format of a class of useful automated messages that we receive regularly: password reset requests, delivery notifications, subscription confirmations, and administrative announcements. In 2022, a former employee of the publishing house Simon & Schuster was arrested for masquerading as a publisher or a literary agent to snooker unsuspecting authors and editors into sending him their unpublished manuscripts. Because his requests and the accompanying web links looked similar to what people might expect from an agent or publisher (replacing an "m" with "rn" to create @penguinrandornhouse), leading authors and celebrities, including Margaret Atwood and Ethan Hawke, were fooled. Phishing attacks rely on that sense of familiarity and our tendency to respond quickly in order to get through the deluge of messages. We are not perfect at detecting deviations from what we expect to see—we don't stop and play spot-the-difference with every message.[27]

Phishing emails are the opening move in a complex and costly form of fraud known as business email compromise. Scammers use pilfered employee passwords to gather internal information about how a company works until they have enough to start forging invoices and stealing real money. And though simple, phishing tactics are surprisingly effective. Across 2.9 million test emails sent to employees of several large US healthcare organizations, nearly one out of every seven fraudulent links was clicked. One large-scale field study of ten thousand employees at the Dutch Ministry of Economic Affairs found that about one-third clicked the link in a suspicious email about connecting their phone and password for easier password recovery, and 22 percent entered their password (along with their name and phone number in most cases) on the suspicious website at the other end of the link. In this case, the phishing test had a misspelling in the sender address, a changed logo, an odd way of greeting and addressing the recipient, an unusual extension in the linked web address, and the use of two different fonts. Most people today are generally aware that it's risky to enter their password on suspicious websites, but when we are busy and a phishing attempt looks enough like a real message, any of us can be fooled.[28]

Social engineering hacks work because their familiarity makes us drop our guard. Recognizing the warning signs is key to avoiding the hook. A big step is simply asking yourself whether a familiar-looking message might not be what it seems. Whenever we receive an unexpected message with a link, we should contact the ostensible sender directly. Receive a receipt for something you don't remember buying? Go directly to the store website and check your order history. Get a warning about a problem with your tax return or a text from your credit-card company about possible suspicious charges? Don't reply to the text, click the link, or call the number listed in the message. Instead, look at the government website or the back of your card for the correct number and call it. (And when you do go to a website, be careful entering the address; scammers sometimes set up entire fake websites designed to fool people who make common typos.)

TRANSGRESSING THE BOUNDARIES

In 1993, a team of writers for the satirical magazine *Spy* asked several newly elected members of the US Congress what they would do about the ethnic cleansing then underway in Freedonia. Jay Inslee of Washington, who would go on to become his state's governor in 2013, said, "I'm not familiar with that proposal . . . um, but it's coming to the point now that a blind eye to it for the next 10 years is not the answer." Corrine Brown of Florida said, "We need to take action," while Steve Buyer of Indiana observed, "It's a different situation than the Middle East."[29]

Buyer was closest to being right. Freedonia is indeed different from the Middle East—it's a fictional nation mentioned in the Marx Brothers' 1933 film *Duck Soup*. Inslee, Brown, and others were seduced into recommending US intervention in a nonexistent country based on the familiar form of the question and the situation it referenced (and perhaps on their desire, ironically, not to appear ignorant). Wars in Europe and Africa were top stories at the time, and these harried junior politicians, not yet skilled in discussing international affairs, relied on the similarity between names like Bosnia, Somalia, and Freedonia to make foolish policy statements.

Most hoaxes of this sort are like spear phishing—they mimic familiar tropes of a legitimate interview to lure a specific target into trusting the interviewer more than they should. Hoaxes capitalize on appearing superficially similar to the real thing. Even academic scientists have tried to punk one another with phony journal articles to make points about declining standards and rising bullshit. In perhaps the most famous modern academic hoax, physicist Alan Sokal published a nonsensical academic article in the humanities journal *Social Text*. His paper, titled "Transgressing the Boundaries: Toward a Transformative Hermeneutics of Quantum Gravity," had the familiar trappings of a genuine postmodern article, but in place of any attempt at meaningful content, it included a lot of nonsense that would sound impressive to a credulous reader. Sokal announced the hoax several weeks after its publication and wrote about it in the magazine *Lingua Franca*.[30]

In what some consider to be the greatest literary hoax of the twentieth century, the Australian poets James McAuley and Harold Stewart decided to send up the emerging modernist poetry tradition by inventing a poet named Ernest Lalor Malley. They described Malley as a recently deceased auto mechanic and insurance salesman, untrained as a poet, who had written a range of modernist, surrealist poetry. McAuley and Stewart duped John Reed and Max Harris, the editors of the art and literary journal *Angry Penguins* (trust us, we are not making this up), into publishing Malley's work and hailing him as a genius.[31]

Just as great art forgeries are broadly consistent with an artist's known body of work, Malley's poems plausibly could have been written by a contemporary modernist. In a 1944 statement to the publication *Sydney's Fact*, Stewart and McAuley describe how they created Malley's works:

> We produced the whole of Ern Malley's tragic life-work in one afternoon, with the aid of a chance collection of books which happened to be on our desk—the Concise Oxford Dictionary, collected Shakespeare, dictionary of quotations, etc. We opened books at random, choosing a word or phrase haphazardly. We made lists of these and wove them into nonsensical sentences. We misquoted and made false allusions. We deliberately perpetrated bad verse, and selected awkward rhymes from Ripman's Rhyming Dictionary. In parts we even abandoned metre altogether.[32]

The Australian hoaxers even invented quotations from famous figures to include in Malley's poems:

> *I have been bitter with you, my brother,*
> *Remembering that saying of Lenin when the shadow*
> *Was already on his face: "The emotions are not skilled workers."*

The poems were also partly plagiarized. In their statement, the hoaxers reported, "The first three lines of the poem 'Culture As Exhibit' were lifted straight from an American report on the drainage of breeding-grounds of mosquitoes":

> *"Swamps, marshes, borrow-pits and other*
> *Areas of stagnant water serve*
> *As breeding-grounds . . ." Now*
> *Have I found you, my Anopheles!*

The Ern Malley hoax fooled many in the literary world, including a prominent British literary critic, Herbert Read. It significantly damaged the modernist poetry tradition in Australia for decades. *Angry Penguins* folded just a few years later, and its editor Max Harris was convicted of publishing some obscene content that was in Malley's poems. Yet since the 1970s, Malley's "work" has gained prominence as legitimate surrealist poetry. In an ironic twist, the Ern Malley poems are now more widely read and discussed than those Stewart and McAuley published under their own names.

MAKING THE NATURAL SEEM STRANGE

Just as advertisers work to increase familiarity and name recognition, fraudsters craft situations in which we rely on familiarity to our detriment. If something seems familiar, we should ask ourselves, **"Why does this ring a bell?"** If it's something we feel that we know but can't recall how we learned it, or if it seems pleasant or good for no obvious reason, our evaluation of it might be driven by familiarity rather than logic. There's a chance it is just superficially similar to what we think it is.

Much of the time, our sense of knowing is an accurate signal and serves us well. Few of us can identify the moment when we learned that George Washington was the first president of the United States, that the Korean War began in 1950, that a car's brake pedal is to the left of the accelerator, or that a new coronavirus was infecting people in China. We must rely on information that we just know, even if we don't recall why we know it. But when critical decisions depend on what we "just know," we should—as much as possible—evaluate whether we might instead think we know something that isn't actually so.

When discussing the nature of instincts, William James wrote, "It takes, in short, what [philosopher George] Berkeley calls a mind debauched by learning to carry the process of making the natural seem strange." Making the natural seem strange means defamiliarizing ourselves with something by temporarily setting aside what we know in order to evaluate new information more objectively, to see what it actually means. For example, one of our editors suggested a method of catching mistakes that we hadn't considered: read a document backward—not word by word but sentence by sentence or at least paragraph by paragraph. We tried it and noticed that our expectations about what should come next were disrupted, and we found typos and other errors we had previously missed.[33]

Making the familiar seem new is a common technique in many fields. Artists find it easier to copy a drawing by turning it upside down, effectively reducing the effects of their knowledge by disrupting typical spatial configurations. Writers try to break out of blocks and ruts by changing where and how they work. Chess masters change their openings entirely to gain a new perspective on the game, and their play often improves despite their lack of familiarity with the board positions that arise. The goal, in all these cases, is to evaluate the evidence anew without relying on the sense that we already know the right answers and decisions.[34]

The defamiliarization process can make things look dramatically different. The business professor Michael Roberto asks his students to evaluate this startup pitch:

I'd like to open a new kind of grocery store. We're not going to have any branded items. It's all going to be private-label. We're going to have no television advertising and no social media whatsoever. We're never going to have anything on sale. We're not going to accept coupons. We'll have no loyalty card. We won't have a circular that appears in the Sunday newspaper. We'll have no self-checkout. We won't have wide aisles or big parking lots. Would you invest in my company?

If you haven't already figured it out, this underwhelming idea is the business model of Trader Joe's, one of the most beloved companies in the US retail food industry. Nonetheless, the fact that people aren't impressed by its business plan tells us something. In evaluating a pitch, people might pay too much attention to their stereotypical ideas about successful grocery stores. Or perhaps there is something more to the success of Trader Joe's than its general business idea, and replicating the key aspects of its model won't guarantee replicating its success. Either way, defamiliarizing a story by obscuring names and identities lets us see it in a new light. If we turn Trump and Biden into "Candidate A" and "Candidate B," or Russia and the United States into "Country X" and "Country Y," we can better evaluate the merits of who is right and who is wrong, which policy is wise and which is misguided, and whether either side is obviously corrupt or virtuous.[35]

If we blind ourselves to who said what or did what, we temporarily defamiliarize ourselves with the actors involved. This approach lets us shed our ideological skin and evaluate evidence without being biased by our feelings of familiarity and loyalty. When we do this, we sometimes find that our actual preferences are less aligned with our preferred candidate or party than we previously assumed.[36]

Automated analytics are a formalized way of eliminating familiarity biases. In sports, analytics attempt to quantify the factors that truly matter for winning and then evaluate each player and team according to those criteria. As Michael Lewis documented in his book

Moneyball, analytics helped overcome the effects of familiarity (and long-standing biases about body types and pedigrees) in scouting judgments about the future potential of baseball players. By formally modeling what mattered most in predicting game outcomes, teams could shift their strategies toward what worked rather than relying on what was traditional and familiar. Many sports have adopted analytics to determine the optimal long-run approach, leading to large shifts in how many three-point shots are taken in basketball, where fielders position themselves in baseball, and how often teams try going for first down instead of punting on fourth down in football.[37]

In this chapter, we've explored how a superficial similarity with information and its sources can lead us to trust when we shouldn't. But even when we encounter something for the first time, we can find it more compelling than we should, especially when it seems precise. The more specific, concrete, and detailed a story or argument, the more credible we tend to find it. In the next chapter, we will explore why precision is valued, how it can lead us astray, and what questions we can ask to avoid being lured off track.

CHAPTER 7

PRECISION—TAKE APPROPRIATE MEASURES

People treat precision as a sign of rigor and realism and vagueness as a sign of evasion. When we're given concrete, detailed information, we tend to assume it must be accurate and well researched. To see through this kind of smokescreen, we must vary our perspective and make the right comparisons.

IN HIS NOVEL *THE RESTAURANT AT THE END OF THE UNIVERSE*, Douglas Adams describes something called a "total perspective vortex" machine. When a person enters its small chamber, they see a complete model of the entire universe with a tiny dot labeled "You are here." The crushing revelation of their own irrelevance at this vast scale typically proves fatal. Fortunately for us, we don't need to take such a risk to put things in perspective.

A quantity or number might seem huge or tiny in isolation, but viewing it on the proper scale can help us think about it more clearly. We might balk at paying a few extra cents per gallon at the gas pump, but a difference of a few hundred dollars in the initial cost of a car typically isn't a deal breaker. We might zealously clip grocery coupons that collectively save a few dollars a year on coffee beans but then not think twice about buying daily lattes that add up to much more. We might buy Ivory soap because its advertisements claim that it is 99 44/100 percent pure, but how pure is soap supposed to be?[1]

When we see a single dollar figure, measurement, or percentage in isolation, we do not automatically evaluate it on the right scale or compare it to other relevant values. Anyone looking to deceive us can take advantage of this tendency, and thinking about the right comparison is a critical step if we want to avoid being misled. If an expert says that increased screen time is associated with a significant reduction in happiness, we might be inclined to cut down on screen time. But if we learn that the link between screen time and self-reported well-being is roughly comparable in strength to that between screen time and potato consumption—that is, a trivially small relationship—we might not bother. Instead, we might try to get more sleep, which has a much stronger link to happiness, not to mention health benefits.[2]

When we hear a precise claim, especially one consistent with our expectations and commitments, we tend to idle our critical thinking when we should rev its engine instead. Those looking to fool us often rely on precision because we take precision as a signal of truth. When confronted with a precise claim, cost, or value, we can ask a question. If the number is meant to be impressively large, ask, **"Is that a lot?"** If it is meant to be surprisingly small, ask, **"Is that a little?"** Depending on the nature of the claim, we can ask follow-up questions. Is it still a lot or a little when compared to other things? Is there enough evidence to make such a precise claim? Would I be just as impressed if that number were rounded off (so it wasn't as precise)?

Asking questions like "Is that a lot?" reminds us to compare the cost of a gallon of gas to the other costs associated with driving a car, such as buying the car, financing the purchase, and paying for insurance. It reminds us to think about the total savings from collecting coupons relative to the value of the time we spend doing it. It reminds us to ask whether Ivory is different from any other soap, whether there is enough evidence to report a percentage to two decimal places, and whether we'd be as persuaded if the number were rounded down to 99 percent.[3]

PRECISION MOCKERY

On May 25, 2021, Rand Paul took the floor of the US Senate to argue for a 10 percent cut in the annual budget of the National Science Foundation (NSF). To exemplify the kind of spending he viewed as wasteful, he cited the $874,503 total cost of a single grant on how cocaine changes the sexual behavior of quail. Paul illustrated the project with a comical image of a quail burying its beak in a pile of cocaine. The concreteness of that image, coupled with a cost specific to a single dollar, amplified the impression that the grant truly was a large expense—especially for a study of coked-up quail sex. But that dollar amount represented only a tiny fraction of the budget cut Paul was pushing. Eliminating 10 percent of the NSF's $8.3 billion annual budget—$830 million—would have eliminated not just one but thousands of scientific grants every year.[4]

Paul's fellow senators must be tired of hearing about the quail grant since he has been telling them about it since at least 2018, often showing the same picture, but with different dollar figures attached. He presented it again just four days later, with the dollar figure changed to $356,933.140. This odd numerical format makes it easy to mistake the decimal place as a comma and to thereby misread the cost as more than $356 million. We should be suspicious whenever a big cost is reported with precision to a single dollar, and even more so when it's reported with decimals. When something costs hundreds of thousands of dollars, whether it ends in $3 or $1 is irrelevant, and the fractional-penny precision is an ironic tell that Paul is not really concerned about the cost of a specific research project. Whenever we see a number like this, we should round it and see if it seems less impressive. But that's just the first line of defense—we also need to put those numbers in proper perspective.

By cherry-picking a few grants from thousands, emphasizing their total cost without putting that cost in context, and proposing to cut what sounds like a small percentage of a total budget, Paul relied on our tendency to accept the way facts are framed by a speaker. In isolation, 10 percent sounds small and $874,503 sounds large. Paul did not mention the scale difference between the grant and the entire agency budget, nor did he describe what else would be eliminated by his cuts.

One might argue that $874,503 is too much to spend on a study of sex and drugs in quail, given that it's more than ten times the median family annual income in the United States. We all can imagine other uses for that money that we personally consider more worthy. But we also need to consider how much we value the broader goal of funding science. Inevitably, some projects we don't understand or support will be funded, and a 10 percent cut would never eliminate only those grants we happen to dislike. If we think the government should support science, and we recognize the scale of expenditures necessary to do so, then we need to compare the costs of funding science not to household incomes but to the costs of other comparably large objectives, such as agricultural subsidies, veterans' benefits, and healthcare—everything national governments do is huge in proportion to individual or family budgets. Similarly, if we think the government should not support the arts, we should make that argument on principle, not by pointing to the $200 million budget of the National Endowment for the Arts, which looks like a rounding error when it is compared to the costs of many other government activities, such as $150 billion for transportation infrastructure or $780 billion for defense.

By focusing his audience's attention on the quail grant and a precise dollar amount and leaving unmentioned the total cost of research on drug abuse (let alone the total size of the science budget or US federal spending), Paul also exploited a cognitive pattern known as "denominator neglect." Kimihiko Yamagishi asked students to evaluate the risk to them of each of 11 causes of death, such as homicide, pneumonia, and cancer. Before making their judgment, they saw estimates of how many people die from each cause, either out of 100 people or out of 10,000. For example, they might see a death rate of 12.86 out of 100 (or, equivalently, 1,286 out of 10,000). Participants found all 11 causes riskier when the denominator was 10,000 than when it was 100, even though the death rates were identical. In fact, even when the death rate was somewhat higher in the 100 condition than in the 10,000 condition (such as 24.12 out of 100 versus 1,286 out of 10,000), they still rated death rates out of 10,000 as indicating *greater* risk. The participants were influenced by the size of the numerator (1,286 is much larger than 24.12) without fully correcting for differences in the denominator.[5]

Ironically, if Paul had actually wanted the government to spend less on quail sex research, he should have proposed cuts to the National Institutes of Health (NIH), the popular agency that actually funded that research, not the National Science Foundation. He also should have traveled back in time because the quail sex grant had actually ended in 2016, years before he complained about it.[6]

CONCRETENESS AND PRECISION

Politicians like Rand Paul know intuitively that stories with specific images and precise numbers are persuasive. We have an easier time remembering concrete information because it is stored in memory using both a verbal code and a pictorial one. Abstract ideas, by contrast, don't call to mind specific, universal images. Concrete words like "quail," "sex," and "cocaine" activate regions at the back of the brain that handle visual information. Abstract words like "science," "research," and "addiction" activate the frontal lobes, which process information independent of any particular sense. Concrete words are also better able to trigger strong emotional responses, which strengthen our memory for them.[7]

The appeal of personality typologies, like the Myers-Briggs Type Indicator or the four-color system of Thomas Erikson, endures in part because types are categories, containers with precise boundaries in which everyone shares a concrete set of features. It's easy to think about people if we can precisely label them as one of four colors or sixteen types. Unfortunately, people are not that simple. Studies of personality testing have shown that the type assigned to a person the first time they take a test is likely to be different just a few weeks later—not because their personality has changed dramatically but because their answers on the second test differed by just enough (perhaps due to a change in mood or to the noise inherent in human behavior) to push them across the sharp but arbitrary line dividing one type from another. In reality, personality is less like a distinct category and more like a constellation of many traits, each of which can vary over a wide range, resulting in an explosion of unique combinations.[8]

In a sense, precise numbers—like "$873,503"—are like concrete words or personality types, something we can visualize and compare. That concreteness might help explain why people fell for the misleading infographic on hours of protection from masking: Its message matched their expectations, and it provided exact numbers for different combinations of masks rather than vague statements of more or less protection. It might also explain why ungrounded scientific claims accompanied by exact percentages—for example, that we use only 10 percent of our brain or that 90 percent of communication is nonverbal—are so sticky.

The more precise the numbers, the more persuasive they can be. For example, an analysis of over sixteen thousand home sales in South Florida and Long Island, New York, showed that houses listed with a more precise price (for example, $367,500 versus $370,000) wound up selling for more. The precise starting numbers might create stickier "anchors," meaning that people don't feel there is as much room for negotiation. We can counter that tendency by rounding to a more approximate number before starting a negotiation.[9]

A good cheater knows that maintaining a convincing front over any length of time requires precise, concrete details. Elizabeth Holmes of Theranos, for example, told precise lies about where the US military was deploying her devices and which companies had validated their accuracy. Bernie Madoff paid the high-school-educated employees of his Ponzi hedge fund huge salaries to forge account statements, trading records, and trade confirmations in such minute detail that the prices all matched actual daily stock quotations and the amounts summed to the fictitious account balances at the bottom. Many of his victims did no more than glance at these pages each month, see the precisely reported values, and decide that they looked okay. And con artists who want help recovering their lost riches always state the specific value, form, and currency of the treasure. (Did you ever wonder how they know these details if the treasure has been missing for so long?)

THESE DON'T GO TO FOUR

Measuring twice before cutting once is excellent advice, but it won't help if our measuring device doesn't measure what we think it does. Being fooled by the limits of our own measures or tools is surprisingly common. In the chaos that immediately followed the nuclear reactor explosion at Chernobyl in 1986, the dosimeters on-site registered only 3.6 roentgen per hour, a level that wouldn't warrant evacuating the local population. But 3.6 was the maximum possible reading for those instruments, and that value was reported in an official statement about the situation. Relying on such a device during a nuclear disaster is like weighing yourself with a kitchen scale and concluding that you have met your weight-loss goals. Critical hours passed before better instruments indicated a possible meltdown, making it much harder to contain the disaster and more costly to mitigate it.[10]

The Chernobyl problem is a form of what's known as a false negative, a measurement that reassures us that there's no problem when there really is one. The low roentgen count was mistakenly treated as evidence of low radiation risk. When a device gives a precise answer and we don't know its limits, we must be particularly vigilant about the risk of false negatives. For example, proper negative reports of medical tests, whether for new Covid-19 cases or recurrences of cancer, will use phrases like "none detected" rather than "none present." That's because the tests cannot detect minuscule amounts of virus or the faint early signs of cancer. Without a perfectly sensitive test, it's impossible to prove that something is entirely absent, so it would be improper for the conclusion to be "none present." You could still be infected if the test isn't sensitive enough to detect the infection (for example, if the exposure was so recent that there is not yet enough virus for that test to register it).

The emergency conditions of the early pandemic months saw many other failures to consider the precision and limits of the tools at hand. For example, the UK government's Covid-19 dashboard failed to report 15,841 positive tests that had been conducted during the week of September 25 to October 2, 2020. As a result, people in the UK did not know how much the case numbers had increased in comparison to previous weeks; the corrected numbers turned a flat trend into an upswing. The problem wasn't just an accidental oversight—it was a failure of the measurement tools. Public Health England had gathered log files of results from the private companies that carried out the testing and had merged them automatically into Excel templates, which they then sent to other agencies, including the National Health Service. However, these files used the older Microsoft Excel .xls format, which was limited to a total of 65,536 rows (the current version, .xlsx, can have up to 1,048,576 rows). When the spreadsheet reached its maximum, it stopped adding new test results. The number of reported cases was capped by Excel's own 3.6 roentgen—its row limit—even though the actual number was much higher.[11]

INCREDIBLE PRECISION

Often the hooks that make a claim appealing are precisely what should make it suspect. In a paper published in 2005, which has since been cited more than 3,700 times in the scientific literature, Barbara Fredrickson and Marcial Losada reported discovering what they called a "critical positivity ratio." According to their analysis, people whose ratio of positive to negative emotional experiences exceeds 2.9013 flourish, whereas those with a lower ratio flounder. The uncontroversial notion that people are better off having more positive than negative emotional experiences became eye-catching scientific news because of this exact numerical cutoff for success. The four-decimal-place precision of their positivity ratio implied that the authors had discovered a quantitative law of nature that governs human experience—a rare event in psychology.[12]

Few human behaviors, if any, can be measured accurately to four decimal places. Whenever we see something reported that precisely, we should ask ourselves how much evidence would be needed to support that claim. Would it be a lot? How many experiences would we need from each individual in order to know that the ratio should be precisely 2.9013 and *not* 2.9012 or 2.9014?

The answer is "a lot." We would need to accumulate at least 80,000 negative experiences and about 232,000 positive ones for each person in order to know that the ratio should be 2.9013 and not 2.9014 (or higher). And this is enough only if each experience is unambiguously either positive or negative, we make no errors in counting, and the ratio is identical for every person. (Remember that faulty assumptions can lead to absurd conclusions!) Losada and Fredrickson based their assertion on observations of a comparatively tiny sample of people: interactions among teams of eight executives from sixty companies. With so little data, it's mathematically impossible to conclude that 2.9013 was any more correct than thousands of other equally precise ratios. Would we have found their findings as compelling if the authors had instead concluded that the ratio is "about 3 to 1, but maybe as low as 1 to 1, or perhaps as high as 5 to 1"?[13]

By making a precise claim, Losada and Fredrickson gave their work the impression of greater scientific rigor than it merited. When someone benefits from making an extremely precise claim, we shouldn't grant them a pass if they backtrack and make it more approximate when challenged (in this case, softening the claim to "somewhere around 3"). Calling their positivity ratio "critical" further emphasized the strict boundary between two distinct states (flourish or flounder). Being on the wrong side of a categorical boundary is important—either your army has invaded your neighbor or it hasn't—which is why we take care to map borders precisely.

Not recognizing how much data are needed for a precise answer is an even more common problem outside science. For several years, Twitter estimated in its regulatory filings that 5 percent or fewer of its accounts were operated by bots. Less than a month after concluding his April 2022 agreement to buy the social media company for $44 billion, Elon Musk tweeted that the deal was "temporarily on hold pending details supporting calculation that spam/fake accounts do indeed represent less than 5% of users." To know that percentage with absolute certainty, you'd need to accurately classify virtually all of the more than 214 million unique daily users as bots or nonbots. But Musk proposed a different process: "To find out, my team will do a random sample of 100 followers of @twitter. I invite others to repeat the same process and see what they discover." After a brief legal battle, Musk did eventually buy the company, but the bot dispute still lingered. Would his method have resolved it?[14]

The idea of using a random sample to estimate the true percentage of bots makes sense—it's far more efficient than evaluating every single account. But sampling means you have to take measurement precision into account. If Musk sampled 100 random accounts and found that only 4 were bots, should he be confident that fewer than 10.7 million (5 percent) of the 214 million daily users are bots?

For the sake of argument, let's assume that 7 percent of Twitter users are bots, enough for Musk to want to scuttle the deal. With a random sample of one hundred users and this true bot rate of 7 percent, he would observe five or fewer bots 29 percent of the time—that is, he would have a roughly three-in-ten chance of making a decision that would be wrong by his own criteria!

If the true bot rate were indeed 7 percent, Musk would need to sample more than six hundred accounts to be 99 percent sure that he wouldn't mistakenly observe fewer than 5 percent bots. More precise answers require more data. If Musk wanted to be 99.99 percent sure that he wasn't spending $44 billion to own a platform populated by more than 5 percent bots, and the true bot rate were actually 5.1 percent, he'd need to sample over 332,600 accounts—more than three thousand times as many as he said he would. Moreover, these estimates depend heavily on the bot-detection method being infallible, like a perfectly sensitive Covid-19 test or a perfect classifier of experiences as positive or negative. The numbers would be much higher if the test were imperfect.[15]

MISLED BY MODELS

Fredrickson and Losada's critical positivity ratio was in fact a prediction output by a mathematical model they created, not a value derived from analyzing a sufficiently large sample of human emotional experiences. But like the claim itself, the model assumptions were unjustifiable. Losada apparently applied a set of equations used to model the behavior of fluids to observations of 480 business executives from an earlier study. As Nick Brown, Alan Sokal (the same Alan Sokal who punked a humanities journal), and Harris Friedman explained, the sorts of variables used in the modeling of human emotions do not meet the stringent criteria required to apply those equations. Even if they did, Fredrickson and Losada adapted and tweaked the models in arbitrary ways to generate numerical predictions that came somewhat close to those Losada had reportedly observed in his study of executives. Fredrickson and Losada then presented the model's output as if it were a universal law of human nature.[16]

Brown and colleagues describe the Fredrickson and Losada approach as analogous to "a video of a Rubik's Cube being miraculously solved in five seconds, only for it to be revealed at the end that what was filmed was an ordered cube being scrambled, with the whole sequence then being played back in reverse." In response to this critique, Fredrickson admitted that she had relied on Losada's modeling and "has since come to question it." The journal that had published the original paper issued a correction notice that officially discarded the modeling aspect of the paper from the scientific literature, including "the model-based predictions about the particular positivity ratios."[17]

In part, the positivity-ratio error resulted from treating a mathematical model as if it were a precise description of reality. Instead, models are tools that simplify reality enough to make concrete forecasts and predictions that scientists, companies, and policymakers can then check against reality. Models need not be complex or precise to be useful. For example, "the US stock market returns 7 percent per year" is a model that makes the specific prediction that a $1,000 investment today will be worth $1,967.15 after ten years. Even if this model were correct, we shouldn't expect to end up with that exact amount (because of the noise and inconsistency inherent in financial markets), but we would have good odds of winding up with more than we started with.

Precision does have its virtues. All else being equal, models that make precise predictions are better than models that make vague ones. A model that accurately predicts *how much* your sales will increase as a result of a new marketing campaign is better than one that merely predicts *that* your sales will increase. Knowing that tomorrow will start off rainy before becoming sunny is useful, but knowing the rain will end in time for your 2:00 p.m. outdoor wedding is even better. A precise model is misleading, however, when it provides more precision than is merited by the data or verifiable through observation of the actual results. If the meteorological model lacks accuracy and it rains all day, its precision isn't useful.

Accuracy and precision, though often confused, are fundamentally different concepts. An accurate measuring tool gives something close to the right answer on average. A precise measuring tool gives a detailed, consistent answer, regardless of whether it's right or wrong. The claim of an exact, optimal positivity ratio of 2.9013 has more "truthiness" than truth—it is a precise claim, but that precision can give us the false impression that it's also accurate.

IMPLAUSIBLY PRECISE POLLS

False impressions of accuracy are especially troubling when the subject is public opinion and political preferences. Polls report precise percentages of support for candidates and policies, and they often include a margin of error to indicate some uncertainty. But the estimates can be surprisingly inaccurate when they start with flawed assumptions.

Polls are scientific attempts to say something quantitative about a broad group of people—the voters on election day—without surveying every one of them. If we could somehow poll all the voters in the country in a single survey, we wouldn't need to worry about whether our poll was representative. Whenever we want to claim something about a broad group of people by investigating a smaller subset of them, though, we have to hope that the people we did include are similar *in all relevant ways* to those we excluded.[18]

In political polling, this "representativeness" problem can never be solved completely. The group of people who respond to a poll will never perfectly match the population distribution for all combinations of race, gender, age, education, region, political leaning, willingness to answer calls from an unknown number, and other attributes. Even in the astronomically unlikely event that everyone the pollster calls answers the phone and responds to questions, some segments of society inevitably will be underrepresented and others overrepresented among the respondents.

In order to make their surveys representative of the population as a whole, professional pollsters use weighting schemes to adjust the demographic composition of their samples. If they reach a disproportionate number of older White respondents, they might count each of those responses less in computing their prediction. If they have too small a percentage of young Black voters, each would count more. Still, any two polls, even two samples collected by the same pollster using the same survey on the same day, can produce slightly different predictions.[19]

During the 2016 US presidential election campaign, the *Los Angeles Times* and the University of Southern California ran a tracking poll called Daybreak. Unlike most political polls that survey a new random sample of voters for each new prediction, the Daybreak poll asked the same set of three thousand people—known as a "panel"— about their voting preferences every single day.

The goal of the Daybreak poll was to provide estimates of voting preferences uncontaminated by the noise inherent in changing the sample for each poll. It weighted its sample of three thousand people to match the population demographics as best as it could and recruited people who were willing to state their preference every day. The downside of panels like Daybreak is that if the panel's original composition is odd in some way, the oddities will remain for the life of the poll.[20]

As it turned out, the poll had only two respondents who were young Black men, one a Hillary Clinton supporter and the other a Donald

Trump supporter. Each of them was weighted the same in the overall prediction of who would win the election. But the resulting fifty-fifty split was not representative of how young Black men typically vote in US presidential elections. They tend to overwhelmingly support the Democratic Party candidate. There were so few young Black male Trump voters in the United States that predicting that all young Black male voters would go for Clinton would have been more representative than predicting that 50 percent of them would do so.

Because there were only two such voters in this "group," those two people had an outsized influence on the poll's overall results. Each counted nearly three hundred times as much as the most overrepresented group in the survey (likely older White voters) and about thirty times as much as the average voter in the poll. When that one Trump supporter didn't respond to the pollster on a particular day, the poll's top-line prediction swung by about 1 percent toward Clinton, but when he did respond, it swung 1 percent toward Trump.[21]

HOW MANY PEOPLE DOES IT TAKE TO . . .

The size of the sample in a public opinion poll, market research survey, bot/nonbot classification, or scientific experiment is like the size of the sensor in a camera or the mirror in a telescope—the bigger the sample or sensor, the subtler the differences that we can detect. A precise claim—such as the critical flourishing ratio being 2.9103 positive to negative experiences or there being fewer than 5.00 percent bots on Twitter—requires a large enough sensor to measure it precisely. Similarly, measuring a 90 percent preference for Clinton requires more than two people. In psychology and other social sciences, many studies lack a suitably powerful telescope to provide reliable answers to their empirical questions.[22]

Have you ever wondered whether people who like eggs eat egg salad more often than people who don't like eggs? Neither have we, but a study by decision scientist Joe Simmons and his colleagues confirmed that the answer is yes, they do. Now for the important question: How many people do you think they had to survey in order to reach this conclusion? We could easily mislead ourselves if we asked a few people and the first three happened to like eggs but not egg salad ("Wow, I just discovered something weird!"). Even with the obvious difference in preferences for egg salad they observed between egg lovers and egg haters, we'd have to survey at least forty-seven people each time to have an 80 percent chance of finding the same (or a larger) difference. Testing only ten people would be just slightly better than testing no one at all.[23]

This is the point Simmons was making by carrying out a survey on such obvious relationships. If we have only a small amount of data and we want to draw conclusions any more surprising, definitive, or controversial than "Egg lovers are more likely to enjoy egg salad," we probably don't have enough evidence. Instead, we'd be deceived by a false sense of precision—like looking into a child's toy telescope and concluding that Saturn has no moons.

Imagine that the last two times you were driving to a nearby city, Google Maps suggested an alternative route that would get you there faster. You accepted the suggestion, but each time you soon ran into heavy traffic and arrived even later than you'd originally expected. We've had this experience ourselves, and we've been tempted to opt out of such recommendations in the future or switch to a different navigation app. But are two consecutive errors enough evidence to draw conclusions about a tool you've been using for years? (They might not have been errors—your planned route might also have made you late.) If you happened to pick two good stocks that outperformed an index fund, do you have enough evidence that you can consistently beat the market? If you picked the winner in two Super Bowls, would you quit your job and become a professional sports bettor? Being guided by a tiny sample of recent experiences is the worst way to use data; we almost never have enough evidence for a reliable conclusion, but we always have enough to be fooled.

WHEN ANSWERS ARE PRECISELY WRONG

The more you think about the seductiveness of precision, the more you will notice occasions when people casually throw around precise but impossible numbers. In the first game of a doubleheader on May 8, 2022, the New York Yankees second baseman Gleyber Torres hit the game-winning home run to beat the visiting Texas Rangers. A walk-off homer should be a highlight of any baseball player's season. Yet when speaking to reporters at the end of the day, Rangers manager Chris Woodward poured cold water on Torres's achievement: "Small ballpark, that's an easy out in 99 percent of ballparks . . . just happened to hit it in a little league ballpark to right field." When asked about Woodward's comment, Yankees manager Aaron Boone laughed and wryly observed, "His math is wrong. Ninety-nine percent is impossible. There's only 30 parks."[24]

Just as there can't be 90 percent support for one candidate in a sample of two people, the homer couldn't be an out in exactly 99 percent of ballparks unless there are at least one hundred of them. This sort of mistake—reporting a percentage or average that's impossibly precise—is surprisingly common, and not just for baseball managers. After noticing a number of errors like this in scientific publications they were reading, Nick Brown and James Heathers developed a simple algorithm to check for this form of false precision. They mordantly named it GRIM, for Granularity-Related Inconsistency of Means. The GRIM test checks whether a reported average or percentage is literally impossible given the number of people (or stadiums) that went into it.[25]

Chris Woodward's 99 percent GRIM error was likely intended as an exaggeration for effect, but it was a bad one—Torres's ball traveled 369 feet, so it would, in fact, have been a home run in twenty-six out of the thirty Major League Baseball stadiums (over 86 percent, not 1 percent). In some cases, GRIM inconsistencies result from misunderstanding how to round numbers properly, but in other cases, they reveal more serious problems—percentages or averages that sound plausible but are actually impossible.

It's easy to spot impossible averages like 90 percent of two voters or 99 percent of thirty ballparks. And if you toss a coin exactly ten times, you can't get 5.5 heads. But with other numbers, GRIM errors are less obvious. Imagine a scientific paper that reports asking eleven people to rate their happiness on a 1 to 7 scale, and finding an average of 3.86. This value sounds reasonable enough, but a bit of arithmetic shows that the closest you can get to 3.86 is either 3.81818 or 3.90909, neither of which rounds to 3.86.[26]

Before GRIM, nobody had thought to check systematically whether the averages reported in scientific articles might be mathematically impossible (even though the math involved is no more complicated than basic arithmetic). Brown and Heathers applied GRIM to the averages reported in a large number of articles in prominent psychology journals and found errors far more often than we might expect. Among articles that reported enough information to run the test, about half had at least one GRIM error, and more than 20 percent had multiple errors. When Brown and Heathers examined the original data from these articles, they found that many of the errors were due to sloppiness, but in several cases, the errors were consequential enough that the articles required substantial corrections to their statistical conclusions. By now this should be a familiar pattern; mistaken conclusions and outright fraud in scientific articles are most often detected when people open one or two doors behind the headline and find that the details—in this case, the arithmetic calculations—don't support the claims.[27]

THE TRAP IN EXTRAPOLATION

Just as our attraction to precision can deceive us when we're making inferences from models and from small samples of data, it can give us unwarranted confidence in predictions about the future. The US

Department of Transportation makes regular reports to Congress that estimate the total number of vehicle miles traveled in the country that year and predict road traffic up to twenty years into the future. Year after year, the reports have forecast steady growth in traffic volume. Yet that growth tapered off in the late 1990s, and traffic volume actually declined slightly in the early 2000s. Eric Sundquist, the director of the University of Wisconsin's State Smart Transportation Initiative, analyzed these forecasts in 2013 and discovered that the models had been created based on trends that held true in the 1980s and hadn't been updated since. The financial and societal stakes of using such outdated models are high. Underpredict future traffic, and roads will be clogged and crumbling. Overpredict, as these models did, and we will squander resources on unneeded construction.[28]

Just as political predictions are accurate only if they are based on representative samples, model predictions for the future—or for any new data—are useful only if the model itself is calibrated using similar data. Predicting future outcomes for cases like those you've seen before is relatively safe. Extrapolating beyond what you've seen can be disastrous.

One of our favorite examples of the dangers of extrapolation, and one we use in our teaching, involves a prediction for 100-meter sprint times. Over the past one hundred years, world record times have dropped for both men and women, but the drop has been steeper for women. In 1922, the record 100-meter time was 10.4 seconds for men and 12.8 seconds for women, a gap of 2.4 seconds in favor of men. As of 2022, the records were 9.58 and 10.49 seconds for men and women, a gap of only 0.91 seconds. A scientific article in the journal *Nature* extrapolated the linear improvements in Olympic records for the 100-meter dash since 1900 for men and women (averaging about 0.011 seconds faster per year for men and 0.017 seconds per year for women) into the future, and predicted that women would outperform men by 2156, when it forecast a time of 8.079 seconds for women and

8.098 for men. But we know that this linear trend can't continue unabated into the future. If it did, then by the year 2636, people would be able to finish the 100-meter dash before they started it—and women would achieve this miracle years before men![29]

Extrapolating linear trends is dicey enough, but extrapolating more complex patterns can be even more problematic, in part because we don't intuitively understand them as well. If we are watching a car go down a highway, it's easier to see how fast it's moving (changing location) than to judge how much it is accelerating (changing speed). Numbers that start out small, perhaps too small to attract worry or even notice, can reach disturbing levels faster than we intuitively realize—as the world saw with the exponential spread of Covid-19.

Much as compounding interest amplifies wealth, the exponential (colloquially, "viral") growth of anything amplifies its impact. For instance, if 10 people in your town are newly diagnosed with Covid-19 each day, then after 10 days there will be 100 more cases. The trend is linear at a rate of 10 per day; if we drew a graph with the date on the x-axis and the total number of cases on the y-axis, we would have a straight line going up and to the right. Now imagine instead that there were 10 new Covid-19 cases diagnosed on one day. On the next day, there were 11 new cases, on the third day 12, and then 13 and 14 on days 4 and 5, respectively. We would see the number of new cases increasing every day, but it would be harder to intuit that there would be a total of 145 cases after 10 days and over 200 by day 13. The rate of change is tiny—growth of one more new case each day than the previous day—but the consequence is 45 percent more cases after 10 days than would happen with a constant number of new cases each day. The graph would be curved upward, with the slope increasing as it goes farther to the right, meaning that as time goes by, it will take less and less additional time for the total number of cases to increase by the same amount.

To make a precise forecast in the face of exponential growth, we need to do the math. But to avoid being blindsided by exponential growth, we just need to check whether the rate is increasing over time and know that if it is, it won't take long for the problem to get out of hand. A simple rule of thumb works well: Look for anything that doubles within a short time period. And be especially wary if it takes even less time to double again. We could be seeing a once-in-a-century pandemic—or the business opportunity of a lifetime.

CUBISM

In early May 2020, when the United States still had relatively few documented deaths from Covid-19, the Trump administration pushed to lift public health restrictions, against the recommendations of its own task force and in the face of expert predictions that the country would have 200,000 deaths by June 1. The White House justified its policy by pointing to its own "cubic" model, which predicted that daily deaths would drop to zero by May 15.[30]

The Trump administration's model was created not by an infectious disease expert or epidemiologist but by an economic adviser named Kevin Hassett. He appears to have tried different functions in Microsoft Excel, which can automatically fit trend lines with various shapes to any set of data, until he found one that made rosy predictions.[31]

A cubic model changes direction twice; it starts high, then drops, then climbs, then drops again. Or . . . it starts low, then climbs, then drops, then climbs again. What happens at the start of the curve determines the direction it is going when the data end and extrapolation begins. Their cubic-model prediction that deaths would fall to zero depended on treating the pattern of small fluctuations in daily deaths during the early days of the pandemic as a decreasing trend so that the ensuing trend of increasing deaths would eventually reverse course, leading to a decreasing trend when extrapolated into the future. However, treating those initial days instead as a period of increasing daily deaths would result in an extrapolation that would forecast a large increase in deaths. As we now know, Hassett's prediction of the pandemic's imminent end was wrong. As of mid-May 2020, the United States was experiencing about 1,500 deaths each day.[32]

The Trump administration wasn't alone in making overly rosy predictions. Before the start of the fall 2020 semester, the University of Illinois predicted that its Urbana-Champaign campus would have a "worst-case" total of 700 cases over the course of the entire semester, with no more than 100 infectious people on campus at any time and with daily cases dropping to single digits within weeks. Whenever anyone claims that a prediction or forecast is a worst-case scenario, be wary—there is almost always a worse one. In reality, the campus had 3,923 cases by late November, averaging nearly 40 new cases per day. Unlike the White House's cubic model, the university's models were mathematically rigorous—but like the cubic model, the conclusions stemmed from flawed starting assumptions.[33]

The prediction of a total of 700 cases assumed that undergraduates would comply perfectly with testing and contact tracing and that students would be notified of a positive test result within 24 hours. Not surprisingly for a large public university known for raucous parties, compliance was far less than 100 percent, and during the crucial early weeks of the semester, test results were delayed well over 24 hours.

The problem wasn't with the models. It was with how they were interpreted and used. Perhaps the most egregious aspect of this prediction was its unwarranted precision. The university gave no indication that 700 cases was only one in a vast range of possibilities and that the 700-case prediction depended on critical assumptions about compliance and testing. Using more realistic assumptions, the same models predicted 3,000–8,000 cases.[34]

People who are trying to hook us make precise promises. But we wouldn't find this precision persuasive if the promises didn't already appeal to us. The academic reviewers and editor who evaluated the impossibly precise critical flourishing ratio likely accepted the underlying premise that people who have more positive experiences are more likely to thrive and they wanted to believe in the power of psychological science to derive quantitative laws. Administrators at the University of Illinois who wanted to avoid a semester of fully remote learning were happy to act on the precise "worst case" estimate of seven hundred cases. The Trump administration wanted Covid-19 to be a smaller problem than it was, so they accepted the precise prediction of a rapid drop to zero deaths.

Zero Covid-19 deaths in a few weeks should have seemed too good to be true, and history records that it was. Usually when something is too good to be true, it's both too precise and too impressive, like Charles Ponzi's promise of a return of 50 percent in 90 days. In this chapter, we've seen how easily we can be hooked by precisely stated claims that aren't justified—mistaken inferences drawn from erroneous model assumptions, overgeneralization based on small samples, and too-perfect predictions of future events. In the next chapter, we'll discuss the ways in which we're hooked by claims of potency—offers in which the benefits or effects are out of proportion to the costs or causes involved.

CHAPTER 8

POTENCY—BE WARY OF "BUTTERFLY EFFECTS"

According to the popular science cliché, a butterfly flapping its wings in Brazil can cause a tornado in Texas. We find potency unduly persuasive, when in reality, we should be wary whenever anyone claims that a big effect can come from a small cause.

IN 2021, AMERICAN SOCIAL MEDIA INFLUENCER CAROLINE CALloway launched her own brand of essential oils with a marketing blitz to her more than 600,000 Instagram followers. Calloway had gained infamy for provocative claims and event promotions that seemed to fall through at a high rate—receiving a six-figure book deal and then failing to deliver the book, launching a national workshop tour but failing to reserve venues, and so on—somehow landing on her feet and walking away to the next thing every time. She apparently didn't keep anyone's money—she returned the publisher's advance and refunded the workshop participants—so she's not a scammer in the most egregious sense. But she was sufficiently aware of her own reputation to own it by naming her new product Snake Oil.[1]

From Dr. Pierce's Pleasant Pellets during the 1918 influenza pandemic to frontal lobotomies in the mid-twentieth century to hydroxychloroquine and ivermectin during the Covid-19 pandemic, people in distress often seek unproven, risky medical treatments. Some of these "miracle drugs" are effective for other disorders—hydroxychloroquine is a standard antimalarial and ivermectin an effective antiparasitic. But the alternative uses for such drugs bear the hallmarks of pseudoscience: a founder story in which a lone genius discovers their utility, an evidence base of personal testimonials rather than randomized clinical trials, and unverifiable claims of unprecedented effectiveness in treating a tremendous variety of ailments.[2]

WHY SNAKE OIL SALESMEN DESERVE THEIR REPUTATION—BUT SNAKE OIL DOESN'T

Claims of miracle therapies are commonplace today, but they reached their apex in the patent medicine era of the late nineteenth century. The transcontinental railroad was built in the 1880s, and its construction relied heavily on Chinese immigrants. This backbreaking physical labor was often the only work available to them. In the era before modern medicine, when even aspirin had yet to be discovered, laborers had few ways to quell the pain of aching joints and muscles. The Chinese workers relied on a traditional medicine: snake oil. At the time, snake oil was used throughout the world, most commonly as a muscle relaxant or an anesthetic to deaden joint pain. Chinese snake oil came mostly from water snakes, Europeans used vipers, and Native American tribes used rattlesnakes.[3]

One person is perhaps more responsible for the present reputation of snake oil than anyone else: Clark Stanley, also known as "the Rattlesnake King." At the 1893 World's Columbian Exhibition in Chicago, Stanley set up a booth where he handled snakes and handed out an odd fifty-three-page pamphlet titled *The Life and Adventures of the American Cowboy: True Life in the Far West*. It juxtaposed an initial section on the glories of cowboy life with a second section touting the amazing and wide-ranging health benefits of his snake-oil liniment—which he also offered for sale at the fair.

To promote his snake oil remedy, Stanley followed the pseudoscience script. He claimed to have learned the ancient secret of snake-oil medicine while living among the Moki Indians (now the Hopi tribe) in Walpi, Arizona, for two years in the 1870s. According to his advertisements, Stanley's snake-oil liniment worked far better than other treatments, "banishing pain with a power that has astonished the medical profession." He reported having tried snake oil on friends, and he claimed that it treated "Rheumatism, Neuralgia, Sciatica, Lame Back, Lumbago, Contracted Cords, Toothache, Sprains, Swellings, Frost Bites, Chill Blains, Bruises, Sore Throat, Bites of Animals, Insects and Reptiles," adding that it "kills the poison, relieves the pain, reduces the swelling and heals the wound." He hyped his snake oil as "a wonderful pain destroying compound" and "the strongest and best liniment known for the cure of all pain and lameness."

Whereas modern medical advertising is heavily regulated in most countries and medicines are tested for both efficacy and safety before they can be marketed as a treatment for any ailment, no such rules existed in the United States before 1906, and claims of broad benefits from traditional remedies were commonplace. Dan has a collection of medicine bottles from the late 1800s and early 1900s, offering a diverse sampling of unregulated remedies that claimed potency for a huge and unrelated set of ailments. Hymosa from the Walker Pharmacal Company was "a compound for the treatment of rheumatism, neuralgia, gout, lumbago, sciatica, and all rheumatic affections" (20 percent alcohol). Dr. Hand's Pleasant Physic was intended "for the relief of infants, children, or adults suffering from constipation. It is of especial value during pregnancy, after confinement, and in obstinate constipation. It stimulates the liver, tones the bowels, and does not gripe" (6 percent alcohol). St. Jacob's Oil was touted as "the great German remedy for rheumatism, neuralgia, backache, burns, scalds, sprains, swellings, bruises, corns, bunions, household accidents, and for all diseases of horses and cattle" (no alcohol!). Similar claims can still be found today in the market for supplements and vitamins, which are regulated only as a food and not as a drug by the FDA.[4]

Clark Stanley took advantage of lax regulatory standards to build a successful snake-oil business, with factories in Massachusetts and Rhode Island. Only years later, after the Pure Food and Drug Act of 1906 was passed, were his products investigated. In 1917, he was fined $20 (about $475 today) for deceptive advertising claims. However, the deception for which he was fined was not the claim to cure everything from sciatica to sore throats, nor his dubious discovery story, nor even his hyping of an ineffective treatment. He was fined because his snake-oil liniment contained no actual snake oil![5]

Snake oil might be of use for pain relief even if it is not the cure-all Stanley promoted; there is not much scientific evidence for or against it. But snake-oil salesmen deserve their reputation for hyping the purported effectiveness of products in the absence of evidence and promoting a cure based on mechanisms that could not possibly have the benefits they claim.

We can often spot deceptive claims of extreme potency by asking, **"What's the active ingredient?"** Asking ourselves what part of a product or treatment is doing the work—or whether there may be several active elements aside from the one we've been told about—helps us to see why it might appear to be more effective than it actually is. Most homeopathic remedies, for instance, include no more than a trivial amount of any active ingredient, and any perceived benefits are due to placebo effects and natural recovery. The same is true of Reiki and other "energy therapies" that involve detection and manipulation of energy fields, sometimes over long distances, to diagnose and treat disease. Neither the existence of such fields nor the ability of practitioners to affect them has been demonstrated scientifically.

We might also wonder how the world would be different if a product or service actually were as potent as advertised. The fact that psychics haven't bankrupted every casino and won every lottery means that a preternatural ability to see the future is not involved in their forecasts.

VIDEO GAMES DON'T CURE AGING

Clark Stanley was not the first to be fined for overhyping scientific or medical claims, and he won't be the last. In 2016, Lumos Labs, the maker of the popular "brain-training" program Lumosity, agreed to change their advertising and paid $2 million to settle a charge by the US Federal Trade Commission (FTC) of unsubstantiated advertising claims about the potent, "proven" benefits of its products, such as "Lumosity gives students a boost in classrooms worldwide" and "Healthy adults can benefit from Lumosity training." Other brain-training companies like LearningRx and Carrot Neurotechnology have also settled claims with the FTC for deceptive advertising.[6]

We all want to stave off the cognitive consequences of aging. Everyone would like to be better at focusing attention and remembering names, events, and where they left their keys. The cognitive training industry claims to have found a treatment for mental decline, but it draws on many of the same marketing ploys used by Clark Stanley. Company websites tout their founder's discovery of the therapy or treatment, rely on personal testimonials about the effectiveness of their products, and claim extraordinarily broad benefits from fairly trivial interventions. In our own comprehensive review of the studies these companies have touted as evidence, we found virtually no support for the idea that practicing cognitive tasks improves real-world cognition or makes healthy people smarter.[7]

The notion that a butterfly can cause a tornado to spawn thousands of miles away is the prototype for "a small change makes a

huge difference," which has become a universal template for generating interest, clicks, shares, and all the other rewards that come with
publicity. The few potent yet tiny interventions that actually work
are exceptionally valuable. Vaccines and antibiotics are unicorns:
one time injections or short courses of pills that can make the difference between immediate death and decades of life and can translate
into enormous positive returns in health and longevity for society and
civilization at large. But stories like these are far rarer than we think;
most of the time, life hacks won't change your life, and big effects result from big interventions.[8]

SUSPECT PRIMES

So profound is the appeal of overly potent effects that it can penetrate
the cognitive defenses of people who should know better, including
the researcher most famous for documenting our cognitive foibles,
Nobel Prize winner Daniel Kahneman. In Chapter 4 of his bestselling
book *Thinking, Fast and Slow*, Kahneman described a series of studies
showing how subtle, almost unnoticed influences can substantially
alter our thoughts and behaviors.[9]

One study, for example, reported the "Lady Macbeth effect": After
you watched a short film clip meant to elicit disgust, physically clean-
ing your hands was said to "wash away" that experience and lead you
to judge moral transgressions to be less severe. Another study found
that hanging a picture of eyes in a breakroom increased voluntary
contributions to the use of the communal coffee machine. In the most
famous and influential of these experiments, college students were
asked to create sentences from sets of words. For some participants,
half of the sets included words about being elderly, such as "wrinkle,"
"forgetful," and "Florida." After completing this task, the students left
the laboratory and walked to the elevator. However, the experiment
had not ended; a researcher surreptitiously timed their walk to test
the hypothesis that the people who had been thinking about words

related to old age would be unconsciously "primed" to walk more slowly, as an elderly person would. Sure enough, the students who were primed took one additional second on average to walk the approximately 10 meters to the elevator. This finding made a big splash. If subtle, unnoticed features of the world around us can have such potent influences, then we must have much less control of our actions and decisions than we intuitively believe.[10]

Kahneman knew that these findings would be implausible to skeptical readers, so he made sure to hammer home how strong he thought the evidence was: "The idea you should focus on, however, is that disbelief is not an option. The results are not made up, nor are they statistical flukes. You have no choice but to accept that the major conclusions of these studies are true. More important, you must accept that they are true about *you*." He might be right that none of these findings were "made up." But in the years since Kahneman insisted that these metaphor-driven priming results were beyond question, many have been subjected to independent attempts at replication, and none has emerged unscathed.

Soon after publishing his book in 2011—and not long after an independent laboratory failed to replicate the elderly priming study with more rigorous methods than the original—Kahneman penned a letter to priming researchers imploring them to shore up the foundations of their science by replicating each other's work. He wrote, "Your field is now the poster child for doubts about the integrity of psychological research. . . . I believe that you should collectively do something about this mess."

The letter was met mostly with silence but occasionally with denial and resistance. For example, in an interview with science journalist Ed Yong, the social psychologist Norbert Schwarz argued, "You can think of this as psychology's version of the climate-change debate . . . the consensus of the vast majority of psychologists closely familiar with work in this area gets drowned out by claims of a few persistent priming skeptics." In science, comparing critics to climate-change deniers is an extremely low blow.[11]

Six years later, John Bargh, the senior author of the influential elderly-walking study, published a book arguing that subtle factors have pervasive influences on our actions and thoughts in daily life, even proposing that these priming effects could be harnessed for a new form of psychotherapy. His book contained no evidence of grappling with the failures to replicate his own work and that of others. Instead, it ignored them. He omitted studies that other researchers had failed to replicate—including his elderly priming effect—but included similar, not-yet-replicated studies, many of them from the same scientific papers as the ones he left out of the book. If you read Bargh's book without any foreknowledge, you would have no idea that the main scientific field it covers was a "poster child for doubts about the integrity of psychological research."[12]

In the same year that Bargh published his book, Kahneman reflected on the effects of his letter: "I hoped that the authors of this research would rally to bolster their case by stronger evidence, but this did not happen." If these social priming effects are so potent that they determine our daily thoughts, actions, and behaviors, their adherents should have had little trouble reproducing them in well-controlled laboratory studies. Instead, they spent more effort arguing that independent, direct replication—a bedrock principle of science found in elementary school textbooks—was irrelevant to their field.[13]

HOLDING THE WARMTH EFFECT TO THE FIRE

Although few researchers who had published findings of social priming took up Kahneman's challenge, outsiders did. Like many psychologists, we were intrigued by the remarkable findings of the elderly priming study. In our own discipline, cognitive psychology, priming is an established phenomenon, but there it refers to the notion that seeing one word or image will slightly enhance our ability to see or process an identical or related word or image moments later. A core principle in cognitive psychology is that priming becomes weaker as the difference in meaning between the prime and the target increases; the weaker the association and the more conceptual jumps between them, the weaker the effect. The notion that unscrambling sentences for a few minutes unconsciously spread to the general idea of aging and thence to the association between aging and walking speed, thereby causing someone to walk more slowly in a different place some time later, is implausible in light of what we know from decades of rigorous priming research.[14]

Nonetheless, there was a chance that Bargh had discovered one of those extraordinarily rare butterfly effects. Rather than accept the potency of these metaphorical priming results at face value or dismiss them out of hand, we decided to check for ourselves. We worked with our students to replicate a more recent finding from the Bargh group that followed the same priming logic. That study, published in *Science* in 2008, tested the idea that experiencing physical warmth would activate the concept of warmth, thereby priming other meanings of warmth, including interpersonal warmth, and leading people to judge other people to be "warmer." The paper reported a big effect in each of two experiments. People who held a warm cup of coffee gave "personality warmth" ratings about half a point higher on a 1–7 scale than did people who held a cold cup. And people who briefly held a warm therapeutic pack acted more prosocially than did those who held a cold therapeutic pack. We followed the procedures of both of these experiments as closely as we could, except that we tested more than three times as many participants. We found virtually no effect of holding something warm on how people thought or behaved immediately afterward.[15]

As a scientific journal editor, Dan has overseen replication efforts by independent teams of researchers that scrutinized similar claims of powerful effects from small interventions. Most have not held up. One of these, a 1979 study by Thomas Srull and Robert Wyer, helped to launch the entire literature on such priming effects; it provided a recipe for later researchers to follow and has been cited over 2,400 times. College student participants first rearranged sets of words to form sentences (the same task Bargh used years later to prime elderliness). They then read a brief story in which the main character acted in ways that potentially could be interpreted as hostile. For some participants, most of the word sets could only form sentences that described hostile actions. For others, most formed neutral sentences. Those primed by descrambling hostile sentences rated the story character as three points more hostile on a 0-to-10 scale. When converted to a common statistical scale, that difference in hostility ratings was more than twice as big as such obvious differences as the heights of men and women or the number of years older and younger people expect to work before retiring. Yet in the project Dan edited, across twenty-two replication attempts of that study design, all using a standardized protocol, with more than seven thousand participants in total, the average increase in hostility ratings was a mere 0.08 points.[16]

In 2017, Ulrich Schimmack of the University of Toronto analyzed each of the priming studies that Daniel Kahneman's book had cited as incontrovertible evidence and found that most of those original studies provided little statistical evidence for their claims. Accordingly, replication studies conducted by independent laboratories since 2011 have found that people don't actually walk more slowly after unscrambling sentences related to aging, washing one's hands does not make moral judgments less severe, getting people to recall the Ten Commandments doesn't make them more honest, and flashing images of money does not make people more selfish.[17]

Kahneman later admitted that he had been wrong to place so much trust in "the results of underpowered studies with unreasonably small samples" and that he had blinded himself to their implausible potency: "I knew all I needed to know to moderate my enthusiasm for the surprising and elegant findings that I cited, but I did not think it through." The robustness Kahneman initially saw in social priming research was that of a castle made of sand. But after witnessing six years of failed replications, Kahneman revised his views. He noted that the size of behavioral priming effects "cannot be as large and as robust as my chapter suggested," and he warned that authors like him "should be wary of using memorable results of underpowered studies as evidence for their claims." A Nobel laureate—who had written an influential paper decades earlier about the dangers of putting faith in results from small studies—admitted that he himself had been hooked by the supposed potency of priming.[18]

Had Kahneman approached the priming phenomenon with more skepticism, he might have realized how implausibly big the effects were. One study he cited, for example, claimed that priming people with photographs of classrooms and school lockers made them more likely to vote for additional school funding. The primes were so potent that their effect was larger than the difference in support for school funding between people with and without children! The same logic would have cast doubt on the warmth priming studies that we could not replicate. The original paper reported an impact of holding a warm therapeutic pack on generosity that would be almost 50 percent larger than the difference in charitable contributions made by high- and low-income people. If that were true, then nonprofit organizations would have learned long ago to do all their fundraising on warm summer days—which they don't.[19]

ARE "VOTERS" MORE LIKELY TO VOTE?

If their results were correct, studies showing potent effects of trivial primes on judgments, ratings, and walking speed would be scientifically important. But in the real world, we're rarely asked to do such psychology laboratory tasks as unscrambling sentences or numerically rating someone's warmth on a personality survey. There are studies, however, that have sought ways to address complex societal problems using similar "light-touch" interventions. Many of these interventions have claimed to find much bigger effects for real, important outcomes than the effects associated with more traditional, intensive interventions.

When an electorate is polarized, as it has been in the United States for several cycles, success at the polls depends less on persuading voters to switch their support than on getting the people who already support a candidate to actually cast their ballots. Political campaigns have developed sophisticated techniques to turn out voters likely to support their candidates, because even small increases in turnout can matter. Getting those increases, however, is not easy; even the best messaging techniques have limited benefits. For example, an analysis of multiple studies of door-to-door canvassing found an average turnout benefit of 4.3 percent, roughly one additional voter for every twenty-three people canvassed. A separate meta-analysis found that direct mail applying social pressure to vote increased voting by 2.3 percent. Phone calls from volunteers increased turnout by 2.9 percent, calls from commercial phone banks increased turnout by 0.8 percent, and automated "robocalls" did so by only 0.1 percent.[20]

Since these logical, tried, and tested approaches carry high costs for low returns, it makes sense to be skeptical of interventions claiming dramatically bigger benefits. We certainly were skeptical when we heard about a 2011 paper hypothesizing that people would be more likely to vote if they were primed to think of themselves as someone who votes than if primed to think of the importance of voting.[21]

The paper reported an experiment in California before the 2008 presidential election in which participants who were asked to answer "How important is it to you to *be a voter* in the upcoming election?" were 13.7 percent more likely to vote than were participants asked to answer "How important is it to you to *vote* in the upcoming election?" In a separate experiment with voters in a New Jersey election, those who got the identity-priming "be a voter" version were 11.9 percent more likely to vote than those who got the "to vote" version. This subtle change to the wording of a single survey item appeared to have three times the impact of visiting voters in person and encouraging them to go to the polls.[22]

If this were true, it would make the three words "be a voter" into an elixir for political engagement whose potency appears all the more striking in light of the barrage of other "get out the vote" messages that the participants in these experiments likely heard and viewed between the time of the study and election day. By now you might have anticipated the plot twist in this story. Sadly, it's not really a twist—it's exactly what we have come to expect in cases like this. In 2016, the same journal published a much larger study that found that in Michigan, Missouri, and Tennessee primary elections, voters asked about voting and voters asked about being a voter were about equally likely to vote. And crucially, neither group was more likely to vote than those asked about grocery shopping, a control condition that should have no effect on voting. In other words, neither question about voting had any effect on the likelihood of voting. In contrast, a more traditional get-out-the-vote message increased turnout by about 2.1 percent, in line with prior research on phone-call effects.[23]

Social psychologists and researchers in marketing, consumer behavior, and the branch of applied behavioral science known as "nudging" like to study the effects of these sorts of subtle wording interventions on important, real behaviors and judgments. If they worked, they would yield practical benefits at little cost. But their true effects almost always range from small to nonexistent. In a different domain, a 2011 study reported a big effect of a subtle difference in phrasing: Describing a person who "was shooting" a gun, as opposed to a person who "shot" a gun, led to much higher judgments of criminal intentionality. A later set of twelve independent replications found a tiny effect . . . in the opposite direction. The lack of evidence for subtle wording influences on behavior hasn't deterred political campaigns from using them; prior to the 2022 US election, we both received postcards emphasizing the importance of "being a voter."[24]

Many "too potent to be true" claims promote quick, simplistic fixes for complex societal problems, such as racial disparities in educational attainment and school discipline. For example, a 2011 paper in the journal *Science* reported a 79 percent drop in the grade-point-average gap between White and Black college students following a one-hour classroom intervention. A similarly lightweight self-affirmation intervention purportedly reduced racial disparities in suspensions between Black and White secondary-school students.[25]

Exercises like these, described enthusiastically by their proponents as "wise interventions," have received extensive attention because they are said to yield massive effects with minimal effort—a brief, onetime classroom activity rather than costly changes in the personnel, curriculum, or organization of the school. They purport to quickly counteract the cumulative impact of years of racial, societal, and structural inequalities that collectively contribute to lower academic performance when far more extensive interventions have made little headway.

Whenever you read that a new study shows huge benefits from a single brief experience, remember to compare its "active ingredients" to other, more established approaches to solving the same problems. Complex problems usually require multipronged solutions, if they are solvable at all, and rarely yield to the proverbial "one simple trick." We should meet any claim that contradicts this principle with a demand for the strongest level of evidence.[26]

To be clear, we are not arguing that any of these studies are fraudulent or deliberately deceptive. We are suggesting that you should be skeptical of them and others like them. Even the most responsibly and transparently executed research sometimes gives the wrong answer. But publishers, the media, and the rest of us gravitate to studies showing incredibly potent results. In contrast to laboratory word-priming studies, "wise intervention" studies require resources and access possessed by relatively few research groups. This means few such studies are subjected to replication by independent, disinterested researchers. When they have been, the results have tended to be far less impressive. In the absence of such replication, the best stance is—as usual—to remain uncertain.

Doing so can be challenging because findings of huge effects from tiny interventions are widely promoted and enter the popular consciousness almost instantly, whereas a measured scientific appraisal takes time (if it happens at all). More often than not, those initial, exciting results suffer a thousand cuts over the ensuing years, but they rarely die. As we mentioned in our discussion of precision, robust conclusions usually require much more data than we think they do. Here are a few examples:

- A 2003 study with only 17 participants reported that playing first-person shooter video games improved performance on laboratory cognitive tasks. It was published in *Nature*, has been cited more than 3,500 times, and was followed by extensive popular media coverage, including a TED talk that has been viewed more than eight million times. Independent replications by other labs generally find far smaller effects, and meta-analyses that correct for selective publication show little or no benefit.[27]
- A 2010 study of 42 participants reported that those who held their bodies in two separate "power poses" for one minute each subsequently had increased testosterone levels, decreased cortisol levels, greater risk tolerance, and stronger feelings of power than those in a control group. The study was published in *Psychological Science* and has been cited more than 1,400 times. A TED talk on power posing has been viewed more than sixty-seven million times. Subsequent studies found no evidence

of hormonal changes or risk tolerance, the key findings of the study, and the first author of the original study has since disavowed the results.[28]

- A series of studies and scientific papers in the late 1980s and early 1990s touted the idea that "mastery orientation," which is now known as "growth mindset," helps people overcome adversity. A 2006 book and 2014 TED talk (viewed by more than fourteen million people) brought this work to the mainstream. As the psychologist Stuart Ritchie notes, advocates have claimed vast implications of adopting a growth mindset: Possessing one constitutes a "basic human right" and might even help resolve the Israel-Palestine conflict. Yet a recent meta-analysis shows little evidence that brief interventions designed to instill a growth mindset have any real effect on academic performance, the main focus of the mindset movement.[29]

When an initial finding leads to news headlines, popular books, and TED talks, it will remain widely believed long after scientists know its limitations. That's why a single incredible result (or even a series of them) from a single research team should rarely drive policy.

THE YOUNGMAN TEST

Henny Youngman, the comedian known as "the King of the One-Liners," liked to say, "Someone asked me 'How's your wife?' and I said 'Compared to what?'" The examples in this chapter have highlighted one of the primary ways that marketers, politicians, and even some scientists take us in. Knowingly or unknowingly, they exaggerate the efficacy or impact of a product, service, treatment, policy, or intervention. We are fooled when we evaluate results in isolation without comparing them to anything else. To know whether the benefits of a product or treatment are too good to be true, remember Youngman's joke and ask yourself, **"Compared to what?"**

Compare the potency of what's on offer to that of other things in the same domain. For getting out the vote, compare the effects of minuscule changes in survey wording to more intensive efforts like phone banking and door-to-door canvassing. For claims about the power of a brief intervention, look at the known effects of more sustained interventions, or look at salient factors we know have a meaningful impact and see how large they are. For example, compare the effects of a get-out-the-vote intervention to the difference in turnout of Black voters when Barack Obama was on the presidential ballot (an average of 61.4 percent in 2008 and 2012) to their turnout when he was not (56.1 percent in 2004 and 2016); the difference is just 5.3 percent. A long line of research in behavioral decision-making shows that people evaluate options more accurately when they can see more than one option at a time. [30]

We can also imagine how the world would differ if the claim were true. If politicians could dramatically increase turnout by telling people to think of themselves as voters, wouldn't they have figured that out decades ago? If merely describing an action as "was shooting" rather than "shot" yielded more convictions, wouldn't prosecutors do that every time? If our actions were so heavily influenced by fleeting exposures to physical sensations and words, wouldn't people trying to influence us for a living have gained total control of our actions by now?

DOES GRAND THEFT AUTO MAKE MURDERERS?

Moral panics about new media forms and technologies go back at least to ancient Greece. From the invention of written language to printed books to rock lyrics to the Internet, some people will see social changes as evidence of declining standards and will blame whatever "kids today" are playing, watching, or using. In the 1950s, parents were warned to keep teenagers from watching Elvis Presley because his dancing would inspire promiscuity. In the 2000s, Google and

PowerPoint were said to be making us "stoopid," and smartphones and social media are blamed for current trends in social isolation, depression, and suicide.[31]

Measuring the *actual* consequences of changes in technology use and media consumption is devilishly hard. If social scientists wanted to conduct an experiment to test the popular belief that playing violent games causes actual violence, their ethics committees might not let them measure how often their participants assaulted their research assistants. So researchers in this field use simplified laboratory tasks to measure what they deem to be aggressive behavior. For example, they might measure whether people choose to send an opponent in a game a louder and longer blast of unpleasant noise. In doing so, researchers assume anything that increases "laboratory aggression" would also increase real-world aggression.[32]

We've already discussed the importance of understanding the scale along which things are measured in order to avoid being deceived by overly precise claims. Having a sense of scale is also essential in evaluating potency. For example, we can check whether a reported effect is bigger than the largest effect that could possibly be measured using that scale.

Joe Hilgard applied this logic to critique a prominent 2013 study of the effects of video games on aggression. The participants in that study were randomly assigned to play either a violent or a nonviolent game for a total of one hour spread over three consecutive days. Then they were asked to write what would happen next in a story, and they were given the opportunity to blast their gaming opponents with unpleasant noise. Players of the violent game wrote more aggressive content and blasted their opponents with more noise. A lot more. Hilgard thought the study results were implausible: "If one hour of violent games divided across three days caused such dramatic changes in aggressive thoughts and behavior, we would notice whenever our friends or students purchased a new violent video game." Police would be on alert, and everyone would have figured out to steer clear of gamers for days after a new release dropped.[33]

Hilgard wondered what the largest plausible effect of video games on those story completion and noise blast measures might be, so he conducted a new study of his own. He randomly assigned people to view violent or nonviolent games and then asked them to complete the story by describing what the main character from the video game would do. Some participants wrote about Ethan from Heavy Rain, whom they had just watched calmly draw an architectural sketch; others wrote about Michael from Grand Theft Auto V, whom they had just watched murder twenty people in a strip club. Participants' stories about ultraviolent Michael were *less* aggressive than those written by participants in the original study—where they were asked to write about "a normal person." That is, the original effect was larger than what should be the biggest effect you could possibly find using that measure—a description of what a mass murderer would do—so we shouldn't trust it.[34]

We believe that science has the potential to discover treatments, interventions, and tools that can be game changers for human welfare. It has done so many times in the past, but breakthroughs like movable type, nuclear energy, and the Internet are once-in-a-generation events. We have focused this chapter instead on scientific studies with dubious results, especially claims of implausibly potent effects. Such studies have served as the basis for interventions, policies, and practices with cumulative direct and opportunity costs in the tens or hundreds of billions of dollars. When any product or process is said to have powers that are surprisingly broad, unique, or out of proportion to its cost, our deception detectors should start to tingle. If Nobel Prize winners can be taken in by poorly supported assertions of potency, so can the rest of us.[35]

CONCLUSION

SOMEBODY'S FOOL

When a friend offers you a cookie, you probably don't check whether it's poisoned. We began our exploration of why we get taken in by examining our tendency to assume that people are telling us the truth rather than lying. We noted that this truth bias is both rational and necessary. If we were universally suspicious, we might never be conned, but the vast majority of our daily interactions are straightforward, so extreme skepticism would be counterproductive.

All of us are capable of being fooled, probably in more ways than we realize and more often than we are willing to admit. Over the last eight chapters, we've described some key cognitive patterns that make it easy for us to be fooled—our habits of thought that scammers exploit and the hooks they use to attract us to believe things we shouldn't. Our default tendency to accept first and check later, if ever, is a prerequisite for being taken in, but by learning to ask questions at the right times, we can limit our risk of being duped. Still, people vary in how eager they are to question: Some are more skeptical, and others are more trusting. Not every investor fell for Madoff, Theranos, or BitConnect; not every art collector bought one of the Knoedler's

225

fakes; and not everyone who got a call from someone posing as their company's CEO wired money.

We close our analysis of deception by asking three critical questions: Who among us is most likely to be a victim? How can we know when we are the target? How much should we do to avoid being fooled?

THAT'S JUST BULLSHIT

For social interaction to work at all, we need not only a truth bias but also an even more general assumption that when people communicate with us, they are saying something substantive—whether it's true or not. The strength of this convention explains why we sometimes get fooled by claims that are best described as bullshit. As the philosopher Harry Frankfurt defines the term, "bullshit" is plausible, seductive content that lacks true meaning—think of Ern Malley's line "The emotions are not skilled workers." Bullshitting is concerned neither with truth nor with falsity. As Frankfurt explains, "The bullshitter may not deceive us, or even intend to do so, either about the facts or what he takes the facts to be. What he does necessarily attempt to deceive us about is his enterprise . . . the truth-values of his statements are of no central interest to him." Frankfurt notes that we have "bullshit artists" because, once freed from the constraint of correspondence to reality, bullshit can be more expressive and playful.[1]

One especially engaging form of bullshit is what the psychologist Gordon Pennycook and his colleagues call "pseudo-profound bullshit." Its hallmark is long, fancy words that are vague enough to evoke associations that are broadly scientific, spiritual, or intellectual but that do not correspond to actual scientific or logical propositions.

Pennycook wondered whether some people are more likely than others to treat pseudo-profound bullshit as true. For a 2015 study, they devised a "bullshit receptivity scale" using a website that took words from New Age writer Deepak Chopra's tweets and rearranged them into sentences that were grammatical but otherwise random. These pseudo-Chopraisms—statements like "Hidden meaning transforms unparalleled abstract beauty" and "Wholeness quiets infinite phenomena"—sound remarkably similar to some of Chopra's actual tweets, and the research participants had some difficulty distinguishing between them.[2]

Pennycook's studies showed that people who report trusting their intuitive judgments when making decisions and those who perform worse on cognitive reasoning tasks were more likely to judge the pseudo-Chopraisms to be profound—that is, they were more receptive to bullshit. Although the participants rated Chopra's actual tweets as somewhat more profound than the randomly generated ones, the same individual traits predicted profundity ratings for both the real and pseudo-Chopraisms. That is, the more people rely on intuition and the less skilled they are at analytical thinking, the more impressed they tend to be with statements so nonsensical that they could be neither true nor false. We have come across many cases of successful people who are convinced that they can trust their gut instincts about other people and make quick, confident decisions based on intuition alone—they are easier to fool.

This gets to the heart of the problem with bullshit—its lack of a relationship to actual truth and the corresponding difficulty we can have in evaluating it. Just as some claims are so vaguely stated that they are "not even wrong," bullshit is not even false. If you ask yourself the question we suggested at the start of this book for computing truth bias—"Is that really true?"—and you can't figure out what concrete evidence would convince you one way or the other, you may be dealing with bullshit. If that happens, ask, **"Could this even be false?"** Try replacing the abstract platitudes and complex words with simple, concrete ones that convert an obscure claim into an easily understandable one. For example, to test the statement "Wholeness quiets infinite phenomena," try to imagine an infinite phenomenon . . . perhaps an irrational number like pi, whose digits go on forever without repeating. Then, think about whether "wholeness" could apply to it. If it could, is there any concrete sense in which pi is noisy and could be quieted? If we can't readily come up with a concrete interpretation that could be assigned a truth value, it's likely bullshit. If you are looking for deep thoughts, consult the writings of Jack Handey instead.

EXPERTISE VERSUS DECEPTION

Experts are great bullshit detectors, at least within their areas of expertise, and expertise provides one of the best defenses against uncritical acceptance of what we're shown. Rupert Murray's 2005 documentary *Unknown White Male* provides a vivid example. On July 3, 2003, photography student Doug Bruce found himself in a New York City subway car headed toward Coney Island. He had bumps on his head and a throbbing headache, but he had no memory of how he had gotten there or anything since the evening before.

Doug then realized that he had no idea where he was, or even who he was. He searched his backpack for clues to his own identity and, finding none, went to a police station for help. From there he was taken to a hospital, where he was diagnosed with retrograde amnesia—loss of memory for his own past. Eventually, he called a phone number written on a scrap of paper he had, and a woman he had met a few weeks earlier came to the hospital and brought him back to his Manhattan apartment.

Murray's film documents Doug's attempts to recover his memories, not only of his identity and past but also of simple sensory experiences like snow and ocean waves. He visited his family in Spain, some friends in London, and a previous home in Paris. With no definitive explanation for his amnesia or resolution of his symptoms, he resumed photography school, began a relationship with a fashion model, and adopted a less cynical, more childlike outlook on life and all its (brand-new) wonders.

Unknown White Male has an arresting style, with camera angles, sound design, time shifts, and visual effects that help the audience experience Doug's sense of dislocation and confusion. When we show the film in our psychology classes, the majority of our students are convinced that Doug's memory loss is genuine—as were all the people in the film whom Doug knew before and after the onset of his amnesia. That makes sense because according to studies we have conducted, about 75 percent of the general public believes that amnesia involves forgetting one's own identity.[3]

Yet experts on memory and neuroscience generally do not accept Doug's story because they know this sort of memory failure almost never happens. In the rare cases where people forget their past or lose their sense of self, a physical brain injury is readily apparent, and the self-knowledge tends to return quickly. Skills and facts are seldom lost. A driver might not remember the hours or days right before a car crash, but the earlier in life a memory was formed, the less likely it is to vanish. What takes longer to return (and sometimes never does) in actual cases of amnesia is the ability to form *new memories*. Doug had no difficulty doing that. In fact, his ability to pick and choose which elements of his past he wants to add back into his memory and which ones he wants to leave behind is the emotional core of the film's narrative.

Most documentary filmmakers are not propagandists; they do not deliberately mislead their audiences. Likewise, autobiographies and memoirs are written not to convince historians, memory experts, and journalists but to appeal to their authors' fans and followers. Still, in picking what to show and what to omit, what to highlight and what to mention in passing, and even what kind of soundtrack to play, documentarians convey a chosen message. In fact, Murray's film may have omitted information from Doug's story that suggests he was malingering all along.[4]

As cognitive scientists, we are not the target audience for *Unknown White Male*. For us, it is a demonstration of the ways people misunderstand how memory works, not a case study of how memory actually breaks down. Experts in any topic can recognize and interpret more patterns than novices do, so they have a keener sense of when to be suspicious. Their greater knowledge lets them spot bullshitters who only act as though they know their subject. That's how chess masters deduced that the John von Neumann who entered the World Open wasn't a good chess player.

But experts are not immune to being fooled. Their expertise itself consists partly of strong expectations about how things should work, which skilled con artists can exploit by being careful to satisfy them. "John Drewe" fabricated documentation of the provenance of John Myatt's forged paintings and left it right where experts would expect to find it. Diederik Stapel got his many fraudulent papers through scientific peer review by generating results that fit with what experts in his field expected to see. And although they weren't attempting to con anyone, Trafton Drew and his colleagues showed that practicing radiologists were so good at finding tumors on CT scans (the thing that they expected to see) that they often missed tumor-sized gorillas that had been mischievously inserted into the images.[5]

When experts stray too far from their specialty without realizing it, they can be exploited by cons that meet their expectations but don't fool true experts. Some leaders in the technology industry repeatedly proclaim the imminence of artificial general intelligence—the development of entities that are at least as capable as human beings across a wide swath of intelligent behavior. Their expertise in developing sophisticated computational models is genuine, but it is not the expertise necessary to evaluate whether a model's output constitutes generally intelligent behavior.

People who make these predictions appear to be swayed by the most impressive examples of how well new machine learning models like ChatGPT and DALL-E do in producing realistic language and generating beautiful pictures. But these systems tend to work best only when given just the right prompts, and their boosters downplay or ignore the cases where similar prompts make them fail miserably. What seems like intelligent conversation often turns out to be a bull session with a bot whose cleverness comes from ingesting huge volumes of text and responding by accessing the statistically most relevant stuff in its dataset. A bot has no commitment to telling the truth because its code does not incorporate the concept of truth. The way people react to technology that Gary Marcus calls "autocomplete on steroids" might say more about how people infer deep, meaningful causes from superficial patterns than about the intelligence of the underlying model. So seductive are these demonstrations that a Google employee made headlines in 2022 for his belief that the firm's LaMDA interactive language model had become "sentient" and deserved legal personhood (as well as its own lawyer). Always keep in mind that—like current examples of artificial intelligence—human expertise is limited, not general: It provides a big advantage in a small domain.[6]

THEY COME TO YOU BY CHANCE

Once a con is exposed and dissected, it often seems that only the gullible and ignorant could have fallen for it. If bullshit receptivity makes us more vulnerable but expertise can protect us, how do scammers know who among us to target? Sophisticated frauds might take precise aim at an individual or group, but in many cases, scammers rely on their victims to identify themselves.

If you've been on the Internet long enough, you've likely received emails from a "Nigerian prince" opening with a tantalizing line such as "I do not come to you by chance" and offering to deposit vast riches into your bank account if you first send a small amount of cash. In

2006, the *New Yorker* profiled a Massachusetts psychotherapist in his fifties who was invited by one "Captain Joshua Mbote" from Africa to help recover a lost fortune of $55 million. Over the next year and a half, he ended up losing $80,000, and as the scam also involved cashing bad checks and passing on some of the funds, he was later sentenced to two years in US prison for bank fraud and other crimes. This poor fellow comes across as intelligent and well-meaning, yet he fell hard for the scam. He was far from the only victim in the 2000s; according to the Dutch firm Ultrascan, advance-fee scams, of which the Nigerian prince is only one variety, collectively took in $9.3 billion in 2009 alone.[7]

Like savvy politicians, advance-fee fraudsters don't let a good crisis go to waste. On March 24, 2022, one month into the Russian invasion of Ukraine, Dan received an email with the enticing subject line "Business Matter." In poorly punctuated English, someone calling himself "Mr. Bahren Shani" offered to invest up to €200 million on behalf of wealthy Russian individuals if Dan could propose a "convincing business project." Dan briefly considered proposing a partnership to distribute a book about how not to be victimized by scammers. In the end, he didn't respond because he was sure that at some point before receiving the investment, he would be asked to help these rich folks pay some minor expenses, probably because their overseas funds had all been frozen by sanctions—except, somehow, the €200 million "investment."

Unlike many phishing attempts that superficially mimic the appearance of legitimate queries, these "out of the blue" emails make transparently ridiculous pitches. That seems counterproductive, which is why the information security researcher Cormac Herley asked in the title of a 2012 paper, "Why Do Nigerian Scammers Say They Are from Nigeria?"[8] Herley explained that the obviousness is the point. It costs the scammers virtually nothing to spam the world, but it costs them a lot to conduct all the follow-up necessary to reel a victim in. The people behind "Captain Mbote" spent six months pursuing their quarry before he started wiring money to them. By declaring at the outset, "This is another absurd instance of the well-known Nigerian scam," the fraudsters sift out doubters, automatically selecting only the most vulnerable to progress to one-on-one interaction. Ironically, if a higher proportion of people receiving the emails know that they're spam, that's better for the scammers—because a higher proportion of those who do respond will be gullible enough to send money. If you're the sort of person who instantly recognizes such emails as a scam, "Captain Mbote" wants to make it easy for you to opt out without wasting any of his valuable time.

MASTERS OF SELECTION

Mentalists, magicians, and other performers regularly rely on a similar selection process to get the best volunteers to identify themselves. No stage hypnotist wants to bring up an audience member who will be unaffected by their persuasion techniques. So most start their routine by creating a not-so-subtle filter. For example, they might ask everyone in the audience to engage in a brief meditation by closing their eyes and holding their arms out in front of them. They might then say, "Imagine that a helium balloon is tied to the index finger on your left hand and that your right hand is holding a brick." After a few minutes of this structured imagining, the most compliant people in the audience will be reaching for the sky with their left hand and the ground with their right. Those people are the most likely to be hypnotizable, so they're the ones invited to the stage, where the hypnotist continues the selection process until whoever remains will do whatever they are asked.

Business models that seem dubious on the surface sometimes turn out to work by incorporating clever selection tactics. Have you ever been offered a free dinner or other inducement to attend a "seminar" that is actually a sales pitch for a financial manager or a course on real estate investing? Have you been offered a free trip if you'll agree to listen to a pitch to buy into a time-share property? Those who reply to the initial message are announcing that they are more ready to be convinced by a hard sell. Robocalls about extending your car's warranty (extended warranties rarely make financial sense) or buying your house immediately for cash (why not put it on the market and take the best bid?) work the same way.

Fringe groups can turn from communities or movements into cults by purifying their ranks through the same kind of selection process. Did the followers of Harold Camping, the Christian radio pastor who prophesied the end of the world in 2011, believe the rapture was imminent because he talked them into it from a standing start? More likely they were a hard-core, committed subset who remained after Camping said more and more implausible things, up to identifying the precise date and time when hell on earth would commence. Teachers laugh about the *Doonesbury* comic in which a professor is dismayed to realize that his students will unquestioningly scribble down whatever he says, no matter how outrageous it becomes. Cult leaders would see this cartoon as a recipe for success.[9]

Keith Raniere was the founder of NXIVM, a multilevel marketing organization that offered self-improvement courses but became infamous for enticing women into master-slave relationships and branding their bodies with a special logo. He proclaimed himself the smartest person in the world, so anyone willing to follow him would already regard him with awe. Toni Natalie, an early member of Raniere's circle, wrote later, "Someone smart enough to attract the attention of *Guinness World Records* must have great wisdom to impart—or so I believed." Even what looked from the outside like horrible publicity was not necessarily bad for the cohesiveness of the group. Leaders of NXIVM turned the questions raised by negative news reports into a tool to ferret out wobblers and keep only the most ardent believers.[10]

If you find yourself continually agreeing with a politician, pundit, or self-styled thought leader, ask yourself whether they might be deliberately attempting to lead you down a path to an extreme or nonsensical conclusion, and get off before you get there.

EVADING SELECTION

Most efforts to reduce Internet fraud focus on reducing the number of people who reply to scammers by educating users or by algorithmically filtering out scam emails. But some attacks inevitably slip through, and some Internet neophytes fall prey to them. By looking at the Nigerian scam from the viewpoint of the scammers, Herley's analysis suggested a more effective way to fight back: Increase the number of people who respond to scam emails but never send money, forcing the scammers to waste time on unproductive interactions, thereby reducing their profits. Such "scam baiters" already exist—the website "419 Eater," named after the Nigerian law that governs fraud, offers tips and support, and comedians have chatted with scammers to gather material for their acts. The more scam baiters, the lower the average return to the scammers on an interaction, and the less incentive they have to continue the scam.[11]

When we find ourselves in high-stakes situations, we should remember that scammers have a different perspective and different goals than we do. Whereas we tend to focus on the information we see and not the information that's absent, the scammer has *all* the information. So no matter how appealing the proposition, we should pause to ask ourselves three questions that can help us avoid deception by selection.

First, ask **"Why me?"** Think about whether you really are the sole focus of their attempt at persuasion or whether you are being swept up in a massive attempt to get people to volunteer.

Second, ask **"What am I doing?"** to think about whether your actions and judgments reflect *your* goals as opposed to those of your interlocutor. Is it likely that the thing they want you to do is exactly the thing you should be doing right now?

Third, ask **"How did I get here?"** to evaluate whether you are in a situation or place where deception is more likely. If a scammer could reach many people like you with little effort, or if the environment is filled with potential scammers, you should be wary.

For example, imagine you're on a cruise and you notice a shop on board called "Rare Artistic Masterpieces." A look in the window reveals that it offers limited-edition "giclée prints" of works by famous artists like Picasso and Dalí. It would be great to have an artist of that stature on your wall! Before buying anything, remember that investing in art was not why you got on a big boat, masterpieces are usually sold at auction or in high-end galleries, not cruise-ship malls, and you now know how people fall for scams that earn money by selecting a few victims from among the thousands of people who see a marquee. If an offer doesn't smell right, or you can think of any concrete reasons why it's dubious, you can walk away without worrying that you have missed a big opportunity.[12]

If an intriguing advertisement for a new cryptocurrency exchange lands in your inbox or social media feeds, ask if it was really intended for you in particular or if many other people received it too. Next ask what you'd be doing by following the guidance in the advertisement. Given your age and financial circumstances, does it make sense to put any money into such a high-risk asset class? Finally, ask yourself whether this is the right outlet for this sort of investment. Why invest *here*, with a brand-new company, rather than going to an established and likely more trustworthy financial firm? Following this simple thought process might have kept ordinary investors from losing billions when the crypto markets plunged in 2022 and several high-flying firms disappeared, along with their customers' assets.

If you stumble upon a Facebook quiz that tells you that your porn-star name is the combination of your first pet's name and the street you grew up on, you should ask why you are being prompted to put that information on a public page. Does whoever created it want to provide a bit of fun for everyone, or might there be an ulterior motive? What else might you be doing by typing in these names? You could be contributing to a coordinated effort by an organization attempting to compile information on people from many similar quizzes. In this case, you're giving them the answer to two of the most common password-recovery questions.

One more step you can take to avoid getting scammed is to perform a "blunder check." Chess players often evaluate many possible moves and countermoves, thinking deeply about strategy and tactics, only to miss the most obvious of errors. Coaches advise that taking a moment after all of that thinking to scan the board and ask, "Am I making a simple mistake?" can help you avoid some of those blunders. You can ask the same question before finalizing any critical decision.

The decision scientist Gary Klein described a similar process he called the "premortem." Before starting a project, agreeing to a deal, or making a big investment, ask yourself, "If this goes horribly wrong, what will be the most likely reason(s)?" Imagine what signs of fraud you might uncover after a deal goes badly, and then look for them before you make the deal.[13]

Performing a blunder check or conducting a premortem on our own can be hard when we're immersed in the moment and lack the objectivity of an outsider. So consider asking someone else to do an independent check. Just as a "red team" can catch critical mistakes before we make them, a disinterested party can raise concerns or suspicions we haven't taken seriously or even considered. In 2016, the owner of a French wine company was contacted by someone posing as the defense minister of France, Jean-Yves Le Drian. The caller asked for €300,000 to help rescue hostages being held overseas. The owner was on the verge of complying when a friend walked in, heard a few moments of their Skype conversation, and said, "That's a scam." The rethink prompted by that one outside comment saved the winemaker from joining dozens of wealthy victims who lost about $90 million to the "faux Le Drian."[14]

Of course, for the ask-a-friend method to work, you have to be open to changing your opinion in response to the advice you get. Leslie Wexner, the billionaire founder of the L Brands fashion company, admitted in 2019 that the swindler and sex offender Jeffrey Epstein had "misappropriated" $46 million from him (a number some observers think is a fraction of the true amount). Before Wexner gave Epstein extensive power over his finances, he was warned by the vice chairman of his own company that Epstein was a con artist, but Wexner chose to trust his gut feelings over the advice of someone with a more objective sense of what was happening.[15]

WHEN ACCEPTING BEATS CHECKING

The last time Chris shopped at a Target store, he was offered an extended warranty on an $8 pair of disposable electric toothbrushes. He laughed, and the cashier did too. By now most people know that extended warranties on small appliances are a bad deal. We should think about preventing fraud in the same way. Is the cost of ensuring that you're not being deceived balanced appropriately against the pain you would suffer if you were?

Many large companies build into their budgets the estimated cost of settling frivolous lawsuits; they see it as an unfortunate but necessary part of doing business. Settling rather than fighting means accepting that they might have been bilked, which can be morally repugnant but financially wise. Similarly, a store that wants to prevent all shoplifting would have to lock down its entire inventory, but doing so would likely alienate too many of its customers. In both cases, the marginal cost of preventing additional cheating outweighs the benefits.

You too should consider whether it would be better both for your pocketbook and for your peace of mind to avoid sweating the small stuff and accept that you're bound to be fooled once in a while. Is it possible that the cash register didn't give you the discounted price?

Sure. Is it worth checking every line on your receipt every time you shop to verify that each price was correct to the penny? Perhaps not.

Many organizations fail to properly balance the costs and benefits of checking; they don't do the calculation to determine whether the cost of fraud prevention is worth it. They might even spend more money establishing policies and enforcing compliance to prevent fraud than the fraud itself costs them. Often the people who create new rules to prevent or reduce misconduct reap the benefits of appearing to take action, but they bear only a small portion of the cost and effort involved in complying with those policies.

Well before he was convicted for trying to profit from his power to appoint a new US senator after Barack Obama was elected president, Governor Rod Blagojevich signed into law the Illinois State Officials and Employees Ethics Act. That law requires approximately 175,000 state employees and appointees to take one work hour every year to complete an online ethics course that addresses everything from hiring and purchasing rules to restrictions on lobbying the government right after serving in it to timecard cheating. Ethics instruction sounds sensible—who could object to reminding everyone once a year about how to be an honest public servant? But this training costs the state millions of dollars each year just from the lost hour of productivity, not even counting the costs of developing and distributing the course, reminding people to complete it, enforcing consequences for noncompliance, and so on.[16]

To judge whether the mandated ethics training is financially worthwhile, we need to know several things. First, does educating workers prevent any inadvertent misconduct? If so, how costly is that misconduct? Second, does the training eliminate any deliberate misconduct? For instance, will the sort of person who tries to solicit bribes to sell a Senate seat be less likely to do so after completing an hour-long course about what gifts can and cannot be accepted from vendors? Third, does the state benefit, financially or otherwise, from being able to claim that all employees completed an ethics training course? Finally, would investing those funds in other things such as audits and investigations prevent more cheating than annual training does? To our knowledge, if these questions were asked, the answers haven't been publicly reported. But without asking and answering such questions, how can we determine whether mandating training about ethical violations is worthwhile?[17]

Sometimes when organizations deploy measures to deter or catch cheating, they inadvertently provide a road map for getting away with it. In March 2022, Jamie Petrone, a former administrator in the emergency medicine department of Yale New Haven Hospital, pleaded guilty to embezzling more than $40 million over a period of eight years. Yale's medical school made it relatively easy for authorized employees to make purchases up to $10,000, but amounts over that triggered additional oversight. Petrone ordered computers, iPads, and other equipment, purportedly for use by medical students, organizing the purchases so that each one fell below the cutoff. She then shipped the gear to a company in New York that resold it and wired the proceeds to her own company. Yale relied on the cutoff to limit the scope of its losses, but that cutoff made it easy for someone like Petrone to hide thousands of fraudulent purchases from scrutiny. Only when a whistleblower tipped off Yale officials that Petrone was loading computer gear she had ordered into her car did they investigate her past purchase orders.[18]

Banks in the United States are required to report deposits of more than $10,000 in cash to the federal government for similar reasons. Unlike Yale's hospital, banks have automated systems to detect when people slice a transaction larger than that into several smaller ones. "Structuring" deposits in that way is illegal because the only logical reason to split them so that they fall below the cutoff is to hide other illegal activity, such as money laundering.[19]

Most organizations lack the resources to implement the systems banks use to prevent fraud. Yale undoubtedly would have preferred not to lose $40 million to an embezzler, but could it really prevent it from happening again? It could lower the criterion for further scrutiny to, say, $1,000 in order to make it harder for someone like Petrone to steal so much so quickly. But doing so would require more bureaucracy for the entire organization and its employees, the vast majority of whom don't commit serious purchasing fraud. As with the Illinois ethics training law, preventing deception can have adverse short- and long-term consequences for employee efficiency and morale. It's the grown-up equivalent of punishing an entire middle school class because one jerk is acting out.

Anytime there's an established cutoff, some people will attempt to beat it. We previously discussed how Benford's law revealed minor tax cheating: People were more likely to report an income just under a $50 cutoff than slightly over it if that meant reducing their taxes by a tiny amount. Similarly, the CDC undoubtedly knew the fifteen-minute cutoff for contact tracing would leave some people who were at risk of Covid-19 infection uninformed of their risk. But some standard must be established in order for contact tracing to be feasible, and some people will subvert the intent of any standard. For example, schools in Billings, Montana, shuffled student seating arrangements every fifteen minutes, avoiding the CDC threshold but possibly increasing the likelihood of spread within classrooms.[20]

Establishing new rules to prevent cheating can start an upward spiral of regulation. Professional cyclists like Lance Armstrong got away with doping in the Tour de France and other races for years because they knew how to break the rules without being detected by the tests in use at the time. When new tests made a drug detectable, riders who wanted to cheat switched to other drugs. If they knew when they would be tested, they scheduled their doping so that it still benefited them but would not show up in their urine at test time. They also started using doping methods that amplified levels of substances their bodies naturally produce, like testosterone, a tactic that meant tests had to answer the murkier question of whether those levels were too high relative to expected baselines. As the arms race of testing and evading continued, new assays of old samples sometimes caught cheating that had happened years earlier. But there have always been and probably will always be ways of avoiding any regulation. A constant cycle of new rules and new evasions is an inevitable consequence of the economic incentives for successful cheating. But the fact that scams are constantly evolving doesn't mean you have to be a victim.[21]

NOBODY'S FOOLPROOF

Earlier in this book, we described trust as a type of commitment—a sticky, enduring assumption that a particular person or group will always tell the truth or act in our interests. Trust is an assumption that can be enhanced or accelerated via familiarity and other social vectors.

Industries, societies, and communities vary in their average level of trust. Sometimes it is too high, as it was in our field of psychological science until about ten years ago. And the result was an excess of misleading, unreplicable, unsupported, and sometimes fraudulent claims. The level of trust can also be too low, as it would be in a society where transactions were all in cash and people could not borrow money. The result would likely be much less fraud but also too little commerce, growth, and progress. We need to strike a balance—to minimize the most profitable opportunities for cheaters while enabling the trustworthy to interact with few impediments.

In working on this book, we've studied frauds and cheaters from all walks of life. We've read books and articles, watched documentaries, listened to podcasts, conducted interviews, and analyzed data. We now spot opportunities for being fooled more often than we used to.

But we also recognize that our immersion in the world of deception has, at least for now, given us an unrepresentative perspective on human behavior and experience. We all develop expectations for base rates—what things are common and what things are rare—based on what we experience or hear about the most. For example, each summer we might hear a lot about shark attacks, but that doesn't mean they are common. Now that you've nearly finished this book, the risk of being fooled is likely central in your thoughts. But fortunately, we don't encounter many Ponzi schemers or art forgers in our daily lives. There's always some risk of being fooled, but long cons and megafrauds are rare, and most of our interactions are with honest people. And even when we are cheated, the consequences are often minor.

We went into detail about massive frauds not because they are common but because they illustrate cognitive mechanisms that make it easy for us to be fooled in more mundane situations. By understanding how infamous fraudsters capitalized on our habits and hooks, we can be better prepared to detect the sorts of scams that we *are* likely to encounter.

We hope that the ideas and stories in this book will help you focus more on the frauds "in the middle," those that are consequential enough to be worth evading and common enough that they are worth watching for. For us as researchers, that sort of deception might be a scientific collaborator making up data. For small business owners, it might be an employee siphoning funds. If you like to buy fine art, sports memorabilia, designer clothes, or antiques, you should be concerned about their authenticity. And we can all be tricked by false advertising, fake news, and political lies.

When the consequences of a potential fraud would be significant, in addition to checking more, we should try to think like the scammer. If someone stands to make a large profit by ripping us off, they may go to great lengths to convince us that they're trustworthy. Someone knowingly selling forged art for millions of dollars has the incentive to spend a lot of time, money, and effort faking its provenance. But someone selling giclée prints on a cruise ship doesn't have to go to great lengths. They can count on finding some people who will buy without checking.

By becoming better at evaluating risk, we can take proactive steps to avoid being fooled in the most personally and professionally consequential ways. When investing with a large firm like Morgan Stanley, Fidelity, or Vanguard, we probably don't need to spend much time or energy making sure it won't steal our life savings. But if we're considering investing in new, unregulated markets like cryptocurrency, we should check carefully. Unless you are a blockchain expert with a sophisticated understanding of math and computer science, investing in crypto means you likely are being influenced by the hook of familiarity and hoping that following a herd will lead you to riches. Would you regret it if the crypto market crashed (again)? Do you have any actual evidence that it won't? What if the company you gave your money to turned out to be an outright scam like the Ponzi schemes that inevitably populate unregulated financial sectors? Even when we're doing routine things like hiring a small company or money manager to handle our investments, it makes sense to check them out thoroughly and to continue doing so on occasion even after we've worked with them a while. The same logic applies to every other area of life.

This brings us back to the first cognitive habit we discussed—focus. We've described the patterns of fraud and our vulnerability to them based on hundreds of historical examples, but we have no information on cases that have never been detected. There may be other frauds, even cleverer than the ones we've discussed, that are still in operation or that flew under the radar and closed shop before anyone got wise to them. It is impossible to know the true rate of fraud in any field because we never find out about the most successful ones. We haven't written an instruction manual for avoiding all forms of fraud because such a book would itself be fraudulent!

We can't know whether undetected frauds differ in meaningful ways from the ones we've described. Scammers are always coming up with new ways to cheat us, and there could be types of fraud that have yet to be detected or invented. Still, even new scams likely will rely on the principles we've described, because these cognitive inclinations enable us to navigate our world efficiently and effectively. A scheme that didn't use a single one of these methods to lower our guard probably could not succeed. Our hope is that knowing how scammers currently co-opt these tendencies will spur critical thinking if we encounter something new.

We began this book with this quotation: "Once in a while, we can all be fooled by something." James Mattis was correct that we can all be fooled—everyone is susceptible given the right circumstances and the right deception. It is the "once in a while" part that we have tried to elucidate. We described four habits of thought that serve us well most of the time and four hooks that we quite reasonably find appealing, and we showed how all of them can be used against us. We also provided strategies to avoid being fooled. But we can't always ask more questions, always dig deeper, always withhold judgment, and always follow every lead to its source.

It's not easy to find the right balance between accepting and checking. Being nobody's fool doesn't mean avoiding *all* deception—it only means recognizing when it might happen and avoiding it when it matters. We hope you will keep the ideas in this book in mind while you go about the world and that they help you avoid the worst consequences of being cheated. But please don't decide that life is so full of fraud that you can't enjoy it. That would be a foolish conclusion.

ACKNOWLEDGMENTS

We began thinking about writing a book on this topic about ten years ago, and we've been gathering ideas and examples ever since. The vast majority were relegated to our notebooks and file drawers alongside several book proposals that we abandoned when our agent, Jim Levine, convinced us they wouldn't work. We could not have written this book without Jim's insight and guidance, and we thank him for helping us avoid fooling ourselves. We'd also like to thank the rest of the team at the Levine Greenberg Rostan Literary Agency, especially Michael Nardullo, who handled all of the international rights sales.

We'd also like to thank our editor, T. J. Kelleher, and our publisher, Lara Heimert, for taking on this project at Basic Books and for helping us find a structure and organization that achieved our goals. Special thanks to Tisse Takagi, who edited two drafts of the manuscript and gave excellent advice on the book's organization and feedback on its prose. Jordan Simons and Jeffrey Ohl read a complete draft and gave detailed and insightful comments throughout. They helped us find and fix many passages that were perfectly lucid to us but would have been confusing to our readers. Pat Simons read the near-final version of the book, and her extensive copyediting made the final version far more readable. Finally, eagle-eyed proofreader Kathy Richards spotted many typos and unclear phrases in the page proofs. If you liked the book, you can thank all of these folks for improving it. (If you didn't, please blame only us.)

Sanga Sung, Tamara Gjorgjieva, Michael Bennett, and especially Jeffrey Ohl provided invaluable assistance with research for the book. We are also grateful for helpful discussions with Jonathan Segal and Pronoy Sarkar.

Well before we began writing this book, we co-curated an exhibition at the Museum of Old and New Art (MONA) in Hobart, Australia, and wrote two essays for the exhibition catalog. Our discussions with David Walsh, Pippa Mott, Jane Clark, Beth Hall, and others at MONA helped inform our writing about art fraud.

In developing the ideas in this book, we talked with many experts in a variety of fields who gave us guidance about their own areas of expertise. Some of those people spoke with us off the record about suspected fraud, and others anonymously gave personal insights into better-known cases. Many of their thoughts helped us frame our discussion. We thank all of them immensely for their help.

During the writing process, we communicated with a number of experts who gave us important information, corrected our misconceptions, and helped us ensure the accuracy of our descriptions. If any errors remain, they are our fault for not listening carefully enough. We are thankful to (in alphabetical order) Max Bazerman, Bill Brewer, Joanne Byars, Susan Clancy, Gary Dell, Daniel Edelman, Shane Frederick, Jennifer Golbeck, Joshua Hart, Diana Henriques, Joe Hilgard, David Laibson, Bosse Lindquist, Andrew Metrick, Scott Myers, Kenneth Norman, Peter Pagin, Ron Rensink, Katie Rothstein, Jamie Shovlin, Joe Simmons, David Smerdon, Larry Taylor, Åsa Wikforss, Mike Wilkins, Katherine Wood, Rene Zeelenberg, and Rolf Zwaan. Nick Brown and Matt Tompkins each read multiple passages and provided detailed feedback.

We would both like to thank our family members, friends, and colleagues for all of their support, encouragement, and understanding throughout the long process of creating this book. Dan especially thanks Kathy Richards, Jordan Simons, Ellix Simons, David Simons,

Pat Simons, and Paul Simons. Chris especially thanks Michelle Meyer, Caleb Meyer-Chabris, Daniel Chabris, and the members of the Knowledge Resistance Project.

Finally, for piquing our curiosity about the subject of this book and helping us to stay motivated as we worked on the project, we thank everyone who has ever fooled us.

NOTES

Introduction

1. Quotation from James Mattis in interview with Judy Woodruff, *PBS News-Hour*, September 2, 2019 [https://www.youtube.com/watch?v=5LZlJmb8cmY].

2. The following two podcasts devoted to the Theranos story and the criminal trial of Elizabeth Holmes include extensive quotations from depositions and trial testimony on the aspects of the case that we discuss in this book: *The Dropout* (ABC News, 2021–2022) [https://abcaudio.com/podcasts/the-dropout/] and *Bad Blood: The Final Chapter* (John Carreyrou, 2021–2022) [https://podcasts.apple.com/us/podcast/bad-blood-the-final-chapter/id1575738174]. The story is narrated in J. Carreyrou, *Bad Blood: Secrets and Lies in a Silicon Valley Startup* (New York: Knopf, 2018). At the end of her fifteen-week trial in early 2022, Theranos founder Elizabeth Holmes was found guilty on four charges related to defrauding investors [https://www.justice.gov/usao-ndca/pr/theranos-founder-elizabeth-holmes-found-guilty-investor-fraud], and she was sentenced to 135 months in prison [https://www.justice.gov/usao-ndca/pr/elizabeth-holmes-sentenced-more-11-years-defrauding-theranos-investors-hundreds]. Her onetime boyfriend and chief operating officer of Theranos, Ramesh Balwani, was also convicted on twelve counts later in 2022 [https://www.washingtonpost.com/technology/2022/07/07/theranos-trial-verdict/].

3. P. Pagin, "The Indicativity View," in *The Oxford Handbook of Assertion*, ed. S. Goldberg (New York: Oxford University Press, 2020); D. Sperber, "Epistemic Vigilance," *Mind & Language* 25 (2010): 359–393 [https://doi.org/10.1111/j.1468-0017.2010.01394.x]; T. R. Levine, *Duped: Truth-Default Theory and the Social Science of Lying and Deception* (Tuscaloosa: University of Alabama Press, 2020). For an argument that truth bias and "gullibility" result from bugs in generally useful cognitive systems, see H. Mercier, *Not Born Yesterday: The Science of Who We Trust and What We Believe* (Princeton, NJ: Princeton University Press, 2020).

4. Gilbert Chikli and the president scam are described in Evan Ratliff's podcast, *Persona: The French Deception* (Wondery, 2022) [https://wondery.com /shows/persona/] and in E. Kinetz, T. Goldenberg, D. Estrin, and R. Satter, "AP Investigation: How Con Man Used China to Launder Millions," AP News, March 28, 2016 [https://apnews.com/article/business-middle-east-israel-europe-africa -7500da6eb1d94e1dbb7e5650d1c20bd6].

5. Writers like Maria Konnikova, Dan Davies, George Akerlof, Robert Shiller, Eugene Soltes, and Edward Balleisen have covered these topics well in recent years. We recommend the following books: M. Konnikova, *The Confidence Game: Why We Fall for It . . . Every Time* (New York: Viking, 2016); D. Davies, *Lying for Money: How Legendary Frauds Reveal the Workings of the World* (New York: Scribner, 2021); G. A. Akerlof and R. J. Shiller, *Phishing for Phools: The Economics of Manipulation and Deception* (Princeton, NJ: Princeton University Press, 2015); E. Soltes, *Why They Do It: Inside the Mind of the White-Collar Criminal* (New York: PublicAffairs, 2016); and E. J. Balleisen, *Fraud: An American History from Barnum to Madoff* (Princeton, NJ: Princeton University Press, 2018).

6. C. F. Chabris and D. J. Simons, *The Invisible Gorilla and Other Ways Our Intuitions Deceive Us* (New York: Crown, 2010).

7. Fraud on the rise: "The True Cost of Fraud Study," LexisNexis, 2022 [https:// risk.lexisnexis.com/insights-resources/research/us-ca-true-cost-of-fraud -study]; "Investment Scam Complaints on the Rise—Investor Alert," US Securities and Exchange Commission, December 14, 2020 [https://www.investor.gov /introduction-investing/general-resources/news-alerts/alerts-bulletins/investor -alerts/investment-0]. Encouraging insider trading: S. Kolhatkar, *Black Edge: Inside Information, Dirty Money, and the Quest to Bring Down the Most Wanted Man on Wall Street* (New York: Random House, 2018). Rigged ratings: For example, when hotels have nearby competitors, those competitors tend to have many more fake negative reviews, according to D. Mayzlin, Y. Dover, and J. Chevalier, "Promotional Reviews: An Empirical Investigation of Online Review Manipulation," *American Economic Review* 104 (2014): 2421–2455 [https://doi.org/10.1257/aer.104.8.2421]. Companies facilitate student cheating: S. Adams, "This $12 Billion Company Is Getting Rich Off Students Cheating Their Way Through Covid," *Forbes*, January 28, 2021 [https://www.forbes.com/sites/susanadams/2021/01/28/this-12-billion-company -is-getting-rich-off-students-cheating-their-way-through-covid]. A shadowy firm known as "Cheat Ninja" or "Chicken Drumstick" took in about $76 million by developing "cheat hacks" for popular online video games, including Call of Duty and Overwatch. See J. Tidy, "Police Bust 'World's Biggest' Video-Game-Cheat Operation," BBC News, March 30, 2021 [https://www.bbc.com/news /technology-56579449]; L. Franceschi-Bicchierai, "Inside the 'World's Largest' Video Game Cheating Empire," *Vice*, June 1, 2021 [https://www.vice.com /en/article/93ywj3/inside-the-worlds-largest-video-game-cheating-empire].

8. Quotation from Donald J. Trump, interview with *Barstool Sports*, July 23, 2020 [https://www.youtube.com/watch?v=Hois8NpBiw0].

9. The original viral Facebook story described and evaluated: D. Mikkelson, "All 8 Supreme Court Justices Stand in Solidarity Against Trump SCOTUS Pick?," Snopes.com, March 27, 2017 [https://www.snopes.com/fact-check/supreme -court-justices-stand/]. Factcheck.org checked the story: C. Wallace, "Justices Didn't Oppose Gorsuch," FactCheck.org, April 4, 2017 [https://www.factcheck .org/2017/04/justices-didnt-oppose-gorsuch/].

10. Baruch Spinoza argued in the seventeenth century that we cannot comprehend a statement or proposition at all without first accepting it, at least temporarily, as true. Two centuries later, the Scottish philosopher Alexander Bain wrote, "We begin by believing everything; whatever is, is true." In the twentieth century, the psychologist Daniel Gilbert and the philosopher Eric Mandelbaum were the main advocates of this "Spinozan model" of belief. B. Spinoza, *The Ethics and Selected Letters*, ed. S. Feldman, trans. S. Shirley (1677; repr., Indianapolis, IN: Hackett, 1982); A. Bain, *The Emotions and the Will* (London: Longmans, Green, 1859); D. T. Gilbert, "How Mental Systems Believe," *American Psychologist* 46 (1991): 107–119 [https://doi.org/10.1037/0003-066X.46.2.107]; E. Mandelbaum, "Thinking Is Believing," *Inquiry: An Interdisciplinary Journal of Philosophy* 57 (2014): 55–96 [https://doi.org/10.1080/0020174X.2014.858417]. In support of this general notion, readers in one study were found to judge sentences to be true about half a second faster than they judged them to be false or uncertain: S. Harris, S. A. Sheth, and M. S. Cohen, "Functional Neuroimaging of Belief, Disbelief, and Uncertainty," *Annals of Neurology* 63 (2008): 141–147 [https://doi.org/10.1002 /ana.21301].

11. C. N. Street and D. C. Richardson, "Descartes Versus Spinoza: Truth, Uncertainty, and Bias," *Social Cognition* 33 (2015): 227–239 [https://doi.org/10.1521 /soco.2015.33.2.2].

12. The Twitter experiment is Study 7 in G. Pennycook et al., "Shifting Attention to Accuracy Can Reduce Misinformation Online," *Nature* 592 (2021): 590–595 [https://doi.org/10.1038/s41586-021-03344-2]. Pennycook's group did a total of 20 experiments of this sort with over 26,000 participants from 2017 to 2020 and reported that overall, prompts regarding accuracy decreased sharing of false stories by about 10 percent but did not increase sharing of true stories. See G. Pennycook and D. G. Rand, "Accuracy Prompts Are a Replicable and Generalizable Approach for Reducing the Spread of Misinformation," *Nature Communications* 13 (2022): 2333 [https://doi.org/10.1038/s41467-022-30073-5].

13. The IRS doesn't arrest people for small tax bills, and if it did, it would not use local police forces to do so. For an excellent report on a massive India-based call-center scam that resulted in the 2016 indictment and arrest of hundreds of people in the United States and abroad for stealing tens of millions

of dollars with calls like these, see "Scam Likely," Season 4 of the podcast *Chameleon* (Campside Media, 2022) [https://www.campsidemedia.com/shows/chameleon-scam-likely]; US indictment of 61 people and entities [https://www.justice.gov/opa/pr/dozens-individuals-indicted-multimillion-dollar-indian-call-center-scam-targeting-us-victims].

14. Binjamin Wilkomirski affair: S. Maechler, *The Wilkomirski Affair: A Study in Biographical Truth* (New York: Schocken, 2001); "Fragments of a Fraud," *Guardian*, October 14, 1999 [https://www.theguardian.com/theguardian/1999/oct/15/features11.g24]. Belle Gibson's cancer cure story: B. Donnelly and N. Toscano, *The Woman Who Fooled the World: Belle Gibson's Cancer Con, and the Darkness at the Heart of the Wellness Industry* (London: Scribe, 2018).

15. Madoff sources: Interview with SEC Inspector General David Kotz, appendix to audiobook of H. Markopolos, *No One Would Listen: A True Financial Thriller* (New York: Wiley, 2010); Michael Ocrant, quoted by Markopolos, p. 82; Madoff quotation from video "Roundtable Discussion with Bernard Madoff," October 20, 2007 [https://www.youtube.com/watch?v=ab1NTIlO-FM]. For more on how confidence works, see Chapter 3 of *The Invisible Gorilla*.

16. Rick Singer pleaded guilty to charges of racketeering conspiracy, money laundering conspiracy, conspiracy to defraud the United States, and obstruction of justice on March 12, 2019, and agreed to cooperate with the Department of Justice investigation [https://www.justice.gov/usao-ma/investigations-college-admissions-and-testing-bribery-scheme]. The college admissions scandal is described in detail by the reporters who covered the story for the *Wall Street Journal*: M. Korn and J. Levitz, *Unacceptable: Privilege, Deceit, and the Making of the College Admissions Scandal* (New York: Portfolio/Penguin, 2020). Note that Rick Singer was an anomaly in a legitimate business: There are many consultants and advisers who help high school students figure out how to get into good colleges, but without Singer's guarantees. And unless the topic is death or taxes, you should be skeptical whenever anyone uses the word "guarantee"—it should prompt more checking, not less.

17. See *Flawed Science: The Fraudulent Research Practices of Social Psychologist Diederik Stapel*, Joint Report of the Levelt Committee, Noort Committee, and Drenth Committee investigating Stapel, November 28, 2012 [https://www.rug.nl/about-ug/latest-news/news/archief2012/nieuwsberichten/stapel-eindrapport-eng.pdf].

18. Some of the most egregious and best-known examples of journalistic fraud involved more than embellishment: writing fiction, including fabricating people, places, and events, and passing it off as straight reporting. For example, Stephen Glass, over the course of contributing twenty-seven later retracted articles to the *New Republic*, invented many memorable characters and scenes—like a seventeen-year-old hacker sitting across the negotiating table from a group of adult

managers at "Jukt Microelectronics," demanding cash payments and all sorts of extra perks in return for promising not to invade their computer system. Whenever suspicions were raised about Glass's facts or sources, he fabricated notes and other materials to back them up, relying on his experience as a fact-checker to create exactly the kind of documentation that a real reporter would be expected to possess. See B. Bissinger, "Shattered Glass," *Vanity Fair*, September 5, 1998 [https://www.vanityfair.com/magazine/1998/09/bissinger199809]. According to Duke University's newspaper, Glass gave a talk in which he discussed repaying some of the magazines that had paid him for his fabricated stories. This article discusses his admission of wrongdoing and the remorse he feels now: A. Ramkumar, "Discredited Journalist Stephen Glass Reveals $200,000 Repayments to 4 Magazines," *Chronicle*, March 28, 2016 [https://www.dukechronicle.com/article/2016/03/discredited-journalist-stephen-glass-reveals-200000-repayments-to-4-magazines].

19. *Wired* had New York University science journalism professor Charles Seife conduct an independent investigation into Lehrer's blogging: C. Seife, "Jonah Lehrer's Journalistic Misdeeds at Wired.com," *Slate*, August 31, 2012 [https://slate.com/technology/2012/08/jonah-lehrer-plagiarism-in-wired-com-an-investigation-into-plagiarism-quotes-and-factual-inaccuracies.html]. In an editorial statement, *Wired* concluded that Lehrer's blog posts did not meet its journalistic standards: E. Hansen, "Violations of Editorial Standards Found in WIRED Writer's Blog," *Wired*, August 31, 2012 [https://www.wired.com/2012/08/violations-of-editorial-standards-found-in-wired-writers-blog/]. Lehrer gave a talk, for which he was paid by the Knight Foundation, in which he apologized for some of his transgressions. A version of that talk/apology appears on his website: Jonah Lehrer, February 2012. Lehrer's made-up quote from Teller: S. Myers, "Another False Quotation Found in Jonah Lehrer's 'Imagine,'" *Poynter*, August 10, 2012 [https://web.archive.org/web/20140722023144/http://www.poynter.org/latest-news/media wire/184700/another-false-quotation-found-in-jonah-lehrers-imagine-penn-teller/]. Lehrer's distorted retelling of Festinger's study appeared in his book *Imagine: How Creativity Works* (Boston: Houghton Mifflin, 2012) as well as this earlier blog post: J. Lehrer, "The Psychology of Conspiracy Theories," *Wired*, August 4, 2010 [http://www.wired.com/wiredscience/2010/08/the-psychology-of-conspiracy-theories]. Seth Mnookin pointed this out in a blog post: S. Mnookin, "Jonah Lehrer's Missing Compass," *Panic Virus*, August 3, 2012 [https://web.archive.org/web/20120803193135/http://blogs.plos.org/thepanicvirus/2012/08/03/jonah-lehrers-missing-compass/].

20. When Jonah Lehrer was caught for plagiarism and fabrication, his publishers removed two of his books from the shelves. But by then, Lehrer had already established himself as a writer, and he has continued to publish books and profit from the renown he had gained. Lehrer's books published after he was caught plagiarizing:

S. Benartzi and J. Lehrer, *The Smarter Screen: Surprising Ways to Influence and Improve Online Behavior* (New York: Portfolio, 2015); J. Lehrer, *A Book About Love* (New York: Simon & Schuster, 2016); J. Lehrer, *Mystery: A Seduction, a Strategy, a Solution* (New York: Simon & Schuster, 2021). Ironically, one of the main endorsers of Lehrer's latest book, *Mystery*, is the British writer Johann Hari, who was himself exposed as a plagiarist and quotation mechanic even before Lehrer was; he describes *Mystery* as "rigorous." We have had experiences with plagiarism, and not just in our roles as college professors. Our previous book has sold well over 2.5 million copies if you count the parts of it that were included without attribution in the 2.5 million copies sold of Rolf Dobelli's 2012 book *The Art of Thinking Clearly* [http://blog.chabris.com/2013/09/similarities-between-rolf-dobellis-book.html]. In 2013, in a statement on his website, Dobelli acknowledged using direct quotations from our book without citation or attribution [https://www.dobelli.com/book-corrections/].

21. The FTX terms of service are described here: B. Dale and F. Salmon, "FTX's Terms-of-Service Forbid Trading with Customer Funds," *Axios*, November 13, 2022 [https://www.axios.com/2022/11/12/ftx-terms-service-trading-customer-funds]. The events of FTX's implosion are summarized here: A. Osipovich et al., "They Lived Together, Worked Together and Lost Billions Together: Inside Sam Bankman-Fried's Doomed FTX Empire," *Wall Street Journal*, November 19, 2022 [https://www.wsj.com/articles/sam-bankman-fried-ftx-alameda-bankruptcy-collapse-11668824201].

22. Ironies abound in the study of deception. For example, the noted accounting firm Ernst & Young paid a $100 million fine because its auditors cheated on an ethics test: K. Gibson, "Ernst & Young Hit with $100 Million Fine After Auditors Cheat on Ethics Exam," CBS News, June 28, 2022 [https://www.cbsnews.com/news/sec-fines-ernst-young-100-million-auditors-cheat-on-ethics-exam/]. And several psychics were victimized by people stealing their account information on Instagram and then charging for their "fake" psychic readings: A. Merlan, "Psychics and Tarot Readers Are Under Siege by Instagram Scammers and Online Fatigue," *Vice*, June 18, 2022 [https://www.vice.com/en/article/n7zb88/psychics-and-tarot-readers-are-under-siege-by-instagram-scammers-and-online-fatigue]. And plagiarism has been detected in writings about plagiarism: R. A. Posner, *The Little Book of Plagiarism* (New York: Pantheon Books, 2007), 8.

Chapter 1: Focus—Think About What's Missing

1. The series *John Edward Cross Country* aired on WE tv for three seasons from 2006 to 2008 [https://www.imdb.com/title/tt0848540/]. Chris transcribed this dialog from a video of one episode of the show.

2. A. Corneau, "Kim Kardashian Realizes Marriage Is Over via Psychic Medium John Edward," *Us Weekly*, January 23, 2012 [https://www.usmagazine

.com/entertainment/news/kim-kardashian-realizes-marriage-is-over-via -psychic-medium-john-edward-2012231/]. *South Park*'s dissection of John Edward in Season 6, Episode 15 (2002), has its own Wikipedia page [https://en.wikipedia .org/wiki/The_Biggest_Douche_in_the_Universe].

3. Mentalists using stooges: J. Hitt, "Inside the Secret Sting Operations to Expose Celebrity Psychics," *New York Times Magazine,* February 26, 2019 [https://www.nytimes.com/2019/02/26/magazine/psychics-skeptics-facebook .html].

4. The trick was invented by Harry Hardin and was first formally described in print by T. N. Downs, *The Art of Magic,* ed. J. N. Hilliard (Chicago: Arthur P. Felsman, 1921), 80–85 [https://archive.org/details/cu31924084451008/page /n87/mode/2up?q=princess+card]. A variant of the Princess Card Trick has also been used as a way of modeling psychotic experiences, e.g., T. Ward, P. A. Garety, M. Jackson, and E. Peters, "Clinical and Theoretical Relevance of Responses to Analogues of Psychotic Experiences in People with Psychotic Experiences With and Without a Need-for-Care: An Experimental Study," *Psychological Medicine* 50 (2020): 761–770 [https://doi.org/10.1017/S0033291719000576].

5. A. Abad-Santos, "This Is What Happens When Talk-Show Psychics Talk About Kidnap Cold Cases," *Atlantic,* May 7, 2013 [https://www.theatlantic.com /national/archive/2013/05/sylvia-browne-cleveland-kidnapper/315507/]; "Celebrity Psychic Told Berry's Mom Her Daughter Was Dead," CBS News, May 9, 2013 [https://www.cbsnews.com/news/celebrity-psychic-told-berrys-mom-her -daughter-was-dead/]. When psychics like Browne fail spectacularly, it's often because they mistakenly assumed that they could get away with a specific prediction about an unsolved cold case—because nobody would ever be able to challenge it. Chris used to show his classes a video clip of Sylvia Browne getting nothing right about a caller's dead father, but when he went back to YouTube the next year, the video was gone.

6. Boston Dynamics parkour video: "More Parkour Atlas," September 24, 2019 [https://www.youtube.com/watch?v=_sBBaNYex3E].

7. For an example of research on "one-pixel attacks" on deep neural networks for image recognition, see J. Su, D. V. Vargas, and K. Sakurai, "One Pixel Attack for Fooling Deep Neural Networks," *IEEE Transactions on Evolutionary Computation* 23 (2019): 828–841 [doi.org/10.1109/TEVC.2019.2890858].

8. Theranos's null-protocol demo: T. De Chant, "Theranos Devices Ran 'Null Protocol' to Skip Actual Demo for Investors," *Ars Technica,* October 20, 2021 [https://arstechnica.com/tech-policy/2021/10/theranos-devices -ran-demo-apps-that-blocked-error-messages-during-investor-pitches/]. Volkswagen emissions scandal: J. Lanchester, "Fraudpocalypse," *London Review of Books,* August 4, 2022 [https://www.lrb.co.uk/the-paper/v44/n15/john-lanchester /fraudpocalypse].

9. We have been using this example in talks and teaching for more than a decade. In addition to becoming a Twitter meme, it has been discussed in several recent popular science books, including Jordan Ellenberg's excellent book about statistical thinking, *How Not to Be Wrong: The Power of Mathematical Thinking* (New York: Penguin, 2014). The details of the Wald story, along with the iconic plane image, are described well in the Wikipedia article "Abraham Wald" [https://en.wikipedia.org/wiki/Abraham_Wald]; details about Black Thursday can also be found at "Boeing B-17 Flying Fortress," Wikipedia [https://en.wikipedia.org /wiki/Boeing_B-17_Flying_Fortress].

10. Dave Rubin's tweet, November 12, 2021 [https://twitter.com/RubinReport /status/1459163836905234437].

11. M. Gladwell, *The Tipping Point: How Little Things Can Make a Big Difference* (Boston: Little, Brown, 2000). We critiqued this example in more depth in *The Invisible Gorilla*, and Duncan Watts analyzes it in his book *Everything Is Obvious*: *Once You Know the Answer* (New York: Crown Business, 2011).

12. For discussion of the underappreciated role of chance in success, see N. N. Taleb, *Fooled by Randomness: The Hidden Role of Chance in Life and in the Markets*, 2nd ed. (New York: Random House, 2008); R. H. Frank, *Success and Luck: Good Fortune and the Myth of Meritocracy* (Princeton, NJ: Princeton University Press, 2016).

13. The study of reasoning about likely business unicorns: G. Lifchits, A. Anderson, D. G. Goldstein, J. M. Hofman, and D. J. Watts, "Success Stories Cause False Beliefs About Success," *Judgment & Decision Making* 16 (2021) [http://journal .sjdm.org/21/210225/jdm210225.pdf]. In this study, the small amount of the payments involved—a handful of participants got an extra dollar—is less important than the fact that the study was "incentive compatible." This term from economics refers to a situation where people's incentives are compatible with revealing their true beliefs. In this case, even though the amount at stake was small, there was no reason for the participants to do anything other than pick which kind of founder they thought was most likely to succeed. Without the "bets" and payouts, more people might answer randomly or in some other fashion.

14. See Fig. 1 of J. Wai, S. M. Anderson, K. Perina, F. C. Worrell, and C. F. Chabris, "The Most Successful and Influential 'Outlier' Americans Come from a Surprisingly Narrow Range of Elite Educational Backgrounds," submitted to *PLoS ONE*, 2022. A list of "unicorns" in 2015 was published in S. Austin, C. Canipe, and S. Slobin, "The Billion Dollar Startup Club," *Wall Street Journal*, February 18, 2015 [https://www.wsj.com/graphics/billion-dollar-club/].

15. The philosopher Åsa Wikforss made this point in her chapter "The Dangers of Disinformation," in *The Epistemology of Democracy*, ed. H. Samaržija and Q. Cassam (London: Routledge, 2023).

16. Browne's conviction: J. Nickell, "Psychic Sylvia Browne Once Failed to Fore-see Her Own Criminal Conviction," *Skeptical Inquirer*, November–December 2004 [https://web.archive.org/web/20050727083155/http://www.findarticles.com/p/articles/mi_m2843/is_6_28/ai_n6361823]. Review of psychic performance: R. Saunders, "The Great Australian Psychic Prediction Project," *Skeptic* 41 (2021): 20–31 [https://www.skeptics.com.au/wp-content/uploads/magazine/The%20Skeptic%20Volume%2041%20(2021)%20No%204%20(Cover).pdf]; R. Palmer, "The Great Australian Psychic Prediction Project: Pondering the Published Pre-dictions of Prominent Psychics," *Skeptical Inquirer*, March–April 2022 [https://skepticalinquirer.org/2022/02/the-great-australian-psychic-prediction-project-pondering-the-published-predictions-of-prominent-psychics/].

17. This logic also animates the popular finance literature about how to pick stocks whose value will increase by a factor of one hundred ("hundred-baggers," an order of magnitude better than the already desirable "ten-baggers"). For example, C. W. Mayer, *100-Baggers: Stocks That Return 100-to-1 and How to Find Them* (Bal-timore, MD: Laissez-Faire Books, 2015); T. W. Phelps, *100 to 1 in the Stock Market: A Distinguished Security Analyst Tells How to Make More of Your Investment Oppor-tunities* (New York: McGraw-Hill, 1972).

18. Hedge fund manager Clifford Asness points out another flaw in the think-ing that you need to find only one Amazon in order to succeed as an investor: You also need to keep riding it all the way up, clairvoyantly knowing to keep it while selling everything else that is destined not to be as big ten years in the fu-ture [https://twitter.com/cliffordasness/status/1529635310677655553?s=21&t=XxESK_H6RnNusIgcyn5zQQ].

19. "Great Moments in Intuition: A Timeline," *O: The Oprah Magazine*, August 2011 [https://www.oprah.com/spirit/a-history-of-intuition-intuition-timeline].

20. S. Shane, J. Preston, and A. Goldman, "Why Bomb Suspect's Travels Didn't Set Off More Scrutiny," *New York Times*, September 23, 2016 [https://www.nytimes.com/2016/09/24/nyregion/how-ahmad-khan-rahami-passed-through-a-net-meant-to-thwart-terrorists.html]; note that this article documents Rahami's travel pattern without saying it is correlated with terrorism.

21. We used this example of thoughts and phone calls in this essay on the law of attraction and its proponents: C. F. Chabris and D. J. Simons, "Fight 'The Power,'" *New York Times*, September 26, 2010 [https://www.nytimes.com/2010/09/26/books/review/Chabris-t.html].

22. M. Lindstrom, "You Love Your iPhone. Literally," *New York Times*, September 30, 2011 [https://www.nytimes.com/2011/10/01/opinion/you-love-your-iphone-literally.html]; see also this response signed by forty-five neuroscientists: R. Poldrack, "The iPhone and the Brain," *New York Times*, October 4, 2011 [https://www.nytimes.com/2011/10/05/opinion/the-iphone-and-the-brain.html?_r=1].

23. Nikola's video was removed from YouTube but is still available at the Internet Archive: "Nikola Motor Company—Nikola One Electric Semi Truck in Motion" [https://web.archive.org/web/20201004133213/https://www.youtube.com/watch?v=IAToxJ9CGb8]. See also T. B. Lee, "Nikola Admits Prototype Was Rolling Downhill in Promotional Video," *Ars Technica*, September 14, 2020 [https://arstechnica.com/cars/2020/09/nikola-admits-prototype-was-rolling-downhill-in-promotional-video/]. By showing an unrepresentative and, in this case, fabricated example of autonomous driving and referring to proprietary AI technology, Nikola made it harder for viewers to ask what was missing. In July 2021, with Nikola's first product yet to reach the market, Trevor Milton was indicted by the US government on fraud charges, mainly for lying about Nikola's products and business in an effort to prop up its stock price while taking the company public. He purportedly claimed that Nikola built batteries in-house that it had actually purchased from other firms, and he allegedly took an ordinary Ford truck, rebadged it with Nikola's logos, and claimed to have built it from scratch [https://www.justice.gov/usao-sdny/pr/former-nikola-corporation-ceo-trevor-milton-charged-securities-fraud-scheme]. Milton was convicted in October 2022: J. Ewing, "Founder of Electric Truck Maker Is Convicted of Fraud," *New York Times*, October 14, 2022 [https://www.nytimes.com/2022/10/14/business/trevor-milton-nikola-fraud.html]. The SEC also charged Nikola Corporation with defrauding investors, and the company agreed to pay $125 million to resolve those fraud charges [https://www.sec.gov/news/press-release/2021-267]. More on Nikola and the fraud investigation: A. Rice, "Last Sane Man on Wall Street," *New York*, January 20, 2022 [https://nymag.com/intelligencer/2022/01/nathan-anderson-hindenburg-research-short-selling.html].

24. Even if you find a plausible connection between hiring Larry Taylor and an improvement in retention, there is no proof that his intervention caused that improvement. Business results aren't like the randomized controlled trials used to evaluate medical treatments. There is no control group that got a "placebo consultation" against which to compare the success of Taylor's clients. You would never expect that kind of data from firms pitching for your business, but you should keep in mind that only that kind of data can truly reveal how effective those firms are.

25. E. Yong, "America Is Zooming Through the Pandemic Panic-Neglect Cycle," *Atlantic*, March 17, 2022 [https://www.theatlantic.com/health/archive/2022/03/congress-covid-spending-bill/627090/].

26. Dan has a section on his vita headed "Not Making Progress" that includes many projects and papers that, for whatever reason, are perpetually on the back burner.

27. Bessemer Venture Partners' anti-portfolio is on their website [https://www.bvp.com/anti-portfolio] and is discussed in detail here: E. Newcomer, "The Anti-Portfolio," *Newcomer*, July 27, 2021 [https://www.newcomer.co/p/the

-anti-portfolio]. Version One also keeps an anti-portfolio [https://versionone.vc /the-version-one-anti-portfolio-the-opportunities-we-missed/]. We have yet to see an anti-portfolio that features investments that flamed out spectacularly, but those should be much harder to forget.

Chapter 2: Prediction—Expect to Be Surprised

1. "CBS News Admits Bush Documents Can't Be Verified," Associated Press, September 20, 2004 [https://www.nbcnews.com/id/wbna6055248]. CBS News president Andrew Heyward said, "Based on what we now know, CBS News cannot prove that the documents are authentic, which is the only acceptable journalistic standard to justify using them in the report. We should not have used them." Dan Rather added, "If I knew then what I know now—I would not have gone ahead with the story as it was aired, and I certainly would not have used the documents in question," and "That was a mistake, which we deeply regret." See "Dan Rather Statement on Memos," CBS News, September 20, 2004 [https://web.archive.org /web/20041230094523/http://www.cbsnews.com/stories/2004/09/20/poli tics/main644546.shtml]. See also "Killian Documents Controversy," Wikipedia [https://en.wikipedia.org/wiki/Killian_documents_controversy].

2. M. Z. Barabak, "Gov. Bush Denies Illegal Drug Use in Last 25 Years," *Los Angeles Times*, August 20, 1999 [https://www.latimes.com/archives/la-xpm -1999-aug-20-mn-1962-story.html]. In the late 1990s, Bush claimed that he hadn't used drugs for the past twenty-plus years, although some reports disputed that, and the wording of his answers to questions about his drug and alcohol use was carefully constructed to leave wiggle room. He had admitted to heavy drinking prior to age forty.

3. Tom Phinney, an expert on fonts and typography [https://www.thomas phinney.com/about/], concluded that the memos were created using Microsoft Times Roman font on a modern word processor. Australian *Desktop* magazine came to the same conclusion in 2004; see "Killian Documents Authenticity Issues," Wikipedia [https://en.wikipedia.org/wiki/Killian_documents_authenticity _issues]. Phinney's analysis: T. Phinney, "Bush Guard Memos Used Times Ro-man, Not Times New Roman," *Typekit*, August 3, 2006 [https://blog.typekit .com/2006/08/03/bush_guard_memo/]. Hannity interview on Fox News, "Kil-lian: CBS Docs Smear My Father," September 15, 2004 [https://www.foxnews .com/transcript/killian-cbs-docs-smear-my-father].

4. Thornburgh report: D. Thornburgh and L. D. Boccardi, *Report of the Indepen-dent Review Panel on the September 8, 2004 60 Minutes Wednesday Segment "For the Record" Concerning President Bush's Texas Air National Guard Service*, January 5, 2005 [http://wwwimage.cbsnews.com/htdocs/pdf/complete_report/CBS _Report.pdf]. Among the many reporting failures identified by the panel, the fi-nal report concluded that CBS had "failed to obtain clear authentication of any

of the Killian documents," had not adequately scrutinized the background of its source, Bill Burkett, and had failed to corroborate the claims. See S. Kiehl and D. Zurawik, "CBS Fires 4 Executives, Producers over Bush–National Guard Report," *Baltimore Sun*, January 11, 2005 [https://www.baltimoresun.com/entertainment/tv/bal-te.to.cbs11jan11-story.html].

5. J. Carreyrou, *Bad Blood: Secrets and Lies in a Silicon Valley Startup* (New York: Knopf, 2018). Carreyrou reports that he wanted to publish the story as soon as possible after he filed it, but his editor "cautioned patience," explaining that the "story was a bombshell and we needed to make sure it was bulletproof when we went to press with it" (see pp. 265–273 for these quotations and the timeline between his filing the story and its ultimate publication).

6. H. Arendt, "Lying in Politics: Reflections on the Pentagon Papers," *New York Review of Books*, November 18, 1971 [https://www.nybooks.com/articles/1971/11/18/lying-in-politics-reflections-on-the-pentagon-pape/].

7. The history and practice of "red teaming" is described in these books: M. Zenko, *Red Team: How to Succeed by Thinking Like the Enemy* (New York: Basic Books, 2015); and B. G. Hoffman, *Red Teaming: How Your Business Can Conquer the Competition by Challenging Everything* (New York: Crown Business, 2017). The story of the red team in the Osama Bin Laden mission is on pp. 191–199 of P. Bergen, *Manhunt: The Ten-Year Search for Bin Laden from 9/11 to Abbottabad* (New York: Crown, 2012).

8. C. Ansberry, N. Subbaraman, and J. R. Brinson, "Why Cloth Masks Might Not Be Enough as Omicron Spreads," *Wall Street Journal*, January 11, 2022 [https://www.wsj.com/articles/cloth-face-mask-omicron-11640984082]. The graph was created by the ACGIH Pandemic Response Task Force [https://www.acgih.org/pandemic-task-force], an organization focused on occupational environmental health solutions. The task force that developed these "Effectiveness of Face Coverings for Preventing SARS-COV-2 Transmission" guidelines consists of "a group of volunteers focused on developing fact sheets and resources for industrial hygienists, other health and safety professionals, and their managers." They do not appear to have expertise in infectious disease or epidemiology. One member has a master's degree in industrial hygiene, another is an industrial hygienist with a bachelor's degree in environmental science, and a third is a consultant and certified hygienist. Their "hours of protection" infographic has now been seen by millions.

9. The "hours of protection" were calculated as follows. For two people wearing non-fit-tested N95s, the table assumed filtration of 90 percent for each mask, so 10 percent of viral particles would get through. Multiply 0.1 x 0.1 for the two masks to get 0.01. Take the inverse of that, for reasons that are unclear, to get 100, and multiply by 15/60 (minutes each hour). The result is 25 hours. The calculation depends on nothing but an assumption about 15 minutes and the known particle filtration level of the mask.

10. "Scientific Brief: SARS-CoV-2 Transmission," Centers for Disease Control and Prevention, May 7, 2021 [https://www.cdc.gov/coronavirus/2019-ncov/science/science-briefs/sars-cov-2-transmission.html].

11. For an in-depth discussion of misleading science communication, see C. T. Bergstrom and J. D. West, *Calling Bullshit: The Art of Skepticism in a Data-Driven World* (New York: Random House, 2020).

12. Kahan et al. study: D. Kahan, E. Peters, E. Dawson, and P. Slovic, "Motivated Numeracy and Enlightened Self-Government," *Behavioural Public Policy* 1 (2017): 54–86 [doi.org/10.1017/bpp.2016.2]. Kahan and Peters conducted a replication of this study with another 1,600-person sample: D. Kahan and E. Peters, "Rumors of the 'Nonreplication' of the 'Motivated Numeracy Effect' Are Greatly Exaggerated," Yale Law & Economics Research Paper No. 584, August 26, 2017 [http://dx.doi.org/10.2139/ssrn.3026941]. For information on how people read such "contingency tables," see W. C. Ward and H. M. Jenkins, "The Display of Information and the Judgment of Contingency," *Canadian Journal of Psychology* 19 (1965): 231–241 [https://doi.org/10.1037/h0082908]; R. E. Nisbett and L. Ross, *Human Inference: Strategies and Shortcomings of Social Judgment* (Englewood Cliffs, NJ: Prentice-Hall, 1980).

13. The concept of "motivated reasoning" refers to the idea that we often deploy reasoning skills only when we are motivated to do so—most often to defend a belief that we already have—rather than to figure out what is the right conclusion to draw from the evidence we have; see Z. Kunda, "The Case for Motivated Reasoning," *Psychological Bulletin* 108 (1990): 480–498 [https://doi.org/10.1037/0033-2909.108.3.480]. Some scholars have pushed this idea a step further and argued that the main purpose of our reasoning ability is to win arguments and convince others to our side, so the cognitive ability of logic exists to serve a social purpose: H. Mercier and D. Sperber, *The Enigma of Reason* (Cambridge, MA: Harvard University Press, 2017).

14. J. H. Anderson, "Let's Shed the Masks and Mandates—Omicron Stats Show We Can Stop Living in Fear," *New York Post*, January 9, 2022 [https://nypost.com/2022/01/09/omicron-stats-show-we-dont-need-mask-mandates-or-vaccine-requirements/]. Analysis used in the *New York Post* story: J. H. Anderson, "Do Masks Work? A Review of the Evidence," *City Journal*, August 11, 2021 [https://www.city-journal.org/do-masks-work-a-review-of-the-evidence]. Randomized study on masking in Bangladesh: J. Abaluck et al., "Impact of Community Masking on COVID-19: A Cluster-Randomized Trial in Bangladesh," *Science* 375 (2021), eabi9069 [doi.org/10.1126/science.abi9069].

15. A. Gampa, S. P. Wojcik, M. Motyl, B. A. Nosek, and P. H. Ditto, "(Ideo)Logical Reasoning: Ideology Impairs Sound Reasoning," *Social Psychological and Personality Science* 10 (2019): 1075–1083 [https://doi.org/10.1177/1948550619829059]. The other two studies in this paper showed that the pattern holds with items

worded less like logic puzzles and more like natural speech. The example syllogism comes from study 1 materials posted at Open Science Framework [https://osf.io /a496s/].

16. The spreadsheet kerfuffle is explained here: J. Cassidy, "The Reinhart and Rogoff Controversy: A Summing Up," *New Yorker*, April 26, 2013 [https://www.newyorker.com/news/john-cassidy/the-reinhart-and-rogoff -controversy-a-summing-up]. The bestseller that contained the erroneous analysis is C. M. Reinhart and K. S. Rogoff, *This Time Is Different: Eight Centuries of Financial Folly* (Princeton, NJ: Princeton University Press, 2009). The paper in which the spreadsheet error was reported, along with other criticisms of possible expectation-driven bias in the Reinhart-Rogoff analysis, is T. Herndon, M. Ash, and R. Pollin, "Does High Public Debt Consistently Stifle Economic Growth? A Critique of Reinhart and Rogoff," *Cambridge Journal of Economics* 38 (2014), 257–279 [https://doi.org/10.1093/cje/bet075]. Reinhart and Rogoff acknowledged the Excel error in a letter but disputed other concerns about their data analysis: M. Gongloff, "Reinhart and Rogoff's Second Response to Critique of Their Research," *Huffington Post*, April 17, 2013 [https://www.huffpost.com/entry /reinhart-rogoff-research-response_b_3099185].

17. B. Mellers, R. Hertwig, and D. Kahneman, "Do Frequency Representations Eliminate Conjunction Effects? An Exercise in Adversarial Collaboration," *Psychological Science* 12 (2001): 269–275 [https://doi.org/10.1111/1467-9280.00350].

18. "Driscoll Middle School Trick Play," YouTube [https://www.youtube.com /watch?v=0UIdI8khMkw]. These norm violations are not rule violations, but some expert commentators dislike them: F. Deford, "Middle School Trick Play Is No Laughing Matter," *Sports Illustrated*, November 17, 2010 [https://www.si.com /more-sports/2010/11/17/driscoll-middleschool]. In this case, some of the deception came from the actions of an assistant coach, and experts felt it was poor sportsmanship for a coach to deceive other middle schoolers in this way.

19. Our 1999 *Gorillas in Our Midst* video is on YouTube [https://www.you tube.com/watch?v=vJG698U2Mvo], as is Dan's 2010 *Monkey Business Illusion* [https://www.youtube.com/watch?v=IGQmdoK_ZfY]. See D. J. Simons and C. F. Chabris, "Gorillas in Our Midst: Sustained Inattentional Blindness for Dynamic Events," *Perception* 28 (1999): 1059–1074 [doi.org/10.1068/p281059]; D. J. Simons, "Monkeying Around with the Gorillas in Our Midst: Familiarity with an Inattentional-Blindness Task Does Not Improve the Detection of Unexpected Events," *i-Perception* 1 (2010): 3–6 [doi.org/10.1068/i0386].

20. Canon's project was called "Decoy" and was part of a larger series called *The Lab* [https://www.youtube.com/watch?v=F-TyPfYMDK8].

21. As it turns out, Montalban knew the principle in real life as well. In the 1980s, he appeared in a series of advertisements for Chrysler automobiles in which he touted their "fine Corinthian leather," among other luxury features. There was

no such thing as Corinthian leather: "Corinthian Leather," Wikipedia [https://en.wikipedia.org/wiki/Corinthian_leather].

22. D. A. Stapel and S. Lindenberg, "Coping with Chaos: How Disordered Contexts Promote Stereotyping and Discrimination," *Science* 332 (2011), 251–253 [doi.org/10.1126/science.1201068], and retraction notice [doi.org/10.1126/science.1201068]; A. K. Leung et al., "Embodied Metaphors and Creative 'Acts,'" *Psychological Science* 23 (2012): 502–509 [doi.org/10.1177/0956797611429801]; L. E. Williams and J. A. Bargh, "Experiencing Physical Warmth Promotes Interpersonal Warmth," *Science* 322 (2008), 606–607 [doi.org/10.1126/science.1162548]; A. Dijksterhuis and A. Van Knippenberg, "The Relation Between Perception and Behavior, or How to Win a Game of Trivial Pursuit," *Journal of Personality and Social Psychology* 74 (1998): 865–877 [https://doi.org/10.1037/0022-3514.74.4.865]; S. W. Lee and N. Schwarz, "Bidirectionality, Mediation, and Moderation of Metaphorical Effects: The Embodiment of Social Suspicion and Fishy Smells," *Journal of Personality and Social Psychology* 103 (2012): 737–749 [https://doi.org/10.1037/a0029708].

23. Stapel received the Career Trajectory Award from the Society of Experimental Social Psychology, but the award was rescinded after the discovery of his fraud: "Career Trajectory Award Recipients," Society of Experimental Social Psychology [https://www.sesp.org/content.asp?admin=Y&contentid=146]. See also the final investigation report: Levelt Committee, Noort Committee, and Drenth Committee, "Flawed Science: The Fraudulent Research Practices of Social Psychologist Diederik Stapel," November 28, 2012 [https://www.rug.nl/about-ug/latest-news/news/archief2012/nieuwsberichten/stapel-eindrapport-eng.pdf]. See the following for an overview of the case: Y. Bhattacharjee, "The Mind of a Con Man," *New York Times Magazine*, April 26, 2013 [https://www.nytimes.com/2013/04/28/magazine/diederik-stapels-audacious-academic-fraud.html]. Psychologist Yoel Inbar described his firsthand knowledge of the Stapel case in an episode of the podcast *Two Psychologists, Four Beers* titled "The Replication Crisis Gets Personal" [https://www.fourbeers.com/4]. Stapel's memoir, *Faking Science: A True Story of Academic Fraud*, was published in Dutch in 2012 and translated into English by Nicholas J. L. Brown in 2016 [http://nick.brown.free.fr/stapel/FakingScience-20161115.pdf].

24. Wansink study: B. Wansink, D. R. Just, and C. R. Payne, "Can Branding Improve School Lunches?," *Archives of Pediatric and Adolescent Medicine* 166 (2012): 967–968 [https://doi.org/10.1001/archpediatrics.2012.999]; retraction notice in *JAMA Pediatrics* 171 (2017), 1230 [doi.org/10.1001/jamapediatrics.2017.4603]. LaCour study: M. McNutt, "Editorial Retraction," *Science* 348 (2015): 1100 [doi.org/10.1126/science.aac6638]. Hauser study: M. D. Hauser, D. Weiss, and G. Marcus, "RETRACTED: Rule Learning by Cotton-Top Tamarins," *Cognition* 117 (2010): 106 [https://doi.org/10.1016/j.cognition.2010.08.013]. See also "Findings of Research Misconduct," Office of Research Integrity, US Department of Health

and Human Services, September 10, 2012 [https://grants.nih.gov/grants/guide/notice-files/not-od-12-149.html].

25. According to the investigation report by Harvard and the NIH, "Findings of Scientific Misconduct," December 13, 2001 [https://grants.nih.gov/grants/guide/notice-files/not-od-02-020.html], "Dr. Ruggiero engaged in scientific misconduct by fabricating data." Examples of Ruggiero's retracted papers: K. M. Ruggiero, J. P. Mitchell, N. Krieger, D. Marx, and M. L. Lorenzo, "RETRACTED: Now You See It, Now You Don't: Explicit Versus Implicit Measures of the Personal/Group Discrimination Discrepancy," *Psychological Science* 11 (2000): 511–514 [https://doi.org/10.1111/1467-9280.00298]; K. M. Ruggiero and D. M. Marx, "RETRACTED: Less Pain and More to Gain: Why High-Status Group Members Blame Their Failure on Discrimination," *Journal of Personality and Social Psychology* 77 (1999): 774–784 [https://doi.org/10.1037/0022-3514.77.4.774].

26. In a completely different field of expertise, basketball legend Kobe Bryant spotted this pattern in 2012 when describing "Linsanity," the sudden and unexpected rise to stardom that season of second-year NBA player Jeremy Lin: "It just means that we probably haven't been paying attention to him. It seems like it come out of nowhere, but if people go back and take a look, that skill level was probably there from the beginning. It just went unnoticed." In Lin's case, it's possible that his talents were underrated because he was an Asian American graduate of an Ivy League school, not a common background for an NBA player. Kobe Bryant's quotation and a list of Lin's accomplishments during the "Linsanity" period in 2012 are described in K. Peters, "Jeremy Lin Proving That He's the Real NBA Deal," *Palo Alto Online*, February 16, 2012 [https://www.paloaltoonline.com/news/2012/02/16/jeremy-lin-proving-that-hes-the-real-nba-deal].

27. Retraction Watch Leaderboard [https://retractionwatch.com/the-retraction-watch-leaderboard/].

28. L. L. Shu, N. Mazar, F. Gino, D. Ariely, and M. H. Bazerman, "Signing at the Beginning Makes Ethics Salient and Decreases Dishonest Self-Reports in Comparison to Signing at the End," *Proceedings of the National Academy of Sciences* 109 (2012): 15197–15200 [https://doi.org/10.1073/pnas.1209746109]; retraction notice, September 13, 2021 [https://doi.org/10.1073/pnas.2115397118].

29. Honesty declaration quotation: US Form 1040 for tax year 2019. The odometer study approach was clever because it did not require the company to laboriously inspect thousands of cars to determine the true readings; one can assume that because reporting higher values is not in the driver's interest, the ethical "nudge" from signing first must have resulted in greater honesty.

30. Simmons and colleagues reported their discovery of the fraudulent data in "Evidence of Fraud in an Influential Field Experiment About Dishonesty" on their blog *Data Colada*, August 17, 2021 [https://datacolada.org/98]. The investigation of the original data was inspired by the failure of some of the original authors to

replicate their own findings: A. S. Kristal, A. V. Whillans, M. H. Bazerman, and D. Ariely, "Signing at the Beginning Versus at the End Does Not Decrease Dishonesty," *Proceedings of the National Academy of Sciences* 117 (2020): 7103–7107 [https://doi.org/10.1073/pnas.1911695117]. We both know Dan Ariely personally. Chris collaborated with Ariely on research projects in the early 2000s, Ariely wrote an endorsement for our last book, and Ariely introduced us to our literary agent. Dan has corresponded with Ariely about multiple studies and replication efforts. Over the years, we both have been impressed by his ability to apply behavioral science to everyday life. Coincidentally, Dan has been involved in other cases in which researchers have reexamined older studies in which Ariely was involved and raised questions about their replicability and about some of the method details. For example, Dan served as the editor for a large-scale attempt to replicate one of Ariely's more famous studies, a finding that priming people by having them list the Ten Commandments led to reduced cheating. That attempt by many laboratories using a carefully vetted protocol did not find such a reduction in cheating. For more details, see S. M. Lee, "A Famous Honesty Researcher Is Retracting a Study over Fake Data," *BuzzFeed News*, August 20, 2021 [https://www.buzzfeednews.com/article/stephaniemlee/dan-ariely-honesty-study-retraction]. In his response to the odometer fraud story, Ariely said that the data in question came to him directly from the insurance company, and he committed to "developing new policies to ensure that our data collection and analysis meets the highest standards." It's worth noting that honesty nudges are hard to test in the real world, but one group recently did manage to test whether signing first would increase honest reporting of claims by insurance customers in a Nordic country. Unlike the fraudulent odometer study, they found no benefit of signing first: J. B. Martuza, S. R. Skard, L. Løvlie, and H. Thorbjørnsen, "Do Honesty-Nudges Really Work? A Large-Scale Field Experiment in an Insurance Context," *Journal of Consumer Behaviour* 21 (2022): 927–951 [https://doi.org/10.1002/cb.2049].

31. An Exact Fishy Test [https://macartan.shinyapps.io/fish/].

32. It's akin to the famous graphic identifying the many coincidences and parallels between Presidents Lincoln and Kennedy—if you give yourself enough options, you'll find intriguing patterns. Wikipedia gives a good summary: "Lincoln–Kennedy Coincidences Urban Legend" [https://en.wikipedia.org/wiki/Lincoln%E2%80%93Kennedy_coincidences_urban_legend].

33. Card naming: J. A. Olson, A. A. Amlani, and R. A. Rensink, "Perceptual and Cognitive Characteristics of Common Playing Cards," *Perception* 41 (2012), 268–286 [https://doi.org/10.1068/p7175]. Coin tossing: If you flip a fair coin five times, you should get a run of either five heads or five tails over 6 percent of the time, but the sequences people generate include far fewer long runs than they should.

34. J. Golbeck, "Benford's Law Applies to Online Social Networks," *PLoS ONE* 10 (2015): e0135169 [https://doi.org/10.1371/journal.pone.0135169].

35. J. Golbeck, "Benford's Law Can Detect Malicious Social Bots," *First Monday* 24 (2019) [https://doi.org/10.5210/fm.v24i8.10163]. Note that constructing a bot network so that the collection of follower counts for the bots themselves adhered to Benford's law might not be that hard. But ensuring that the accounts followed by those bots also had follower counts that adhered to Benford's law would be especially challenging.

36. *Radiolab* discussion of misapplications of Benford's law to the 2020 US presidential election: Latif Nasser, "Breaking Benford," November 13, 2020 [https://radiolab.org/episodes/breaking-benford].

37. M. J. Nigrini, *Benford's Law: Applications for Forensic Accounting, Auditing, and Fraud Detection* (Hoboken, NJ: Wiley, 2012).

38. Quotation from J. Levitt, *Contemplating Comedy* (Conrad Press, 2020). Avoiding being deceived by one's own expectations is critical to the art of forecasting future events. See P. E. Tetlock and D. Gardner, *Superforecasting: The Art and Science of Prediction* (New York: Crown, 2015).

Chapter 3: Commitment—Be Careful When You Assume

1. The original London and New York exhibitions of Shovlin's Lustfaust creation are reviewed here: A. Jones "It's Only Mock 'n' Roll but We Like It," *Independent*, May 1, 2006 [https://www.independent.co.uk/arts-entertainment/music/features/it-s-only-mock-n-roll-but-we-like-it-6102224.html]; "Art in Review; Lustfaust—A Folk Anthology, 1976–1981," *New York Times*, July 21, 2006 [https://www.nytimes.com/2006/07/21/arts/art-in-review-lustfaust-a-folk-anthology-19761981.html]. Shovlin told us in a short email interview about the people who recalled having seen Lustfaust in the 1970s. After the 2006 exhibitions, Shovlin "revived" the band, undoubtedly convincing even more people that it really had existed before he fabricated it.

2. Fiona Broome's original website for the Mandela Effect [https://mandelaeffect.com/].

3. For a good explanation of the memory mechanisms associated with the Mandela Effect, see: M. Triffin, "Your Whole Life Is a Lie: It's BerenstAin Bears, Not BerenstEin Bears," *Yahoo Health*, August 13, 2015 [https://www.yahoo.com/lifestyle/your-whole-life-is-a-lie-its-berenstain-bears-126604020432.html]. *Good Housekeeping* magazine has compiled a set of fifty examples of divergent memories that have been cited as instances of the "effect": "50 Mandela Effect Examples That Will Make You Question Everything," May 25, 2022 [https://www.goodhousekeeping.com/life/entertainment/g28438966/mandela-effect-examples/]. There is also a 2019 science fiction film called *The Mandela Effect* (directed by David Guy Levy) based on the idea. Two examples of the self-published literature

that takes the effect seriously—as an indication of large-scale disturbances in the universe rather than readily explicable memory distortions—are S. Eriksen, *The Mandela Effect: Everything Is Changing* (CreateSpace, 2017); T. S. Caladan, *Mandela Effect: Analysis of a Worldwide Phenomenon* (CreateSpace, 2019). For a recent psychological study of this phenomenon, see D. Prasad and W. A. Bainbridge, "The Visual Mandela Effect as Evidence for Shared and Specific False Memories Across People," *Psychological Science*, 2022 [https://doi.org/10.1177/095679 7622110894].

4. Evidence of mistaken beliefs about memory: D. J. Simons and C. F. Chabris, "Common (Mis)Beliefs About Memory: A Replication and Comparison of Telephone and Mechanical Turk Survey Methods," *PLoS One* 7 (2012): e51876 [https://doi.org/10.1371/journal.pone.0051876]. Ironically, a converse misbelief about memory—the belief that if you don't remember doing something, you must not have—was probably responsible for a widespread belief that people were being entrapped into some kind of fraud or worse regarding shipments of seeds that they received from China in 2020. People were surprised to get seeds in the mail and came up with several possible explanations, including biological warfare and Amazon.com scams, when the most plausible explanation is that they (1) bought seeds online, (2) didn't realize the companies they were buying seeds from were Chinese companies, and (3) forgot they had bought the seeds by the time they arrived, after long pandemic-related delays. See C. Heath, "The Truth Behind the Amazon Mystery Seeds," *Atlantic*, July 15, 2021 [https://www.theatlantic.com/science /archive/2021/07/unsolicited-seeds-china-brushing/619417/].

5. Claims that the Middle Ages never happened: J. Elledge, "Did the Early Medieval Era Ever Really Take Place?," July 4, 2022 [https://jonn.substack.com/p /did-the-early-medieval-era-ever-really]. Claims that Wyoming doesn't exist: J. Goodrick, "Growing Online Theory Says Wyoming Doesn't Exist," AP News, November 22, 2020 [https://apnews.com/article/wyoming-coronavirus -pandemic-gillette-d7d2bbf5e2040b4e1e5498c8131bc376]. Even some scientists have argued that what is true about the world inherently fades away over time as a result of some mystical, unexplained force. See J. Lehrer, "The Truth Wears Off," *New Yorker*, December 5, 2010 [https://www.newyorker.com/magazine/2010/12/13 /the-truth-wears-off]; for a rebuttal, see J. Lehrer and C. F. Chabris, "Jonah Lehrer Interviews Christopher Chabris," *Creativity Post*, August 1, 2012 [https://www .creativitypost.com/article/jonah_lehrer_interviews_christopher_chabris].

6. More on this point in this YouTube video [https://www.youtube.com /watch?v=dQw4w9WgXcQ].

7. Anonymous comment on October 24 on this post: S. Alexander, "Kolmogorov Complexity and the Parable of Lightning," *Slate Star Codex*, October 23, 2017 [https://slatestarcodex.com/2017/10/23/kolmogorov-complicity-and -the-parable-of-lightning/].

8. M. Heffernan, *Willful Blindness: Why We Ignore the Obvious at Our Peril* (New York: Bloomsbury, 2011).

9. R. Revsbech et al., "Exploring Rationality in Schizophrenia," *BJPsych Open* 1 (2015): 98–103 [doi.org/10.1192/bjpo.bp.115.000224]; D. Mirian, R. W. Heinrichs, and S. M. Vaz, "Exploring Logical Reasoning Abilities in Schizophrenia Patients," *Schizophrenia Research* 127 (2011): 178–180 [https://doi.org/10.1016/j.schres.2011.01.007].

10. N. Merchant, "US Intel Predicted Russia's Invasion Plans. Did It Matter?," AP News, February 24, 2022 [https://apnews.com/article/russia-ukraine -vladimir-putin-business-europe-8acc2106b95554429e93dfee5e253743]; "2 in 5 Russians Believe War with Ukraine Likely—Poll," *Moscow Times*, December 14, 2021 [https://www.themoscowtimes.com/2021/12/14/2-in-5 -russians-believe-war-with-ukraine-likely-poll-a75816]; M. Mirovalev, "Why Most Ukrainians Don't Believe Biden's Warnings, Distrust West," Al Jazeera, February 21, 2022 [https://www.aljazeera.com/news/2022/2/21/why-ukrainians -dont-believe-in-war-with-russia-distrust-west]; V. Hopkins, N. MacFarquhar, S. Erlanger, and M. Levenson, "100 Days of War: Death, Destruction, and Loss," *New York Times*, June 3, 2022 [https://www.nytimes.com/2022/06/03/world/europe /russia-ukraine-war-100-days.html].

11. Chris estimated people's discount rates for future amounts of money with a twenty-seven-question test in which participants could be randomly chosen to receive the outcome of one of their choices, so they had an incentive to respond honestly about whether they would prefer the smaller amount today or the larger amount in the future. These studies are reported here: C. F. Chabris, D. I. Laibson, C. L. Morris, J. P. Schuldt, and D. Taubinsky, "The Allocation of Time in Decision-Making," *Journal of the European Economic Association* 7 (2009), 628–637 [https://doi.org/10.1162/JEEA.2009.7.2-3.628]; C. F. Chabris, D. I. Laibson, C. L. Morris, J. P. Schuldt, and D. Taubinsky, "Individual Laboratory-Measured Discount Rates Predict Field Behavior," *Journal of Risk and Uncertainty* 37 (2008): 237–269 [https://doi.org/10.1007/s11166-008-9053-x]. Note that discount rates are more meaningful measures when people believe the money will appear in their bank accounts on the specified dates without their having to do anything to receive it and that rigorously estimating people's discount rates can be more complicated than our example implies.

12. N. Augenblick, J. M. Cunha, E. D. Bó, and J. M. Rao, "The Economics of Faith: Using an Apocalyptic Prophecy to Elicit Religious Belief in the Field," *Journal of Public Economics* 141 (2016): 38–49 [https://doi.org /10.1016/j.jpubeco.2016.07.004]. Augenblick et al. tested just 52 participants (23 prophecy believers and 29 Seventh Day Adventists); normally this would be a small sample from which to draw strong conclusions, but in this

case, the difference between the two groups was huge: 22 out of 23 believers rejected $500 after the rapture date, but 29 of 29 comparison participants selected it.

13. Pew survey: Pew Research Center, "Jesus Christ's Return to Earth," July 14, 2010 [https://www.pewresearch.org/fact-tank/2010/07/14/jesus-christs -return-to-earth/]; Cohen quotation: D. Cohen, *Waiting for the Apocalypse* (New York: Prometheus Books, 1983), p. 72.

14. P. Johansson, L. Hall, S. Sikström, and A. Olsson, "Failure to Detect Mismatches Between Intention and Outcome in a Simple Decision Task," *Science* 310 (2005): 116–119 [https://doi.org/10.1126/science.1111709]. The same choice blindness happens for taste preferences: L. Hall, P. Johansson, B. Tärning, S. Sikström, and T. Deutgen, "Magic at the Marketplace: Choice Blindness for the Taste of Jam and the Smell of Tea," *Cognition* 117 (2010): 54–61 [https://doi .org/10.1016/j.cognition.2010.06.010]. In another study, the choice blindness researchers asked voters in two Swedish cities to rate how much they agreed or disagreed with the positions associated with the major political coalitions prior to a national election. Using a gimmicked clipboard, the experimenters then showed them a modified version that made it appear that their ratings aligned more closely with the opposite side. Ninety-two percent of the participants accepted this altered summary score as if it were their own, and nearly half indicated that they were open to changing which coalition they would support in the election. See L. Hall, T. Strandberg, P. Pärnamets, A. Lind, B. Tärning, and P. Johansson, "How the Polls Can Be Both Spot On and Dead Wrong: Using Choice Blindness to Shift Political Attitudes and Voter Intentions," *PLoS One* 8 (2013): e60554 [https://doi .org/10.1371/journal.pone.0060554]. If you're having trouble imagining how voters could be so unfamiliar with the issues and so uncommitted to particular positions and candidates, consider this: The morning after the 2016 US presidential election, one of us overheard two workers in a sandwich shop trying to figure out what candidates had been running, which one had won, and why either of them should really care.

15. This general idea is also supported by research on framing effects in judgments, e.g., P. Slovic, "The Construction of Preference," *American Psychologist* 50 (1995): 364–371 [https://doi.org/10.1037/0003-066X.50.5.364].

16. E. Trouche, P. Johansson, L. Hall, and H. Mercier, "The Selective Laziness of Reasoning," *Cognitive Science* 40 (2016): 2122–2136 [https://doi.org/10.1111 /cogs.12303].

17. The Magic of Consciousness Symposium, Association for the Scientific Study of Consciousness, 2007 [https://web.archive.org/web/20070519203333 /http://assc2007.neuralcorrelate.com/index.php?module=pagemaster&PAGE _user_op=view_page&PAGE_id=7].

18. Some scammers will exploit the same tendency—to commit to, rather than reexamine, old inferences—by starting out with a couple of legitimate transactions in order to build up to a large theft.

19. Frank Casey's story is related on pp. 126–128 of J. Campbell, *Madoff Talks: Uncovering the Untold Story Behind the Most Notorious Ponzi Scheme in History* (New York: McGraw-Hill, 2021).

20. The opposite of the degenerate view is the canonical view, which is the view of an object that shows the most information that is useful in distinguishing it from other objects. This is often from a 45-degree angle to the side and above the object. Anamorphic art—drawings or sculptures that look like real scenes or objects only from a single point of view—work in the same way but reversed; when we see it from that one critical vantage point, we're getting a degenerate view. And we don't realize how distorted it would be from every other viewpoint.

21. J. Kirby, "What to Know About the 'Raw Water' Trend," *Vox*, January 4, 2018 [https://www.vox.com/science-and-health/2018/1/4/16846048/raw-water-trend-silicon-valley]. For more on preferences for the natural, see A. Levinovitz, *Natural: How Faith in Nature's Goodness Leads to Harmful Fads, Unjust Laws, and Flawed Science* (Boston: Beacon Press, 2020).

22. Paolo Macchiarini's criminal conviction is reported here: G. Vogel, "Disgraced Italian Surgeon Convicted of Criminal Harm to Stem Cell Patient," *Science* 376 (2022): 1370–1371 [https://doi.org/10.1126/science.add6185]. For more information on the case, see E. Ward and C. Anderson, "A High-Flying Italian Surgeon's Fall from Grace," *New York Times*, June 17, 2022 [https://www.nytimes.com/2022/06/17/world/europe/macchiarini-windpipe-surgeon-deaths.html]; A. Ciralsky, "The Celebrity Surgeon Who Used Love, Money, and the Pope to Scam an ABC News Producer," *Vanity Fair*, January 5, 2016 [https://www.vanityfair.com/news/2016/01/celebrity-surgeon-nbc-news-producer-scam]. Bosse Lindquist's film about Macchiarini, *Fatal Experiments*, aired on Swedish television and on the BBC in 2016.

23. Bullshit asymmetry principle: The pioneering economist Frédéric Bastiat formulated an early version of this idea in his 1845 book *Economic Sophisms*: "We must confess that our adversaries have a marked advantage over us in the discussion. In very few words they can announce a half-truth; and in order to demonstrate that it is incomplete, we are obliged to have recourse to long and dry dissertations." Even earlier, Jonathan Swift wrote, "Falsehood flies, and the truth comes limping after it; so that when men come to be undeceived, it is too late; the jest is over, and the tale has had its effect." *Examiner [afterw.] The Whig Examiner* [by J. Addison] (United Kingdom: n.p., 1710). Original "hard to read" study: A. L. Alter, D. M. Oppenheimer, N. Epley, and N. Eyre, "Overcoming Intuition: Metacognitive Difficulty Activates Analytic Reasoning," *Journal of Experimental Psychology: General* 136 (2007): 569–576 [https://doi.org/10.1037/0096-3445.136.4.569]. This study has been cited favorably in books by Malcolm Gladwell (*David and Goliath*), Daniel

Kahneman (*Thinking, Fast and Slow*), and Alter himself (*Drunk Tank Pink*). Replication attempt: A. Meyer et al., "Disfluent Fonts Don't Help People Solve Math Problems," *Journal of Experimental Psychology: General* 144 (2015): e16 [https://doi.org/10.1037/xge0000049].

24. S. Benartzi and J. Lehrer, *The Smarter Screen: Surprising Ways to Influence and Improve Online Behavior* (New York: Portfolio, 2015), 127. The time-reversal heuristic was proposed in a blog post by Andrew Gelman, "The Time-Reversal Heuristic—a New Way to Think About a Published Finding That Is Followed Up by a Large, Preregistered Replication (in Context of Claims About Power Pose)," *Statistical Modeling, Causal Inference, and Social Science,* January 26, 2016 [https://statmodeling.stat.columbia.edu/2016/01/26/more-power-posing/].

25. L. Magrath, and L. Weld, "Abusive Earnings Management and Early Warning Signs," *CPA Journal*, August 2002, 50–54. Kenneth Lay's indictment lays out the nature of the manipulation used to beat estimates [https://www.justice.gov/archive/opa/pr/2004/July/04_crm_470.htm]; he was convicted in 2006 [https://www.justice.gov/archive/opa/pr/2006/May/06_crm_328.html]. SEC action against Coca-Cola [https://www.sec.gov/litigation/admin/33-8569.pdf].

26. Thaddeus's analysis of Columbia's ranking: M. Thaddeus, "An Investigation of the Facts Behind Columbia's U.S. News Ranking," Department of Mathematics, Columbia University, February 2022 [https://www.math.columbia.edu/~thaddeus/ranking/investigation.html]. Response from Columbia: A. Hartocollis, "U.S. News Ranked Columbia No. 2, but a Math Professor Has His Doubts," *New York Times*, March 17, 2022 [https://www.nytimes.com/2022/03/17/us/columbia-university-rank.html]. Thaddeus also investigated Columbia's engineering rankings: "The U.S. News Ranking of Columbia's Online Engineering Programs," Department of Mathematics, Columbia University, April 2022 [http://www.math.columbia.edu/~thaddeus/ranking/engineering html]. *U.S. News* ranking changes and other misrepresented data: R. Morse, "U.S. News Rankings Update: Find Out About the Schools That Misreported Data to U.S. News," July 7, 2022 [https://www.usnews.com/education/articles/us-news-rankings-updates]; A. Hartocollis, "U.S. News Dropped Columbia's Ranking, but Its Own Methods Are Now Questioned," *New York Times*, September 12, 2022 [https://www.nytimes.com/2022/09/12/us/columbia-university-us-news-ranking.html]. In a similar scandal, the dean of Temple University's business school was convicted of conspiring to fabricate data over five years in order to push his school up the rankings: A. Lukpat, "Former Temple U. Dean Found Guilty of Faking Data for National Rankings," *New York Times*, November 29, 2021 [https://www.nytimes.com/2021/11/29/us/temple-university-moshe-porat-fraud.html]. The effects of test-optional college admissions: H. Wainer, *Uneducated Guesses: Using Evidence to Uncover Misguided Education Policies* (Princeton, NJ: Princeton University Press, 2011), ch. 1.

27. B. I. Koerner, "The Cheating Scandal That Ripped the Poker World Apart," *Wired*, September 21, 2020 [https://www.wired.com/story/stones-poker -cheating-scandal/].

28. J. Maysh, "How an Ex-Cop Rigged McDonald's Monopoly Game and Stole Millions," *Daily Beast*, July 28, 2018 [https://www.thedailybeast.com /how-an-ex-cop-rigged-mcdonalds-monopoly-game-and-stole-millions].

29. Fyre Festival: G. Bluestone, *Hype: How Scammers, Grifters, and Con Artists Are Taking Over the Internet—and Why We're Following* (Toronto, ON: Hanover Square Press, 2021). Repeat fraudsters in reports on the Office of Justice Programs website: "White Collar Crime and Criminal Careers," 1993 [https://www.ojp.gov /ncjrs/virtual-library/abstracts/white-collar-crime-and-criminal-careers] (PDF of report linked on this page), and the Oversight website: N. L'Heureux, "The Value of Identifying the Repeat Offender," March 22, 2021 [https://www .oversight.com/blog/the-value-of-identifying-the-repeat-offender]. For another example of a convicted fraudster launching a new fraud as soon as he was out of prison, see J. Bullmore, "Château La Thief," *Air Mail*, May 14, 2022 [https://air mail.news/issues/2022-5-14/chateau-lathief].

30. Orlando Basquiat exhibition website [https://web.archive.org/web /20220609201252/https://omart.org/exhibitions/heroes_monsters_jean_michel _basquiat_the_venice_collection_thaddeaus_mumford_jr/]. FBI raid: B. Sokol and M. Stevens, "F.B.I. Raids Orlando Museum and Removes Basquiat Paintings," June 24, 2022 [https://www.nytimes.com/2022/06/24/arts/design/fbi-orlando -museum-basquiat.html]. *New York Times* reporter Brett Sokol published two lengthy articles on the questions around the discovery: "In Orlando, 25 Mysterious Basquiats Come Under the Magnifying Glass," *New York Times*, February 16, 2022 [https://www.nytimes.com/2022/02/16/arts/design/basquiat-painting -orlando-mumford-museum.html], and "F.B.I. Investigates Basquiat Paintings Shown at Orlando Museum of Art," *New York Times*, May 29, 2022 [https:// www.nytimes.com/2022/05/29/arts/design/fbi-basquiat-paintings-orlando -museum.html].

31. J. Settembre, "Forget West Elm Caleb—We Were Duped by 'Psycho' Dating Nightmare Long Island Kevin," *New York Post*, July 12, 2022 [https://nypost .com/2022/07/12/singles-warn-long-island-kevin-is-worse-than-west-elm-caleb/].

Chapter 4: Efficiency—Ask More Questions

1. J. Benjamin and H. Scott, *Winning the World Open: Strategies for Success at America's Most Prestigious Open Chess Tournament* (Alkmaar, the Netherlands: New in Chess, 2021).

2. The "John von Neumann" affair was reported in several chess magazines in 1993. See especially J. Watson, "Yermolinsky Wins World Open . . . but von Neumann Steals the Show," *Inside Chess* 6 (1993): 3–10; D. Vigorito, "1993

World Open," *Chess Horizons* (September–October 1993): 23–24; J. Benjamin, "Yerminator on Top of the World . . . Open," *Chess Chow* (July–August 1993): 5–14; M. Shibut, "Macon a Contribution to Chess Theory," *Chess Chow* (September–October 1993): 3–4. We have supplemented those accounts with interviews of several people who were at the event.

3. Chris co-organized a series of human-versus-computer tournaments called the Harvard Cup from 1989 through 1995. In 1992, the best computer program of the five that competed scored three points against five grandmasters. Therefore, if von Neumann had been accurately transmitting and receiving computer moves and was never caught, he could have contended for one of the top overall prizes and won thousands of dollars. These tournaments are described in a series of articles, especially C. F. Chabris, "The Harvard Cup Man-Versus-Machine Chess Challenge," *ICGA Journal* 16 (1993): 57–61 [https://doi.org/10.3233/ICG-1993 -16113]; C. F. Chabris and D. Kopec, "The 4th Harvard Cup Human Versus Computer Chess Challenge," *ICGA Journal* 16 (1993): 232–241 [https://doi .org/10.3233/ICG-1993-16410].

4. Von Neumann returned to the tournament later on the final night and offered to play anyone to prove he was not a fraud. Macon Shibut, a local master who was hanging around after the tournament, was selected for a quick game, but after three moves, von Neumann sank into deep thought. The spectators started to wander off, and, realizing he could be there for hours, Shibut got up and left as well.

5. Guardian Sport, "Chess Grandmaster Admits to Cheating with Phone on Toilet During Tournament," *Guardian*, July 13, 2019 [https://www.the guardian.com/sport/2019/jul/13/igors-rausis-cheating-phone-tournament -scandal]. Photo of Rausis on the toilet with his phone: S. Dorn, "Chess Grandmaster Allegedly Caught Cheating on Toilet During Tournament," *New York Post*, July 13, 2019 [https://nypost.com/2019/07/13/chess-grandmaster-allegedly-caught -cheating-on-toilet-during-tournament/]. In September 2022, the world champion dropped out of an elite tournament for the first time in his career after losing to a grandmaster he suspected of cheating; see A. Therrien, "Magnus Carlsen and Hans Niemann: The Cheating Row That's Blowing Up the Chess World," BBC News, September 23, 2022 [https://www.bbc.com/news/world-63010107]. Magnus Carlsen later released a statement on Twitter [https://twitter.com /MagnusCarlsen/status/1574482694406565888].

6. It is interesting that cheaters often use bathrooms as part of their schemes. Rausis was not the first to try this in chess (it is actually common, and even though this is well known, bathrooms are still poorly monitored during some tournaments), and we're sure many other students have planted "study aids" there during exams. One question we can ask to help detect cheating is "Where would I be least likely to look for evidence?" (Had Virgil Sollozzo asked this before sitting down to dinner with Michael Corleone, there might never have been a *Godfather: Part*

II.) Privacy norms around bathrooms, changing areas, and similar settings create relatively safe spaces for cheaters. Indeed, the photograph that proved Rausis was cheating was probably taken in violation of local laws, though the photographer was not prosecuted.

7. X. Gabaix and D. I. Laibson, "Shrouded Attributes, Consumer Myopia, and Information Suppression in Competitive Markets," *Quarterly Journal of Economics* 121 (2006): 505–540 [https://doi.org/10.1162/qjec.2006.121.2.505]. Printer production costs have fallen dramatically since the mid-1980s, when the first laser printers were priced at $3,000–7,000.

8. Customers paying more when fees are shrouded: M. Luca, "The Sinister Logic of Hidden Online Fees," *Wall Street Journal*, November 23, 2022 [https://www.wsj.com/articles/the-sinister-logic-of-hidden-online-fees-11669229205].

9. Examples of advertisements: DealDash [https://www.youtube.com/watch?v=DaKsZC0whYc] and Quibids [https://www.youtube.com/watch?v=TCowafeg_-U]. DealDash's fine print also includes hard-to-parse statistics like "54% of auction winners save 90% off Buy It Now prices or more."

10. N. Augenblick, "The Sunk-Cost Fallacy in Penny Auctions," *Review of Economic Studies* 83 (2016): 58–86 [doi.org/10.1093/restud/rdv037].

11. K. Mrkva, N. A. Posner, C. Reeck, and E. J. Johnson, "Do Nudges Reduce Disparities? Choice Architecture Compensates for Low Consumer Knowledge," *Journal of Marketing* 85 (2021): 67–84 [https://doi.org/10.1177/0022242921993186].

12. When you're buying a house, you might think little of raising your offer by $10,000 to close a deal, even if $10,000 is a sum you would agonize over for any other purchase. The extra $10,000 for the house is worth the same as any other $10,000 you might spend! Moreover, if you're financing the purchase, the actual cost at the end of a mortgage will be much greater. At a historically good interest rate of 5 percent, that additional $10,000 would equate to total payments of $19,000 over the course of thirty years, whereas if you invested it with an expected annual return of 5 percent, the same $10,000 would be worth about $43,000 after thirty years. So by that reckoning of the opportunity costs, not adding that $10,000 to your purchase price could make a difference of about $60,000 in your wealth at the end of the mortgage term.

13. J. Liu, "How a Prolific Art Forger Got a New York Gallery Show," *Hyperallergic*, April 11, 2022 [https://hyperallergic.com/723112/how-a-prolific-art-forger-got-a-new-york-gallery-show/].

14. The Knoedler case was covered widely in the press, including a series of articles in the *New York Times*. For an overview, see M. H. Miller, "The Big Fake: Behind the Scenes of Knoedler Gallery's Downfall," *ARTnews*, April 25, 2016 [https://www.artnews.com/art-news/artists/the-big-fake-behind-the-scenes-of-knoedler-gallerys-downfall-6179/]. The account here is based mainly on the podcast *Art Fraud* (iHeart Radio, 2022) and the two documentary films about the

case: *Made You Look: A True Story About Fake Art*, directed by Barry Avrich (2020), and *Driven to Abstraction*, directed by Daria Price (2019).

15. Rosales pleaded guilty to nine counts [https://www.justice.gov/usao-sdny /pr/art-dealer-pleads-guilty-manhattanfederal-court-80-million-fake-art-scam money]; her alleged conspirators were indicted on a total of ten counts [https:// www.justice.gov/usao-sdny/pr/three-defendants-charged-manhattan -federal-court-connection-33-million-art-fraud-scheme].

16. For a longer discussion of the point that forgeries look right in the context of expert assessments of literary forgeries and the value of "gut feelings" in art fraud detection, see D. J. Simons and C. F. Chabris, "The Trouble with Intuition," *Chronicle of Higher Education*, May 30, 2010 [https://www.chronicle.com/article /the-trouble-with-intuition/].

17. The Myatt/Drewe affair is documented wonderfully in L. Salisbury and A. Sujo, *Provenance: How a Con Man and a Forger Rewrote the History of Modern Art* (New York: Penguin, 2009). Other sources include "UK Art Fraudster Found Guilty," BBC News, February 12, 1999 [http://news.bbc.co.uk/1/hi/uk/278413 .stm]; "UK Art Fraudster Jailed," BBC News, February 15, 1999 [http://news.bbc .co.uk/2/hi/uk_news/279937.stm]. As usual, this is just one example of many; e.g., a Norwegian couple was suspected by the Portuguese police in 2010 of creating new works and fake documentation in a similar con: D. Alberge, "An Eclectic Art Fraud in Portugal," *Wall Street Journal*, November 24, 2010 [https://www.wsj .com/articles/SB10001424052748704369304575632801638081746].

18. S. Cain, "'Milli Violini': I Was a Fake Violinist in a World-Class Miming Orchestra," *Guardian*, May 27, 2020 [https://www.theguardian.com/books/2020 /may/27/milli-violini-fake-violinist-miming-orchestra-jessica-chiccehitto -hindman-memoir-sounds-like-titanic]; J. Hindman, *Sounds Like Titanic: A Memoir* (New York: W. W. Norton, 2019).

19. K. Rothstein, "Scam Season Comes for the Orchestra," *Vulture*, February 14, 2019 [https://www.vulture.com/2019/02/a-famous-composer-faked-his-way -through-live-performances.html].

20. Example video from the PBS tour: "Tim Janis, BEAUTIFUL AMERICA FULL PBS Special" [https://www.youtube.com/watch?v=Nu_KwMEl-Kw&t=1460s]; this video credits Hindman as one of the performers at the end.

21. R. Catlin, "The Long Musical Arm of Tim Janis," *Hartford Courant*, November 26, 2001 [https://www.courant.com/news/connecticut/hc-xpm-2001-11 -27-0111270707-story.html].

22. "A Fake Orchestra Performance in 'Sounds Like Titanic,'" NPR.com, February 9, 2019 [https://www.npr.org/2019/02/09/692955821/a-fake-orchestra -performance-in-sounds-like-titanic].

23. The official social media posts issued about the articles, search engine result text, and many other summaries and taglines that reach a vastly larger number of

people than those who "read the whole thing" are commonly written by other people, often specialists in creating online engagement, who have read nothing more than the story itself.

24. Official reports on the Smeesters case: R. A. Zwaan, P. J. F. Groenen, A. J. van der Heijden, and R. te Lindert, "Rapport onderzoekscommissie Wetenschappelijke integriteit: Onderzoek naar mogelijke schending van de wetenschappelijke integriteit" ("Report of the Scientific Integrity Investigation Committee: Investigation into possible violation of scientific integrity"); A. J. van der Heijden, P. J. F. Groenen, R. Zeelenberg, and R. te Lindert, "Report of the Smeesters Follow-up Investigation Committee," January 27, 2014. (English translations were provided to Dan by Renee Zeelenberg.) Smeesters was interviewed about the case: "Smeesters' Side of the Story," *Erasmus Magazine*, September 11, 2012 [https://www.erasmusmagazine.nl/en/2012/09/11/smeesters-side-of-the-story/].

25. J. Liu, D. Smeesters, and D. Trampe, "Effects of Messiness on Preferences for Simplicity," *Journal of Consumer Research* 39 (2012): 199–214 [https://doi.org/10.1086/662139].

26. Scaling the precision of your offer according to its size (bidding in multiples of $1,000 for a car but $5 for a shirt) is not necessarily rational. Every dollar you save by making your offers match the value you put on the purchase is worth the same whether the price is $33 or $33,000.

27. U. Simonsohn, "Just Post It: The Lesson from Two Cases of Fabricated Data Detected by Statistics Alone," *Psychological Science* 24 (2013): 1875–1888 [https://doi.org/10.1177/0956797613480366]. The original study was conducted in the Netherlands, so the amounts were not in dollars, but the same principle applies.

28. M. Enserink, "Rotterdam Marketing Psychologist Resigns After University Investigates His Data," *Science*, June 25, 2012 [doi.org/10.1126/article.27200].

29. Simonsohn interview: E. Yong, "The Data Detective," *Nature* 487 (2012): 18–19 [https://doi.org/10.1038/487018a].

30. G. Spier, *The Education of a Value Investor* (New York: Palgrave Macmillan, 2014). The Farmer Mac story is on pp. 53–57. Having learned the lesson of his wrong initial call on Farmer Mac, Spier later spent over one year researching a company called BYD Auto, a Chinese battery and car maker, before investing his fund's money (pp. 125–126).

31. Shorting means that he borrowed shares and sold them so that he would profit if their price declined by buying them back at the lower price and then returning them to the lender.

32. You can remember this story and its lesson with the helpful phrase "the work required to have an opinion," the value of which is highlighted in an essay titled "The Work Required to Have an Opinion" on the blog *Farnam Street* [https://fs.blog/the-work-required-to-have-an-opinion/].

33. The 2018 documentary film *The China Hustle*, directed by Jed Rothstein, conveys this story and many like it. The group's research report about Orient Paper is available online [https://www.muddywatersresearch.com/research /orient-paper-inc/initiating-coverage-onp/].

34. M. Levine, "Caesars and the $450M 'And,'" *Bloomberg*, May 13, 2014 [https://www.bloomberg.com/opinion/articles/2014-05-13/caesars-and-the -450-million-and]. Levine explains precisely how the bond's terms implied that by selling a small amount of stock, Caesars could relieve a much larger amount of its debt. In 2014, the parent Caesars Entertainment Corporation triggered one of the three events by selling about $6 million of new stock in the subsidiary. The bondholders, fearing a loss of $450 million in value, now had a strong incentive to read all the way to page 106, where they discovered that the three events in the list were joined by the word "and," implying that all three would have to happen for the guarantee to end, while Caesars was treating the list as a set of alternatives, as in A or B or C would be sufficient. The resulting dispute was moot once Caesars went bankrupt later that year.

35. T. Rogers and M. I. Norton, "The Artful Dodger: Answering the Wrong Question the Right Way," *Journal of Experimental Psychology: Applied* 17 (2011): 139–147 [https://doi.org/10.1037/a0023439].

36. "Placebic information" comes from the title of a famous social psychology experiment that revolved around a photocopying machine. The author approached people standing at the copier and interrupted them with a request to make some copies right away. Adding a placebic justification—"because I need to make copies"—was reportedly just as persuasive as a relevant one—"because I'm in a rush." Whether this result is robust and the placebic information truly is just as effective is unclear, but the concept is worth keeping in mind. E. Langer, A. Blank, and B. Chanowitz, "The Mindlessness of Ostensibly Thoughtful Action: The Role of 'Placebic' Information in Interpersonal Interaction," *Journal of Personality and Social Psychology* 36 (1978): 635–642 [https://doi.org/10.1037/0022-3514.36.6.635]. For an example of a randomized clinical trial in which adding a placebic "because" had no persuasive effect, see M. R. Heino, K. Knittle, A. Haukkala, T. Vasankari, and N. Hankonen, "Simple and Rationale-Providing SMS Reminders to Promote Accelerometer Use: A Within-Trial Randomised Trial Comparing Persuasive Messages," *BMC Public Health* 18 (2018): 1–16 [https://doi.org/10.1186/s12889-018 -6121-2]. The phrase "nondenial denial" is attributed to *Washington Post* editor Ben Bradlee and said to have originated in the Nixon administration's interactions with the press during the Watergate scandal.

37. L. Gilbert, "Rothko Specialist and Son Testify They Never Authenticated Fake Painting in Knoedler Trial," *Art Newspaper*, February 2, 2016 [https:// www.theartnewspaper.com/2016/02/02/rothko-specialist-and-son-testify-they -never-authenticated-fake-painting-in-knoedler-trial]; C. Moynihan, "In Knoedler Art Fraud Trial, Expert Testimony on Fakes Weighs Heavily," *New York Times*,

February 1, 2016 [https://www.nytimes.com/2016/02/02/arts/in-knoedler -art-fraud-trial-expert-testimony-on-fakes-weighs-heavily.html].

38. See Chapter 4 of S. A. Clancy, *Abducted: How People Come to Believe They Were Kidnapped by Aliens* (Cambridge, MA: Harvard University Press, 2005). People reported encountering aliens, but not being abducted by them, centuries or longer before 1962. Alien abduction was a new, specific phenomenon tied to TV and film depictions. Although some people claimed to have been abducted prior to 1962, they did not make those claims until after 1962.

39. S. Zito, "Who Is Kathy Barnette?," *Washington Examiner*, May 11, 2022 [https://www.washingtonexaminer.com/opinion/who-is-kathy-barnette].

40. For more examples, see A. Gawande, *The Checklist Manifesto: How to Get Things Right* (New York: Metropolitan Books, 2009).

41. Also see W. Berger, *The Book of Beautiful Questions* (New York: Bloomsbury, 2018).

42. This question was suggested on Twitter by the psychologist Geoffrey Miller.

43. D. A. Redelmeier, E. Shafir, and P. S. Aujla, "The Beguiling Pursuit of More Information," *Medical Decision Making* 21 (2001): 376–381 [https://doi.org/1 0.1177/0272989X0102100504]. This description of the blood pressure study is adapted from C. F. Chabris and D. J. Simons, "Four Ways That Information Can Lead Us Astray," American Express, May 18, 2010 [https://www.americanexpress. com/en-us/business/trends-and-insights/articles/four-ways-that-information -can-lead-us-astray-christopher-chabris-and-daniel-simons/].

Chapter 5: Consistency—Appreciate the Value of Noise

1. *United States of America v. Satish Kurjibhai Kumbhani, aka "Vindee," aka "VND," aka "vndbcc," Defendant*. Indictment filed February 25, 2022, US District Court, Southern District of California [https://storage.courtlistener.com /recap/gov.uscourts.casd.727918/gov.uscourts.casd.727918.1.0_1.pdf]; press release [https://www.justice.gov/opa/pr/bitconnect-founder-indicted-global -24-billion-cryptocurrency-scheme]. Glenn Arcano pleaded guilty to participating in the conspiracy to defraud BitConnect investors [https://www.justice.gov/opa /pr/56-million-seized-cryptocurrency-being-sold-first-step-compensate-victims -bitconnect-fraud].

2. The original publication on Bitcoin is S. Nakamoto, *Bitcoin: A Peer-to-Peer Electronic Cash System*, October 31, 2008 [bitcoin.org/bitcoin.pdf]. See also F. Schär and A. Berentsen, *Bitcoin, Blockchain, and Cryptoassets: A Comprehensive Introduction* (Cambridge, MA: MIT Press, 2020).

3. S. Williams, "The 20 Largest Cryptocurrencies by Market Cap," The Motley Fool, December 15, 2017 [https://www.fool.com/investing/2017/07/20/the-20 -largest-cryptocurrencies-by-market-cap.aspx].

4. T. Frankel, *The Ponzi Scheme Puzzle* (Oxford, UK: Oxford University Press, 2012); see especially ch. 1 for a brief account of Ponzi's original con. A lengthier description and analysis of Ponzi's career and scheme is found in D. Davies, *Lying for Money: How Legendary Frauds Reveal the Workings of the World* (New York: Scribner, 2021), pp. 75–79. Similar schemes were carried out before Ponzi, and indeed described in fiction, but his was the largest—$15 million in 1920 dollars, equivalent to about $220 million as of this writing—and the most publicized, so it became a template for all later cons of its nature, even though many of them had important differences.

5. In multilevel marketing organizations, entrepreneurs recruit other entrepreneurs to sell for them and pay a portion of their proceeds up the chain, all the way to the founder(s). Gifting Tables, a quintessential gifting club pyramid scheme that ran in Connecticut, was investigated by the US government and resulted in several convictions [https://www.justice.gov/usao-ct/pr/two-guilford -women-sentenced-federal-prison-overseeing-gifting-tables-pyramid-scheme].

6. For information about recent examples of Ponzi schemes and a database of documented ones, see Ponzitracker [https://www.ponzitracker.com/about] and the Ponzi Scheme Database [https://dachshund-cheetah-cxaa.squarespace.com /ponzi-database/]. Sources for Celsius: J. Oliver and K. Shubber, "Celsius Chief Feels the Heat After Blocking Withdrawals," *Financial Times*, June 18–19, 2022 [https://www.ft.com/content/18b6fb80-44dd-40ed-b5ea-3f3b f2814c7d]; H. Lang, "Crypto Lender Celsius Network Reveals $1.19 Bln Hole in Bankruptcy Filing," *Reuters*, July 14, 2022 [https://www.reuters.com/business /finance/crypto-lender-celsius-network-reveals-119-billion-hole-bankruptcy -filing-2022-07-14/]. In the intricate world of cryptofinance, Celsius was just one of many firms that got into trouble because it was involved with Three Arrows Capital, a Singapore-based firm that itself went into liquidation in June 2022 after behaving in ways that resembled a Ponzi scheme. See J. Wieczner, "The Crypto Geniuses Who Vaporized a Trillion Dollars," *New York*, August 15, 2022 [https://nymag .com/intelligencer/article/three-arrows-capital-kyle-davies-su-zhu-crash.html].

7. The final balance in the bank account that Madoff used to run his scheme was $222 million on December 10, 2008, the day before his arrest. See J. Campbell, *Madoff Talks* (New York: McGraw-Hill, 2021), 16.

8. Madoff "hedge fund returns" are based on the published 1991–2007 returns of the Fairfield Sentry hedge fund, which invested its clients' money exclusively with Madoff (while pocketing nice management and performance fees for itself) during that period. See C. Bernard, and P. P. Boyle, "Mr. Madoff's Amazing Returns: An Analysis of the Split-Strike Conversion Strategy," *Journal of Derivatives* 17 (2009): 62–76 [https://doi.org/10.3905/jod.2009.17.1.062].

9. These biases can be large: Shane Frederick found that over one-third of the college students he tested stated a preference for receiving $500 for sure rather

than a 15 percent chance of receiving $1 million—an outcome that has an expected value three hundred times as high (0.15 x $1,000,000 = $150,000 = 300 x $500) but an 85 percent chance of not happening and would represent a loss of $500 compared to the sure option. See Figure 3a, p. 34 of S. Frederick, "Cognitive Reflection and Decision Making," *Journal of Economic Perspectives* 19 (2005): 25–42 [https://doi.org/10.1257/089533005775196732].

10. Harry Markopolos, who discovered the Madoff fraud and wrote the memoir *No One Would Listen*, was initially excited that his book was being translated into Romanian and Russian. But then he realized that it was being used as a blueprint for creating Madoff schemes rather than as a manual for detecting and avoiding them. See the final chapter of Campbell, *Madoff Talks*.

11. For the five years ending February 8, 2018, the mean difference between an individual S&P 500 stock's high and low prices within a single day was 1.91 percent (median 1.61 percent). This calculation is based on data from C. Nugent, "S&P 500 Stock Data, 2013–18," Investor's Exchange API, Kaggle, February 2018 [https://www.kaggle.com/datasets/camnugent/sandp500].

12. The graph came from a 2015 experiment in which laypeople were asked which of the four funds they would recommend to a friend. Sixty-eight percent chose the pseudonymous Madoff fund with the impossibly consistent performance record, even though text accompanying the graph noted that the fund was secretive about its strategy and was audited by a small, unknown firm (both of which are warning signs of potential shenanigans and were true of Madoff's fund and many funds that took clients' money and gave it to Madoff to invest). When a separate group of participants were told to think first about whether any of the funds seemed suspicious, more avoided the Madoffesque fund, but 51 percent still chose it. See T. Zhang, P. O. Fletcher, F. Gino, and M. Bazerman, "Reducing Bounded Ethicality: How to Help Individuals Notice and Avoid Unethical Behavior," *Organizational Dynamics* 44 (2015): 310–317 [https://doi.org/10.1016/j.orgdyn.2015.09.009].

13. Alas, Keynes apparently never said this: "When the Facts Change, I Change My Mind. What Do You Do, Sir?," Quote Investigator, July 22, 2011 [https://quoteinvestigator.com/2011/07/22/keynes-change-mind/] (archived at https://archive.ph/wip/5E7jd).

14. Fair play information from "Chess Cheating," Chess.com, October 10, 2022 [https://www.chess.com/article/view/online-chess-cheating]. The most famous case of online cheating was remarkably similar to Chris's lazzir experience: P. Doggers, "Cheating Controversy Results in Most-Watched Chess Stream in History," Chess.com, March 23, 2021 [https://www.chess.com/news/view/most-watched-chess-stream-in-history-dewa-kipas]. Even chess professionals and grandmasters have been caught cheating. A player who was tied for the lead in the online English championship in 2021 was expelled before the tournament ended, and the Armenian Eagles team and their top player,

Tigran L. Petrosian, were disqualified after having won the championship match in the online 2020 PRO Chess League. See L. Barden, "Chess: Keith Arkell Captures Online British Title After Rival Is Disqualified," *Guardian*, August 13, 2021 [https://www.theguardian.com/sport/2021/aug/13/chess-keith-arkell-captures-online-british-title-after-rival-is-disqualified]; PROChessLeague, "Saint Louis Arch Bishops 2020 PRO Chess League Champions; Armenia Eagles Disqualified," Chess.com, October 1, 2020 [https://www.chess.com/news/view/saint-louis-arch-bishops-2020-pro-chess-champions].

15. For example, judges might differ in the sentence they give a defendant despite having the same information about the case. When that happens, at least one defendant is being sentenced unfairly. This type of noise (in the judicial system) should be measured and mitigated. See D. Kahneman, O. Sibony, and C. Sunstein, *Noise: A Flaw in Human Judgment* (New York: Little, Brown Spark, 2020).

16. Leicester City data from "Performance Record of Clubs in the Premier League," Wikipedia [https://en.wikipedia.org/wiki/Performance_record_of_clubs_in_the_Premier_League] and "Leicester City F.C.," Wikipedia [https://en.wikipedia.org/wiki/Leicester_City_F.C.#Premier_League_champions_(2015%E2%80%9316)].

17. *Report of JPMorgan Chase & Co. Management Task Force Regarding 2012 CIO Losses*, January 16, 2013, 128–129 [https://ypfs.som.yale.edu/node/2821]; A. Ahmed, "The Hunch, the Pounce and the Kill," *New York Times*, May 27, 2012 [https://www.nytimes.com/2012/05/27/business/how-boaz-weinstein-and-hedge-funds-outsmarted-jpmorgan.html]; E. Owles, "Timeline: The London Whale's Wake," *New York Times*, March 27, 2013 [https://archive.nytimes.com/www.nytimes.com/interactive/2013/03/27/business/dealbook/20130327-jpmorgan-timeline.html].

18. M. De Vita, "Analysis: Madoff's Returns vs. the Market," in *The Club No One Wanted to Join: Madoff Victims in Their Own Words*, ed. E. Arvedlund and A. Roth (Alexandra Roth Book Project, 2010), 212–219. We obtained the same historical performance data to calculate the year-to-year volatility (standard deviation of returns) for De Vita's sixteen funds and for the Madoff fund (as reported for the Fairfield Sentry feeder fund) from 1991 to 2007. The Sharpe ratio (return over volatility, in each case relative to a risk-free asset, typically US Treasury bills) was 3.02 for Madoff and typically below 0.5 for the non-Ponzi funds.

19. We transcribed the quotation from Agassi's Unscriptd interview, "Andre Agassi Interview | Beat Boris Becker by Observing His Tongue," YouTube [https://www.youtube.com/watch?v=ja6HeLB3kwY] (archived at https://archive.ph/2yofY). The story appears in A. Pattle, "Andre Agassi Reveals He Looked at Boris Becker's Tongue for Serve Clues in Rivals' Clashes," *Independent*, April 30, 2021 [https://www.independent.co.uk/sport/tennis/andre-agassi-boris-becker-tongue-serve-b1840198.html].

20. Some poker professionals wear sunglasses and hats and even zip up hoodies to cover their faces entirely so as not to reveal any facial expressions or breathing patterns. Chris Ferguson advised players to train themselves to use the same amount of time on every decision, or at least to adopt a set minimum time for even the most trivial decision, so that opponents cannot pick up "timing tells." Jonathan Little put it simply in *Secrets of Professional Tournament Poker: The Essential Guide* (D&B Poker, 2021): "Make no unnecessary movements at all." Had Becker known Agassi was getting a tell from his tongue, he could have used that information to deceive Agassi—for example, by positioning his tongue to predict a serve to the middle but actually serving wide.

21. Under the ethical rules of bridge, a partner is not allowed to take advantage of that illicit inference: "Ethics and Discipline," American Contract Bridge League [https://acbl.org/ethics/]. If they do, their opponents could accuse the pair of cheating. Given the inherent challenges of deciding whether a pair benefited from such communication, competitive bridge tournaments have taken steps to prevent other forms of communication. The use of bidding cards that players place on the table was a way to avoid the cheating that was easy when players said their bids aloud. Players could say "a spade" or "one spade" and use that distinction to provide illicit information about their cards to their partner. They could do the same by varying their tone of voice.

22. Sources for the discussion of bridge cheating include the documentary film *Dirty Tricks* (2021), directed by Daniel Sivan; R. Tenorio, "How a Cheating Scandal Brought Down the Michael Jordan of Bridge," *Guardian*, May 5, 2021 [https://www.theguardian.com/sport/2021/may/05/lotan-fisher-bridge-cheating-scandal-2015-documentary]; D. Owen, "Dirty Hands," *New Yorker*, February 28, 2016 [https://www.newyorker.com/magazine/2016/03/07/the-cheating-problem-in-professional-bridge]; J. Colapinto, "Is the Competitive Bridge World Rife with Cheaters?," *Vanity Fair*, February 29, 2016 [https://www.vanityfair.com/culture/2016/02/competitive-bridge-cheating-scandal]; "Fantoni and Nunes Cheating Scandal," Wikipedia [https://en.wikipedia.org/wiki/Fantoni_and_Nunes_cheating_scandal]; "Cheating in Bridge," Wikipedia [https://en.wikipedia.org/wiki/Cheating_in_bridge]; "Fisher and Schwartz Cheating Scandal," Wikipedia [https://en.wikipedia.org/wiki/Fisher_and_Schwartz_cheating_scandal]. If these cheating pairs of players wanted to be extra sneaky, they could occasionally use their tell when they both knew it was meaningless, effectively masking the tell when it was an illegal signal.

23. Some of the prose in these paragraphs on Schön and Sakhai was written for the catalog for an exhibit we co-curated for the Museum of Old and New Art in Hobart, Australia: D. J. Simons and C. F. Chabris, "Fooling Ourselves Most of the Time," in *Gorillas in Our Midst* (Hobart, Australia: Museum of Old and New Art,

2019), 17–44. The same catalog included an essay by curator Jane Clark on the history of fakes and forgeries in the art world.

24. A. Amore, *The Art of the Con* (New York: Palgrave Macmillan, 2015). For a discussion of why people value originals so much, even compared to perfect copies, see P. Bloom, *How Pleasure Works: The New Science of Why We Like What We Like* (New York: W. W. Norton, 2010).

25. Ely Sakhai pleaded guilty to this fraud and was sentenced to forty-one months in prison [http://www.justice.gov/usao/nys/pressreleases/July05/sakhai sentence.pdf].

26. L. Cassuto, "Big Trouble in the World of 'Big Physics,'" *Guardian*, September 18, 2002 [https://www.theguardian.com/education/2002/sep/18/science .highereducation].

27. In response to the Lucent Technologies investigative report that led to his firing, Schön acknowledged mistakes but not fraud: "Although I have made mistakes, I never wanted to mislead anybody or to misuse anybody's trust. I realize that there is a lack of credibility in light of these mistakes, nevertheless, I truly believe that the reported scientific effects are real, exciting, and worth working for." See Lucent Technologies, "Report of the Investigation Committee on the Possibility of Scientific Misconduct in the Work of Hendrik Schön and Coauthors," September 2022 [https://media-bell-labs-com.s3.amazonaws.com/pages/20170403_1709 /misconduct-revew-report-lucent.pdf].

28. Rensink and colleagues' original work on the flicker task: R. A. Rensink, J. K. O'Regan, and J. J. Clark, "To See or Not to See: The Need for Attention to Perceive Changes in Scenes," *Psychological Science* 8 (1997): 368–373 [https://doi .org/10.1111/j.1467-9280.1997.tb00427.x]. We also discussed change blindness in Chapter 2 of our book *The Invisible Gorilla*. Rensink's similarity detection study was described in a book chapter: R. A. Rensink, "Change Blindness: Implications for the Nature of Visual Attention," in *Vision and Attention*, ed. M. Jenkin and L. Harris (New York: Springer, 2001), 169–188.

29. Duplicating data with the goal of passing it off as new has no innocent explanation, and the use of image editing to change data is a deliberate choice to deceive—it's scientific misconduct. Unlike image manipulation, some image duplication can just reflect sloppiness. Dan was coauthor of a paper that accidentally duplicated the same data figure in two places. He had uploaded the same image file twice rather than uploading two separate ones, and the error made it into the final publication. It was obviously an error—the two figures were supposed to be from different experiments with different conditions, so clearly the figures must be different. Yet Dan and his coauthor missed it, as did the journal's copy editor. Everyone makes mistakes, and the scientific literature has mechanisms to correct them. Bik's discovery of the paper mill is described in D. Chawla, "A Single 'Paper Mill'

Appears to Have Churned Out 400 Papers," *Science*, February 27, 2020 [https://doi.org/10.1126/science.abb4930]; E. M. Bik, F. C. Fang, A. L. Kullas, R. J. Davis, and A. Casadevall, "Analysis and Correction of Inappropriate Image Duplication: The *Molecular and Cellular Biology* Experience," *Molecular and Cellular Biology* 38 (2018): e00309-18 [https://doi.org/10.1128/MCB.00309-18].

30. The repeated appearance of 770, as well as a case in which two papers that purportedly tested different participants reported the same results for 17 of 18 outcome measures, was documented in a blog post by Nick Brown: "Strange Patterns in Some Results from the Food and Brand Lab," *Nick Brown's Blog* [http://steamtraen.blogspot.com/2017/03/strange-patterns-in-some-results-from.html]. A more subtle variant of reporting the same results for different studies is known as "salami slicing," the act of reporting different outcomes from a single study across multiple papers. For an investigation of this form of potentially deceptive conduct in studies claiming that action video games increase cognitive abilities, see J. Hilgard, G. Sala, W. R. Boot, and D. J. Simons, "Overestimation of Action-Game Training Effects: Publication Bias and Salami Slicing," *Collabra: Psychology* 5 (2019): 30 [https://doi.org/10.1525/collabra.231].

31. Cornell has not released the full results of its investigations, but the provost issued a statement: "Statement of Cornell University Provost Michael I. Kotlikoff," Cornell University [https://statements.cornell.edu/2018/20180920-statement-provost-michael-kotlikoff.cfm]. A letter from Michael I. Kotlikoff to Nick Brown and others who had investigated Wansink's work [https://www.documentcloud.org/documents/5028990-BrownandFellowSignatories-11-05-18.html] noted that the investigation found "a number of instances of research misconduct" that included "data falsification" and "dual publication."

32. J. Förster and M. Denzler, "Sense Creative! The Impact of Global and Local Vision, Hearing, Touching, Tasting and Smelling on Creative and Analytic Thought," *Social Psychology and Personality Science* 3 (2012): 108–117 [https://doi.org/10.1177/1948550611410890].

33. See "Suspicion of Scientific Misconduct by Dr. Jens Förster," Retraction Watch, September 3, 2012 [http://retractionwatch.files.wordpress.com/2014/04/report_foerster.pdf]. Retraction Watch also provides the LOWI report and a translation: "Förster Report Cites 'Unavoidable' Conclusion of Data Manipulation," Retraction Watch, May 7, 2014 [https://retractionwatch.com/2014/05/07/forster-report-cites-unavoidable-conclusion-of-data-manipulation]; the quotation comes from that translation. In a series of simulations and analyses described in a post titled "Fake-Data Colada: Excessive Linearity" on their blog *Data Colada*, May 8, 2014 [http://datacolada.org/21], Leif Nelson and Uri Simonsohn showed that out of 100,000 simulations, not one produced results as consistently linear as those Förster reported. The same suspiciously consistent pattern emerged in two of his other papers.

34. Avenell's discovery and the subsequent investigation are described in K. Kupferschmidt, "Researcher at the Center of an Epic Fraud Remains an Enigma to Those Who Exposed Him," *Science*, August 17, 2018 [https://www.science.org/content/article/researcher-center-epic-fraud-remains-enigma-those-who-exposed-him].

35. The belief that random things ought to even out (especially in the short run) is the famous Gambler's Fallacy, and the belief that small samples ought to match the population they come from is the fatuous "Law of Small Numbers" described in A. Tversky and D. Kahneman, "Belief in the Law of Small Numbers," *Psychological Bulletin* 76 (1971): 105–110 [https://doi.org/10.1037/h0031322]. It's also a fallacy to think that randomized experiments are invalid unless all of the baseline differences are zero, but the fact that some researchers believe it may account for why fraudsters try to make up results that look that way.

36. M. J. Bolland, A. Avenell, G. D. Gamble, and A. Grey, "Systematic Review and Statistical Analysis of the Integrity of 33 Randomized Controlled Trials," *Neurology* 87 (2016): 2391–2402 [https://doi.org/10.1212/WNL.0000000000003387]. According to an American Academy of Neurology press release, "Study Suggests Probable Scientific Misconduct in Bone Health Studies," November 9, 2016 [https://www.aan.com/PressRoom/Home/PressRelease/1501] (archived at https://archive.ph/wip/Uev5F), "Sato accepted full responsibility, admitting fabrication of the fraudulent Neurology papers, which reported on the effects of therapies to reduce hip fractures both after stroke and in Parkinson's disease patients. Sato stated that none of the coauthors participated in any misconduct and were named as authors on an honorary basis only. Sato requested retraction of the three studies." As often happens with fraudulent studies, when there's one suspicious pattern in a dataset, there are others. In Sato's data, for example, the numbers of participants in each condition were also too consistent. With truly random assignment, we should expect some differences in how many people end up in the treatment and control group. As we have seen, you will rarely (just 8 percent of the time) get exactly 50 heads and 50 tails when you toss a coin 100 times. And there is a surprisingly large chance—over 5.5 percent—that you will get 60 or more heads or tails. Sato's "random assignment" essentially produced the equivalent of 50 heads and 50 tails each time. Of the 30 Sato studies evaluated by Bolland's team, a wildly implausible 27 had identical numbers of participants in each group. In addition to overly consistent sample sizes and outcomes for baseline trials in Sato's studies, some prose and statistics were duplicated across papers that purportedly tested different people.

37. Carlisle's method: J. B. Carlisle, "Data Fabrication and Other Reasons for Non-random Sampling in 5087 Randomised, Controlled Trials in Anaesthetic and General Medical Journals," *Anaesthesia* 72 (2017): 944–952 [https://doi.org/10.1111/anae.13938]. As of September 5, 2022, Fujii had 183 total retractions. The next two people on the retraction leaderboard

[https://retractionwatch.com/the-retraction-watch-leaderboard/], Joachim Boldt with 164 and Hironobu Ueshima with 123, are also anesthesiologists. Yoshihiro Sato sits in fourth place with 110. The fact that the top four most-retracted authors are all from anesthesiology does not mean that this field is especially fraudulent. You'd be deceiving yourself if you came to that conclusion because you looked at what was salient and not at what was absent. It could just be that, due to the influence of Carlisle, the field of anesthesiology research is doing a better job of exposing an alarming level of fraud that exists in many other fields too.

38. McDonald's hamburgers are so consistent from store to store and even country to country that the *Economist* was able to create an index to compare living standards across nations by measuring how many Big Macs the average salary could buy in each country [https://www.economist.com/big-mac-index].

Chapter 6: Familarity—Discount What You Think You Know

1. Artiles has a history of questionable behavior. As Curt Anderson reported, "In 2017, he resigned from the state Senate after using racial slurs in a conversation with two Black legislators in a Tallahassee bar. Then it was revealed Artiles used money from his political committee to hire a former Playboy model and Hooters girl as a consultant." See C. Anderson, "Ex-Florida Senator Charged in Fake Candidate Scheme," AP News, March 18, 2021 [https://apnews.com/article/miami-senate-elections-florida-elections-e8b70ce3270bd170e37a71ca80b5aaae]. Sources for the election story include D. Kam, "Florida Democrats Call for New State Senate Elections Amid Ongoing Campaign Fraud Case," *Orlando Weekly*, March 22, 2021 [https://web.archive.org/web/20210418060352/https://www.orlandoweekly.com/Blogs/archives/2021/03/22/florida-democrats-call-for-new-state-senate-elections-amid-ongoing-campaign-fraud-case]; K. Shepherd, "Ex-Florida State Senator Paid Bogus Candidate to 'Siphon Votes,' Police Say, in Race GOP Narrowly Won," *Washington Post*, March 19, 2021 [https://www.washingtonpost.com/nation/2021/03/19/florida-fraud-artiles-rodriguez-election/].

2. A. Fins, "Palm Beach County Ghost Candidate Exposes 'Lies' Behind Florida Election Reform, Voter Groups Say," *Palm Beach Post*, August 31, 2021 [https://www.palmbeachpost.com/story/news/politics/2021/08/31/palm-beach-county-ghost-candidate-pleads-guilty-election-case/5593843001/]; G. Fox, "Deception and Dark Money: Court Documents Show Scheme of Ghost Candidates in Florida Senate Races," WESH, August 5, 2021 [https://www.wesh.com/article/scheme-ghost-candidates-florida-senate-races/37236133].

3. J. Garcia and A. Martin, "Big Business-Linked Group Gave Over $1 Million to Dark-Money Entity Promoting 'Ghost' Candidates," *Orlando Sentinel*, November 18, 2021 [https://www.orlandosentinel.com/news/os-ne-lets-preserve-the-american-dream-senate-ghost-candidates-20211118-fhplycqaijcixkrr3nipee5qne-story.html].

4. See N. Cooper, F. Maier, and H. Fineman, "LaRouched in Illinois: How to Shred a Ticket," *Newsweek*, March 31, 1986, 22; see also T. Rische, "What's in a Name? Favoritism, Prejudice," *Los Angeles Times*, April 2, 1986 [https://www .latimes.com/archives/la-xpm-1986-04-02-me-2428-story.html] for a discussion of name familiarity effects.

5. C. S. O'Sullivan, A. Chen, S. Mohapatra, L. Sigelman, and E. Lewis, "Voting in Ignorance: The Politics of Smooth-Sounding Names," *Journal of Applied Social Psychology* 18 (1988): 1094–1106 [https://doi.org/10.1111/j.1559-1816.1988 .tb01195.x]. Marsha Matson and Terri Susan Fine investigated how names influenced voting in a low-information, bottom-of-the-ballot 1996 election in Miami-Dade County, Florida. Fifty-seven relatively unknown candidates were running for fifteen open, nonpartisan seats on community advising and zoning boards. Among these largely unknown candidates, those who spent more money generally did better. Overall, candidates with Hispanic names did worse than those with non-Hispanic names (although that effect varied by gender). See M. Matson and T. S. Fine, "Gender, Ethnicity, and Ballot Information: Ballot Cues in Low-Information Elections," *State Politics and Policy Quarterly* 6 (2006): 49–72 [https://doi.org/10.1177/153244000600600103]. Similarly, in a low-information Swiss election, voters were more likely to vote against candidates with non-Swiss names: L. Portmann and N. Stojanović, "Electoral Discrimination Against Immigrant-Origin Candidates," *Political Behavior* 41 (2019): 105–134 [https://doi.org/10.1007/s11109-017-9440-6].

6. L. L. Jacoby, C. Kelley, J. Brown, and J. Jasechko, "Becoming Famous Overnight: Limits on the Ability to Avoid Unconscious Influences of the Past," *Journal of Personality and Social Psychology* 56 (1989): 326–338 [https://doi .org/10.1037/0022-3514.56.3.326].

7. C. D. Kam and E. J. Zechmeister, "Name Recognition and Candidate Support," *American Journal of Political Science* 57 (2013): 971–986 [doi:10.1111 /ajps.12034]. The advantage of appearing first on a list of candidates, especially for down-ballot or nonpartisan races, can be substantial. Based on data from a set of elections in the state of Ohio, the average advantage of being listed first rather than last was 2.33 percentage points. It's not clear how often ballot position actually affects the outcome of a race because in many races, other factors likely contribute more. And in some cases, ballot position is varied to eliminate any overall effects of position. For data and discussion of the effect, see J. M. Miller and J. A. Krosnick, "The Impact of Candidate Name Order on Election Outcomes," *Public Opinion Quarterly* 62 (1998): 291–330 [https://doi.org/10.1086/297848].

8. Note that we should not expect a large effect of this sort of familiarity. Yard signs just aren't that potent, and many other factors contribute to voting choices. This relatively small influence of a pervasive form of advertisement shows why we should be careful not to overstate the possible real-world effects of more subtle

priming effects like the name familiarity effect. See D. P. Green et al., "The Effects of Lawn Signs on Vote Outcomes: Results from Four Randomized Field Experiments," *Electoral Studies* 41 (2016): 143–150.

9. A. R. Pratkanis, A. G. Greenwald, M. R. Leippe, and M. H. Baumgardner, "In Search of Reliable Persuasion Effects: III. The Sleeper Effect Is Dead: Long Live the Sleeper Effect," *Journal of Personality and Social Psychology* 54 (1988): 203–218 [https://doi.org/10.1037/0022-3514.54.2.203]; G. T. Kumkale and D. Albarracín, "The Sleeper Effect in Persuasion: A Meta-Analytic Review," *Psychological Bulletin* 130 (2004): 143–172 [https://doi.org/10.1037/0033-2909.130.1.143].

10. M. Wilson, "Ray's Pizza, 'The' Ray's Pizza, Will Close on Sunday," *New York Times*, October 24, 2011 [https://cityroom.blogs.nytimes.com/2011/10/24/rays-pizza-the-rays-pizza-will-close-on-sunday/]; J. Tierney, "In a Pizza War, It's 3 Rays Against the World," *New York Times*, March 25, 1991 [https://www.nytimes.com/1991/03/25/nyregion/in-a-pizza-war-it-s-3-rays-against-the-rest.html]. The present minichain of Ray's serves excellent garlic knots.

11. J. Torchinsky, "It's Infiniti's 30th Anniversary So Let's Remember When It Had a Vision," *Jalopnik*, November 8, 2019 [https://jalopnik.com/its-infinitis-30th-anniversary-so-lets-remember-when-it-1839724145]; A. Rodriguez, "Why Did a Lumber Company Make the Most Emotionally Gripping Ad to Air During Super Bowl 51?," *Quartz*, February 6, 2017 [https://qz.com/903902/84-lumbers-super-bowl-51-commercial-the-story-behind-the-most-emotionally-gripping-ad-of-the-night]. We estimated the cost of 84 Lumber's commercial based on its length (ninety seconds) and on general reports of the cost of advertising time in the Super Bowl over the years: M. Williams, "Super Bowl Commercial Cost in 2022: How Much Money Is an Ad for Super Bowl 56?," *Sporting News*, February 13, 2022 [https://www.sportingnews.com/us/nfl/news/super-bowl-commercials-cost-2022/v9ytfqzx74pjrcdvxyhevlzd]. Professional soccer doesn't have commercial timeouts, so sponsors build recognition by putting their names and logos on the front of the players' jerseys.

12. D. Davies, *Lying for Money: How Legendary Frauds Reveal the Workings of the World* (New York: Scribner, 2021), 30. The case of Jho Low and 1MDB is described in detail in the 2019 paperback edition of the book *Billion Dollar Whale: The Man Who Fooled Wall Street, Hollywood, and the World* (New York: Hachette Books, 2018) by Tom Wright and Bradley Hope, who reported on the case for the *Wall Street Journal*. Students of financial shenanigans should read Wright and Hope's story for a deep dive into one of the biggest outright thefts of all time. Jho Low was indicted [https://www.justice.gov/opa/pr/malaysian-financier-low-taek-jho-also-known-jho-low-and-former-banker-ng-chong-hwa-also-known]. Former Goldman Sachs investment banker Roger Ng was convicted as part of the bribery and money laundering scheme [https://www.justice.gov/opa/pr/former-goldman-sachs-investment-banker-convicted-massive-bribery

-and-money-laundering-scheme]. Tim Leissner of Goldman Sachs also pleaded guilty in the case, as did Goldman itself, and the prime minister of Malaysia was convicted in Malaysia: M. Goldstein, "The Key to a $4 Billion Fraud Case: A Banker Who Says He 'Lied a Lot,'" *New York Times*, March 13, 2022 [https://www .nytimes.com/2022/03/13/business/tim-leissner-roger-ng-goldman-sachs.html].

13. N. Lafond, "Ex-Sinclair News Director: Promos 'Equivalent to a Proof-of-Life Hostage Video,'" *TPM*, April 4, 2018 [https://web.archive.org /web/20220823073109/https://talkingpointsmemo.com/livewire/former -sinclair-news-director-promos-proof-life-hostage-videos].

14. A. Weiss, "Confessions of a Former Sinclair News Director," *Huffington Post*, April 3 2018 [https://www.huffpost.com/entry/opinion-weiss-sinclair-television -propaganda_n_5ac2c6d4e4b09712fec38b95]; E. Stewart, "Watch: Dozens of Local TV Anchors Read the Same Anti-'False News' Script in Unison," *Vox*, April 2, 2018 [https://www.vox.com/policy-and-politics/2018/4/2/17189302 /sinclair-broadcast-fake-news-biased-trump-viral-video].

15. M. Hall, "USA Today Wrapped Its Newspaper with a Fake Cover About 'Hybrid Babies' with Antlers to Advertise a New Netflix Show," *Insider*, June 5, 2021 [http://archive.today/2021.06.05-022641/https://www.insider.com/usa-today -fake-cover-hybrid-babies-netflix-show-2021-6]. Mobil's program of purchasing op-ed page advertisements was reported by the *New York Times* itself: W. D. Smith, "Advertising," August 22, 1975 [https://www.nytimes.com/1975/08/22/archives /advertising-mobil-finds-speaking-out-pays-ftc-fuelclaim-bar.html]. This research study analyzes the content of Mobil's *New York Times* advertorials from 1985 through 2000: C. Brown and W. Waltzer, "Every Thursday: Advertorials by Mobil Oil on the Op-Ed Page of *The New York Times*," *Public Relations Review* 31 (2005): 197–208 [doi.org/10.1016/j.pubrev.2005.02.019].

16. D. Henriques, *The Wizard of Lies: Bernie Madoff and the Death of Trust* (New York: St. Martin's Griffin, 2017).

17. E. L. Henderson, D. J. Simons, and D. J. Barr, "The Trajectory of Truth: A Longitudinal Study of the Illusory Truth Effect," *Journal of Cognition* 4 (2021): 1–23 [https://doi.org/10.5334/joc.161].

18. As Election Day nears, the repetition that works with voters wears Redford's candidate down, and he starts deliriously mocking his own slogans as he rides from one event to the next: "The Candidate 1972 Robert Redford," YouTube [https:// www.youtube.com/watch?v=b0Dvqxmj5Ps]. First finding of the illusory truth effect: L. Hasher, D. Goldstein, and T. Toppino, "Frequency and the Conference of Referential Validity," *Journal of Verbal Learning and Verbal Behavior* 16 (1977): 107–112 [https://doi.org/10.1016/S0022-5371(77)80012-1]. Increased research on illusory truth: Of the ninety-three papers that Emma Henderson, Samuel Westwood, and Dan reviewed as part of a systematic survey of the literature they conducted in 2020, more than half had been published between 2010 and 2019. See

E. L. Henderson, S. J. Westwood, and D. J. Simons, "A Reproducible Systematic Map of Research on the Illusory Truth Effect," *Psychonomic Bulletin & Review* 29 (2022): 1065–1088 [https://doi.org/10.3758/s13423-021-01995-w].

19. V. Bergengruen, "How 'America's Frontline Doctors' Sold Access to Bogus COVID-19 Treatments—and Left Patients in the Lurch," *Time* magazine, August 26, 2021 [https://time.com/6092368/americas-frontline-doctors-covid-19-misinformation/]. Ivermectin studies were analyzed in detail on the blog *Astral Codex Ten*: "Ivermectin: Much More Than You Wanted to Know," November 16, 2021 [https://astralcodexten.substack.com/p/ivermectin-much-more-than-you-wanted]. Although "real-time meta-analysis" isn't a thing, traditional meta-analyses combine all of the relevant work in a literature to give a quantitative estimate of the overall size of an effect. If all of the studies entering into that estimate are legitimate, the meta-analysis can serve as a basis for planning future research. If misleading or fraudulent studies are included, they can mislead other researchers into thinking effects are larger than they actually are. For example, Sato's fraudulent studies continue to affect the literature: J. Brainard, "'Zombie Papers' Just Won't Die: Retracted Papers by Notorious Fraudster Still Cited Years Later," *Science*, June 27, 2022 [https://www.science.org/content/article/zombie-papers-wont-die-retracted-papers-notorious-fraudster-still-cited-years-later], and a meta-analysis on the effectiveness of nudging included many of Brian Wansink's faulty studies and thereby came to an incorrect conclusion; see S. Mertens, M. Herberz, U. J. J. Hahnel, and T. Brosch, "The Effectiveness of Nudging: A Meta-Analysis of Choice Architecture Interventions Across Behavioral Domains," *Proceedings of the National Academy of Sciences* 119 (2022): e2107346118 [https://doi.org/10.1073/pnas.2107346118]; note that this paper has incorporated significant corrections since its initial publication.

20. Information about the membership of the Theranos board can be found in J. Carreyrou, *Bad Blood: Secrets and Lies in a Silicon Valley Startup* (New York: Knopf, 2018). The quotation about shorting stock was uttered at a conference by an investor who specializes in identifying companies to short—i.e., whose shares he expected would decline because there were dubious elements to their business practices that they were papering over by adding celebrities to their board. The academic study of board composition is Z. Li and M. Rainville, "Do Military Independent Directors Improve Firm Performance?," *Finance Research Letters* 43 (2021): 101988 [https://doi.org/10.1016/j.frl.2021.101988].

21. Experienced authors know that blurbs are part of the game of publishing, and they commonly write blurbs for each other to help with sales and marketing—that's another reason why they can't be taken at face value.

22. The numbers of positive reviews, upvotes, and likes are also biased heavily by the order in which they come in; if the first rating is positive rather than negative, the total rating is more likely to be high even after hundreds of new ratings come

in. That's true even when the first positive, neutral, or negative rating was generated entirely at random. L. Muchnik, S. Aral, and S. J. Taylor, "Social Influence Bias: A Randomized Experiment," *Science* 341 (2013): 647–651 [https://doi.org/10.1126/science.1240466].

23. K. Grind, T. McGinty, and S. Krouse, "The Morningstar Mirage," *Wall Street Journal*, October 25, 2017 [https://www.wsj.com/articles/the-morningstar-mirage-1508946687].

24. Akili Interactive received FDA approval for EndeavorRx as a prescription video game to treat attention-deficit/hyperactivity disorder (ADHD), and immediately promoted it as "FDA cleared" on their website [https://web.archive.org/web/20220906030421/https://www.akiliinteractive.com/]. The use of "Rx" makes an explicit association with the idea of a prescription medication, even though the approval process they used is less rigorous. The product was approved via a De Novo premarket review pathway, which checks "if the data and information provided to the FDA demonstrate that general controls or general and special controls are adequate to provide reasonable assurance of safety and effectiveness, and the probable benefits of the device outweigh the probable risks": "FDA Permits Marketing of First Game-Based Digital Therapeutic to Improve Attention Function in Children with ADHD," US Food and Drug Administration, June 15, 2020 [https://www.fda.gov/news-events/press-announcements/fda-permits-marketing-first-game-based-digital-therapeutic-improve-attention-function-children-adhd]. There are no major risks for a video game (just opportunity costs of spending time playing it), and the objective evidence of effectiveness involved improvements on a laboratory test of attention that is similar to elements of the game itself. Practicing a task typically improves performance on a highly similar task but might not provide much, if any, improvement for real-world attention.

25. T. Abdollah and M. Biesecker, "Hackers Apparently Fooled Clinton Official with Bogus Email," AP News, October 29, 2016. The original email can be found at WikiLeaks [https://web.archive.org/web/20220919052534/https://wikileaks.org/podesta-emails/emailid/34899].

26. The use of "ph" rather than "f" might be an allusion to the repeated "ph" in an earlier form of hacking known as "phone phreaking": "Phishing," Wikipedia [https://en.wikipedia.org/wiki/Phishing].

27. S. Cain, "Literary Mystery May Finally Be Solved as Man Arrested for Allegedly Stealing Unpublished Books," *Guardian*, January 5, 2022 [https://www.theguardian.com/books/2022/jan/06/literary-mystery-may-finally-be-solved-as-man-arrested-for-allegedly-stealing-unpublished-books].

28. Business email compromise: Federal Bureau of Investigation, "Business Email Compromise" [https://www.fbi.gov/how-we-can-help-you/safety-resources/scams-and-safety/common-scams-and-crimes/business-email-compromise].

Healthcare workers click links: W. J. Gordon et al., "Assessment of Employee Susceptibility to Phishing Attacks at US Health Care Institutions," *JAMA Network Open* 2 (2019): e190393 [https://doi.org/10.1001/jamanetworko pen.2019.0393]; A. Baillon, J. de Bruin, A. Emirmahmutoglu, E. van de Veer, and B. van Dijk, "Informing, Simulating Experience, or Both: A Field Experiment on Phishing Risks," *PLoS ONE* 14 (2019): e0224216 [https://doi.org/10.1371/journal.pone.0224216]. People were less likely to freely offer their password after they had experienced phishing once or after they had learned about the nature of phishing, but many still fell for the researchers' second attempt. According to a 2017 survey of US consumers by the Internet security company DomainTools, "91 percent are aware of the existence of . . . spoofed websites or emails of trusted brands": "Majority of Consumers Aware of Online Phishing Scams, Yet Still May Fall Victim This Cyber Monday," November 8, 2017 [https://www.prnewswire.com/news-releases/majority-of-consumers-aware-of-online-phishing-scams-yet-still-may-fall-victim-this-cyber-monday-300551430.html].

29. "Parliament of Suckers," *Spy*, February 1993, 46–47, 51.

30. A. D. Sokal, "Transgressing the Boundaries: Toward a Transformative Hermeneutics of Quantum Gravity," *Social Text* 46/47 (1996): 217–252 [https://doi.org/10.2307/466856]. According to the Google Scholar database (on September 12, 2022), Sokal's hoax paper is the fifth most-cited paper ever published in *Social Text*, with nearly two thousand citations. See also A. Sokal, "A Physicist Experiments with Cultural Studies," *Lingua Franca* 6 (1996): 62–64.

31. We wrote about the Ern Malley case in the exhibition notes for the 2019 *Gorillas in Our Midst* exhibit at the Museum of Old and New Art, Hobart, Australia. The exhibit featured a painting of "Malley" by the well-known Australian artist Sydney Nolan.

32. "'Angry Penguins' Will Be Angrier," *Mail* (Adelaide, SA), June 24, 1944 [https://trove.nla.gov.au/newspaper/article/55882811]. Stewart and McAuley also noted that fabricating Malley's backstory took them more time than composing his works. Malley's poems can be found in *Jacket* magazine [http://jacket magazine.com/17/ern-poems.html].

33. W. James, *The Principles of Psychology* (1890; repr., Cambridge, MA: Harvard University Press, 1983), 1007.

34. Changing where you work: D. Epstein, "A Technique Championed by Russian Writers (and Fraggles) Can Give You a New Perspective," *Range Widely*, November 16, 2021 [https://davidepstein.bulletin.com/308221507559816/].

35. Roberto's discussion of the Trader Joe's case: "Should America Be Run by . . . Trader Joe's?," *Freakonomics* podcast, November 28, 2018 [https://freakonomics.com/podcast/should-america-be-run-by-trader-joes/]). See also D. L. Ager and M. A. Roberto, "Trader Joe's," Harvard Business School Case 714-419, September 2013 (rev. April 2014).

36. You can also use independent websites like ISideWith [https://www
.isidewith.com/political-quiz], Britannica ProCon [https://www.procon.org/],
and Pew Research's political typology quiz [https://www.pewresearch.org
/politics/quiz/political-typology/] to get a relatively objective and more
data-driven idea of which candidates or parties you should be supporting based on
your opinions on a range of issues.

37. M. Lewis, *Moneyball: The Art of Winning an Unfair Game* (New York: W. W.
Norton, 2003). Other sports analytics examples: Stephen Shea, "Analytics and
Shot Selection," ShotTracker [https://shottracker.com/articles/analytics-shot
-selection]; Next Gen Stats Analytics Team, "Introducing the Next Gen Stats Decision Guide: A New Analytics Tool for Fourth Down, Two-Point Conversions,"
NFL.com, September 7, 2021 [https://www.nfl.com/news/introducing-the
-next-gen-stats-decision-guide-a-new-analytics-tool-for-fourth-do].

Chapter 7: Precision—Take Appropriate Measures

1. An example of the Ivory soap advertisement: "Ivory Soap—99 44/100 Pure—
As Real as Ivory—Commercial—1988," YouTube [https://www.youtube.com
/watch?v=t5FJfmOy4Ro].

2. A. Orben, and A. K. Przybylski, "The Association Between Adolescent
Well-Being and Digital Technology Use," *Nature Human Behaviour* 3 (2019):
173–182 [https://doi.org/10.1038/s41562-018-0506-1]. These associations are
just that—associations. It's not appropriate to draw causal conclusions about
the effects of interventions from them. For example, people might sleep more because they have greater well-being rather than the other way around. Or they might
have higher well-being *and* sleep better because they have a more supportive family. The same is true for the smaller effect of technology use: Those who claim detri-
mental effects of technology use often infer causality from associations.

3. Whether 99.44 percent is a lot or a little is a good question, but an equally important one is "99.44 percent of what, exactly?" What is "purity" in this context? Is
it important? Do I really know that pure soap is better soap? Precise numbers and
claims are often used to distract us from wondering whether the thing being (supposedly) measured with such precision is really the thing we should be thinking
about in the first place.

4. Video of Paul's presentation: "Viral Moment: Rand Paul Goes Off in
EPIC Rant About Government Waste," YouTube [https://www.youtube
.com/watch?v=jbUOoMtxX9A&t=140s]. For the scientific rationale behind this grant, see "Cocaine and the Sexual Habits of Quail, or, Why
Does NIH Fund What It Does?," *The Scicurious Brain, Scientific American*, December 28, 2011 [https://blogs.scientificamerican.com/scicurious
-brain/cocaine-and-the-sexual-habits-of-quail-or-why-does-nih-fund-what
-it-does/].

5. K. Yamagishi, "When a 12.86% Mortality Is More Dangerous Than 21.14%: Implications for Risk Communication," *Applied Cognitive Psychology* 11 (1997): 495–506 [https://doi.org/10.1002/(SICI)1099-0720(199712)11:6<495::AID-ACP481>3.0.CO;2-J].

6. P. Bump, "The Various Dishonesties in Rand Paul's Cocaine-Quail Presentation," *Washington Post*, May 28, 2021 [https://www.washingtonpost.com/politics/2021/05/28/various-dishonesties-rand-pauls-cocaine-quail-presentation/]. Paul apparently copied his complaint from Senator Tom Coburn, who had used it to mock wasteful spending when the grant was still active. Coburn had written the amount in 2012 as $356,933 with a footnote "140" superscripted next to the dollar figure. Paul or his staff apparently treated the footnote as a decimal when they made a poster using Coburn's old example. This version of the poster appears at the 0:45 second mark of Paul's May 29, 2021, speech: "Rand Paul's half an hour rant on wasteful government programs," YouTube [https://www.youtube.com/watch?v=DsNDd29azGU&t=45s]. It apparently was the same version he had shown back in February 2018.

7. Some prose in this section was revised from C. F. Chabris and D. J. Simons, "Obama and the Oil Spill: In the Abstract," *Huffington Post*, November 17, 2011 [https://www.huffpost.com/entry/obama-and-the-oil-spill-i_b_619595].

8. T. Erikson, *Surrounded by Idiots: The Four Types of Human Behaviour* (London: Vermilion, 2019); D. J. Pittenger, "Cautionary Comments Regarding the Myers-Briggs Type Indicator," *Consulting Psychology Journal: Practice and Research* 57 (2005): 210–221 [https://doi.org/10.1037/1065-9293.57.3.210].

9. Study 5 in M. Thomas, D. H. Simon, and V. Kadiyali, "The Price Precision Effect: Evidence from Laboratory and Market Data," *Marketing Science* 29 (2010): 175–190 [doi.org/10.1287/mksc.1090.0512]. Consistent with that idea, when people estimate quantitative facts, giving them a rounder starting value (more ending zeroes) leads to greater adjustment away from the starting point: C. Janiszewski and D. Uy, "Precision of the Anchor Influences the Amount of Adjustment," *Psychological Science* 19 (2008): 121–127 [https://doi.org/10.1111/j.1467-9280.2008.02057.x].

10. 3.6 roentgen story: S. Plokhy, *Chernobyl: The History of a Nuclear Catastrophe* (New York: Basic Books, 2018), 107–113. One hunk of corium, a by-product of the meltdown, coagulated over about a week into an eleven-ton hunk of radioactive material now known as the "elephant's foot." According to a report by David Goldenberg, it initially gave off more than 10,000 roentgen per hour, enough to kill a person close to it in minutes. Even fifteen years later, it still produced more than 800 roentgens per hour. See D. Goldenberg, "The Famous Photo of Chernobyl's Most Dangerous Radioactive Material Was a Selfie," *Atlas Obscura*, January 24, 2016 [https://www.atlasobscura.com/articles/elephants-foot-chernobyl].

11. Documentation of the UK error: L. Kelion and R. Cuffe, "Covid: Test Error 'Should Never Have Happened'—Hancock," BBC News, October 5, 2020

[https://www.bbc.com/news/uk-54422505]. Note that people who tested positive did learn their test results, but the reporting error meant that tens of thousands of close contacts didn't learn that they had been exposed. This sort of mistake is especially likely when using an older system that was designed when greater capacities or limits were unanticipated or were too expensive to accommodate. The "Y2K bug," which was caused by old software allocating just two digits rather than four to represent the year in a date value, cost governments and private organizations in the United States alone an estimated $100 billion to fix. See R. Chandrasekaran, "Y2K Repair Bill: $100 Billion," *Washington Post*, November 18, 1999 [https://www.washingtonpost.com/wp-srv/WPcap/1999-11/18/077r-111899-idx.html]. Chris Groskopf has created an excellent guide with red flags that your dataset might have problems of this sort. See C. Groskopf, "The Quartz Guide to Bad Data," *Quartz*, December 15, 2015 [https://qz.com/572338/the-quartz-guide-to-bad-data/]; the latest version is on Github [https://github.com/Quartz/bad-data-guide].

12. B. L. Fredrickson and M. F. Losada, "Positive Affect and the Complex Dynamics of Human Flourishing," *American Psychologist* 60 (2005): 678–686 [https://doi.org/10.1037/0003-066X.60.7.678]; this paper has now been cited over 3,700 times.

13. Our calculations: If you have a total of 312,105 experiences, of which 232,105 are positive and 80,000 negative, then the positive:negative ratio is 2.9013. If one of those 80,000 is switched from negative to positive, the ratio goes to 2.90136, which rounds to 2.9014. So in order to know that the "true" value of the ratio is 2.9013 rather than 2.9014, you need to accurately measure and code hundreds of thousands of experiences.

14. Musk tweeted on May 13, 2022 [https://twitter.com/elonmusk/status/1525291586669531137]; "Twitter Announces First Quarter 2022 Results," April 28, 2022 [https://s22.q4cdn.com/826641620/files/doc_financials/2022/q1/Final-Q1%e2%80%9922-earnings-release.pdf].

15. There are several other problems with Musk's proposed method of checking the prevalence of bots on Twitter. He suggested sampling followers of the @twitter account, but these are not necessarily representative of the full set of Twitter accounts. Neither of us presently follows @twitter, for example, and we have no idea whether bots are more or less likely to follow it than humans are. Second, he suggested skipping the first one thousand accounts that followed @twitter and then checking every tenth one after that. Even after dropping the first one thousand users, his sample would still be biased toward early Twitter adopters. And sampling by regular intervals is not random. Finally, he suggested that other people follow his method and then compare results. In principle, it is always good to have independent investigations arrive at the same conclusion—but applying Musk's exact recipe will not create an independent investigation! It would be better for

Musk's stated objectives if others developed distinct but similarly valid independent methods rather than all copy him. Achieving precision in social science— which is what Musk is undertaking by trying to determine the nature of a large group of entities acting like human beings—is not as simple as it sometimes seems.

16. M. Losada, "The Complex Dynamics of High Performance Teams," *Mathematical and Computer Modelling* 30 (1999): 179–192 [https://doi.org/10.1016/S0895-7177(99)00189-2]. N. J. L. Brown, A. D. Sokal, and H. L. Friedman, "The Complex Dynamics of Wishful Thinking: The Critical Positivity Ratio," *American Psychologist* 68 (2013): 801–813 [https://doi.org/10.1037/a0032850]. This critique describes how Losada applied Lorenz's equations inappropriately.

17. Frederickson's correction notice was published in *American Psychologist* in 2013 [https://doi.org/10.1037/0003-066X.60.7.678]. Other aspects of the paper were not retracted or withdrawn even though the concluding sentence of the abstract was premised on that flawed model.

18. This representativeness issue is the same one Musk faced in trying to identify Twitter bots, but his sample of one hundred accounts was far too small to represent the full spectrum of users.

19. Pollsters can even draw different conclusions from the same survey data. Sites like FiveThirtyEight that collate the predictions of pollsters show that the results produced by some polls consistently lean Republican, while others lean Democrat. Among competent pollsters, those systematic differences typically result from the assumptions going into the weighting methods. And, of course, pollsters can change their weighting algorithms and don't always publicly report their assumptions and procedures.

20. A. Gelman, S. Goel, D. Rivers, and D. Rothschild, "The Mythical Swing Voter," *Quarterly Journal of Political Science* 11 (2016): 103–130 [https://doi.org/10.1561/100.00015031]. The *New York Times* critique of the Daybreak poll: N. Cohn, "How One 19-Year-Old Illinois Man Is Distorting National Polling Averages," *New York Times*, October 12, 2016 [https://www.nytimes.com/2016/10/13/upshot/how-one-19-year-old-illinois-man-is-distorting-national-polling-averages.html]. The *Los Angeles Times* response, though headlined as a rebuttal, more or less confirmed the issues: D. Lauter, "No, One 19-Year-Old Trump Supporter Probably Isn't Distorting the Polling Averages All by Himself," *Los Angeles Times*, October 13, 2016 [https://www.latimes.com/politics/la-na-pol-daybreak-poll-questions-20161013-snap-story.html].

21. Ironically, the Daybreak poll ended up providing more accurate overall percentages for Trump and Clinton than many other polls. (Stopped clocks are precise all the time, even though they're only accurate twice a day!) However, people analyze these polls to find out which subgroups support each candidate, so inaccuracy in those numbers matters.

22. For a discussion of the telescope metaphor in the context of scientific research, see U. Simonsohn, "Small Telescopes: Detectability and the Evaluation of Replication Results," *Psychological Science* 26 (2015): 559–569 [https://doi.org/10.1177/0956797614567341].

23. J. Simmons, "MTurk vs. the Lab: Either Way We Need Big Samples," *Data Colada*, April 4, 2014 [http://datacolada.org/18].

24. The managers' comments were about the first game of a doubleheader on May 8, 2022: "Chris Woodward Jabs at Gleyber Torres' Walk-Off HR, Calls Yankee Stadium 'A Little League Ballpark,'" ESPN, May 9, 2022 [https://www.espn.com/mlb/story/_/id/33886269/chris-woodward-jabs-gleyber-torres-walk-hr-calls-yankee-stadium-little-league-ballpark].

25. If you allow for rounding, you'd need at least 67 ballparks (66/67 = 0.98507, which rounds up to 0.99). See J. Heathers, "The GRIM Test—a Method for Evaluating Published Research," *Medium*, May 23, 2016 [https://jamesheathers.medium.com/the-grim-test-a-method-for-evaluating-published-research-9a4e5f05e870]; N. J. L. Brown and J. A. H. Heathers, "The GRIM Test: A Simple Technique Detects Numerous Anomalies in the Reporting of Results in Psychology," *Social Psychological and Personality Science* 8 (2017): 363–369 [https://doi.org/10.1177/1948550616673876].

26. Nick Brown provided a general version of this idea in our conversations with him: The number of possible two-digit decimal fractions that you can get from a sample of less than 100 is equal to the size of that sample. So if 29 people reported their happiness on a 1 to 7 scale, there are 29 valid two-digit combinations after the decimal point (and 71 invalid ones).

27. The GRIM test alone can't prove definitely that a researcher has committed fraud. Finding a large number of GRIM errors in an article would undermine the validity of any conclusions, though. If the reporting is sloppy enough that the numbers are frequently misreported, we have little reason to trust that the researchers were careful in conducting the study. For example, Brown and his colleagues Tim van der Zee and Jordan Anaya also spotted many GRIM errors in papers by former Cornell professor Brian Wansink, whom we've mentioned before. In one of the GRIM-flagged papers, Wansink had ten people use a rating scale from 1 to 9 to report how physically uncomfortable they were after eating three pieces of pizza. He reported a mean rating of 2.25, which seems superficially reasonable (precise to two decimal places!), but an average of ten integer scores has to have a 0 as the second decimal place. It could be 2.20 or 2.30, but not 2.25. The excess precision made the results that Wansink reported impossible—just like many other values in the same paper. See T. van der Zee, J. Anaya, and N. J. L. Brown, "Statistical Heartburn: An Attempt to Digest Four Pizza Publications from the Cornell Food and Brand Lab," *BMC Nutrition* 3 (2017): 54 [https://doi.org/10.1186/s40795-017-0167-x]; N. Brown, "Strange Patterns in Some Results from the Food

and Brand Lab," *Nick Brown's Blog*, March 22, 2017 [http://steamtraen.blogspot
.com/2017/03/strange-patterns-in-some-results-from.html].

28. Department of Transportation "Status of the Nation's Highways, Bridges
and Transit: Condition and Performance" reports are online [https://www
.transit.dot.gov/research-innovation/status-nations-highways-bridges-and
-transit-condition-and-performance]. Sundquist's analysis: E. Sundquist,
"New Travel Demand Projections Are Due from U.S. DOT: Will They Be Accurate this Time?," State Smart Transportation Initiative, December 16, 2013
[https://ssti.us/2013/12/16/new-travel-demand-projections-are-due-from-u-s
-dot-will-they-be-accurate-this-time/]. Additional discussion: A. Gelman, "The
Commissar for Traffic Presents the Latest Five-Year Plan," *Statistical Modeling,
Causal Inference, and Social Science*, January 21, 2014 [https://statmodeling.stat
.columbia.edu/2014/01/21/commissar-traffic-presents-latest-five-year-plan/];
C. Williams-Derry, "Traffic Forecast Follies: The US DOT Refuses to Learn from
Recent Travel Trends," Sightline Institute, December 23, 2013 [https://www
.sightline.org/2013/12/23/traffic-forecast-follies/].

29. Historical world records from Wikipedia: "Women's 100 Metres World
Record Progression" [https://en.wikipedia.org/wiki/Women%27s_100_metres
_world_record_progression]; "Men's 100 Metres World Record Progression" [https://en.wikipedia.org/wiki/Men%27s_100_metres_world_record
_progression]. Note the improvement in timing precision as well as running speeds.
Prediction of race times: A. Tatem et al., "Momentous Sprint at the 2156 Olym-
pics?," *Nature* 431 (2004): 525 [https://doi.org/10.1038/431525a]. The article did
not report the equation for the line of best fit to these data, but the average yearly
improvements can be extracted from some of the predicted times reported in the
paper. A commentary on the original article noted what would happen by extrapolating to the year 2636: K. Rice, "Sprint Research Runs into a Credibility Gap," *Nature* 432 (2004): 147 [https://doi.org/10.1038/432147b]. This sort of extrapolation
error appears to be common in sports. A more recent article about record times
in the Ironman triathlon constructed a linear model from the seven record times
set since 1987. It then noted that "if you extend that straight line you find that the
current trend predicts a sub-7 Ironman in 2049." Of course, if you extrapolate that
same linear trend further, you can predict that by the year 2494, someone will finish
an Ironman before they start it. See A. Hutchinson, "The Science Says a Sub-Seven-
Hour Ironman Is (Sort of) Possible," *Triathlete*, May 30, 2022 [https://www
.triathlete.com/training/the-science-says-a-sub-seven-hour-ironman-is-sort-of
-possible/].

30. M. Yglesias, "The Trump Administration's 'Cubic Model' of Coronavirus Deaths, Explained," *Vox*, May 8, 2020 [https://www.vox.com/2020/5/8
/21250641/kevin-hassett-cubic-model-smoothing].

31. Perhaps not coincidentally, Hassett was the coauthor of a book published in 1999 that predicted the Dow Jones Industrial Average would reach 36,000 by 2004: J. K. Glassman and K. L. Hassett, *Dow 36,000: The New Strategy for Profiting from the Coming Rise in the Stock Market* (New York: Three Rivers Press, 1999). It reached that level in 2021—an excellent example of a prediction that was very precise but wildly inaccurate.

32. According to "Trends in Number of COVID-19 Cases and Deaths in the US Reported to CDC, by State/Territory," COVID Tracker, Centers for Disease Control and Prevention [https://covid.cdc.gov/covid-data-tracker/#trends_dailydeaths].

33. Dan wrote a detailed analysis of the initial pandemic response at the University of Illinois at Urbana-Champaign: "Fall 2020 Covid Summary," dansimons .com, December 8, 2020 [http://dansimons.com/Covid/fall2020summary.html]. The enrollment was about 33,500, but many students that semester studied remotely because most classes were online. There likely were 20,000–25,000 undergraduates on campus during the semester. The university's forecast discussion: "COVID-19 Briefing Series: Data Modeling," YouTube [https://www.youtube .com/watch?v=VmwK9tyNe8A&t=1734s].

34. The modelers provided a range of possible predictions as a function of different starting assumptions for compliance and testing delays. The details were mentioned only briefly in a video briefing, "COVID-19 Briefing Series: Data Modeling," YouTube [https://www.youtube.com/watch?v=VmwK9tyNe8A&t=1840], by the university's lead modeler, Nigel Goldenfeld, and were not mentioned again by the university administration. In his presentation, Goldenfeld presented a complex graph that, if read correctly, showed the prediction of 700 cases. That same graph showed that a one-day delay in notification of a positive result would lead to a model prediction of just under 4,000 cases for the fall semester. The modeling apparently was just fine, but the university touted a single prediction: It presented an unrepresentative outcome, claimed it was the expected worst case, and neglected to say that actual results may vary.

Chapter 8: Potency—Be Wary of "Butterfly Effects"

1. C. Flanagan, "Caroline Calloway Isn't a Scammer," *Atlantic*, September 27, 2019 [https://www.theatlantic.com/ideas/archive/2019/09/i-get -caroline-calloway/598918/]. The Wikipedia entry on Calloway has a lot more detail about her background and claims: "Caroline Calloway" [https://en .wikipedia.org/wiki/Caroline_Calloway]. Note that "essential oils" are called essential not because they are important or critical for health but only because they are oils that give the plants they come from their "essence," or smell. We suspect that many people have been misled throughout the decades by the word "essential" into thinking these products have been designated as inherently important for

human wellness; perhaps relabeling them "odoriferous oils" would begin to correct this problem.

2. T. Hsu, "A Century After Phony Flu Ads, Companies Hype Dubious Covid Cures," *New York Times*, December 24, 2020 [https://www.nytimes.com/2020/12/24/business/media/dubious-covid-cures.html]. The 1918 influenza pandemic saw many such remedies advertised in newspapers and elsewhere: M. M. Phillips and D. Cole, "Coronavirus Advice Is Everywhere. It Was the Same with Spanish Flu," *Wall Street Journal*, January 22, 2021 [https://www.wsj.com/story/coronavirus-advice-is-everywhere-it-was-the-same-with-the-spanish-flu-6a25d0d4]. Even today, many highly regarded healthcare organizations and medical professionals offer or recommend therapies for which there is no good scientific evidence or physiological mechanism by which they could work.

3. Some types of snakes, including the water snakes used in China, may yield oils with high concentrations of omega-3 fatty acids, which might have some benefits. Rattlesnake oil apparently has far less. See R. A. Kunin, "Snake Oil," *Western Journal of Medicine* 151 (1989): 208 [https://www.ncbi.nlm.nih.gov/pmc/articles/PMC1026931/pdf/westjmed00120-0094a.pdf].

4. See "Questions and Answers on Dietary Supplements," US Food and Drug Administration [https://www.fda.gov/food/information-consumers-using-dietary-supplements/questions-and-answers-dietary-supplements]. Due to an effective lobbying effort, the FDA was explicitly blocked from regulating supplements as drugs in the Dietary Supplement Health and Education Act of 1994; therefore, supplement makers do not have to prove to the FDA that their products are safe and effective before marketing them.

5. Sources for Clark Stanley's story: "Clark Stanley," Wikipedia [https://en.wikipedia.org/wiki/Clark_Stanley]; "Clark Stanley's Snake Oil Liniment," Smithsonian Institution [https://americanhistory.si.edu/collections/search/object/nmah_1298331]; L. Gandhi, "A History of 'Snake Oil Salesmen,'" NPR, August 26, 2013 [https://www.npr.org/sections/codeswitch/2013/08/26/215761377/a-history-of-snake-oil-salesmen].

6. The US Federal Trade Commission announced fines for Lumos Labs [https://www.ftc.gov/system/files/documents/cases/160105lumoslabsstip.pdf], [https://www.ftc.gov/news-events/news/press-releases/2016/01/lumosity-pay-2-million-settle-ftc-deceptive-advertising-charges-its-brain-training-program]; Carrot Neurotechnology [https://www.ftc.gov/system/files/documents/cases/160223carrotneurodo.pdf]; and LearningRx [https://www.ftc.gov/system/files/documents/cases/160518learningrxorder.pdf], [https://www.ftc.gov/system/files/documents/cases/160518learningrxcmpt.pdf], [https://www.ftc.gov/news-events/news/press-releases/2016/05/marketers-one-one-brain-training-programs-settle-ftc-charges-claims-about-ability-treat-severe].

7. Many claims about overly potent interventions capitalize on widely held but mistaken intuitions about untapped potential (see *The Invisible Gorilla*, ch. 6)— the belief that we can "get smart quick" by simply tapping into potential that lurks beneath the surface of our minds. The idea of untapped potential is made most concrete by the prevalence of the myth that we only use 10 percent of our brain. If so, then imagine what we could do if we simply "tapped" the unused potential. This myth helps explain why people are so readily fooled by deceptive brain-training advertisements. It might also explain why scientists have convinced themselves that they've found a butterfly effect, e.g., that listening to Mozart for just ten minutes will increase your IQ by eight to nine points (it doesn't) or that a few minutes of "power posing" can change your levels of testosterone and "the outcomes of your life" (they can't). In 2016, we and our colleagues reviewed all of the studies cited by leading brain-training companies and found that most were so flawed they could not have provided compelling evidence: D. J. Simons et al., "Do 'Brain-Training' Programs Work?," *Psychological Science in the Public Interest* 17 (2016): 103–186 [https://doi.org/10.1177/1529100616661983].

8. The subtitle of Malcolm Gladwell's 2000 book *The Tipping Point*, which may be the bestselling book about social science of all time, is "How Little Things Can Make a Big Difference" (Boston: Little, Brown, 2000).

9. D. Kahneman, *Thinking, Fast and Slow* (New York: Farrar, Straus and Giroux, 2011).

10. Lady Macbeth effect: S. Schnall, J. Benton, and S. Harvey, "With a Clean Conscience: Cleanliness Reduces the Severity of Moral Judgments," *Psychological Science* 19 (2008): 1219–1222 [https://doi.org/10.1111%2Fj.1467-9280.2008.02227.x]. Watching eyes: M. Bateson, D. Nettle, and G. Roberts, "Cues of Being Watched Enhance Cooperation in a Real-World Setting," *Biology Letters* 2 (2006): 412–414 [https://doi.org/10.1098/rsbl.2006.0509]. Priming old age: J. A. Bargh, M. Chen, and L. Burrows, "Automaticity of Social Behavior: Direct Effects of Trait Construct and Stereotype Activation on Action," *Journal of Personality and Social Psychology* 71 (1996): 230–244 [https://doi.org/10.1037/0022-3514.71.2.230].

11. Failed replication of elderly priming: S. Doyen, O. Klein, C. L. Pichon, and A. Cleeremans, "Behavioral Priming: It's All in the Mind, but Whose Mind?," *PLoS ONE* 7 (2012): e29081 [https://doi.org/10.1371/journal.pone.0029081]. Kahneman's letter and Schwarz's response: E. Yong, "Nobel Laureate Challenges Psychologists to Clean Up Their Act," *Nature* 490 (2012): 7418 [https://doi.org/10.1038/nature.2012.11535].

12. J. Bargh, *Before You Know It: The Unconscious Reasons We Do What We Do* (New York: Simon and Schuster, 2017). Ulrich Schimmack critically reviewed the evidence provided by the studies cited in Bargh's book: U. Schimmack, "'Before You Know It' by John A. Bargh: A Quantitative Book Review," Replicability-Index,

November 28, 2017 [https://replicationindex.com/2017/11/28/bargh-book/]. See also I. Shalev and J. A. Bargh, "Use of Priming-Based Interventions to Facilitate Psychological Health: Commentary on Kazdin and Blase (2011)," *Perspectives on Psychological Science* 6 (2011): 488–492 [https://doi.org/10.1177 /1745691611416993].

13. Kahneman's quotation: U. Schimmack, M. Heene, and K. Kesavan, "Reconstruction of a Train Wreck: How Priming Research Went Off the Rails," Replicability-Index, February 2, 2017 [https://replicationindex.com/2017/02/02 /reconstruction-of-a-train-wreck-how-priming-research-went-of-the-rails /comment-page-1/#comment-1454]. Example critiques of replication: J. Mitchell, *On the Evidentiary Emptiness of Failed Replications*, July 1, 2014 [https://web .archive.org/web/20220415162317/https://jasonmitchell.fas.harvard.edu /Papers/Mitchell_failed_science_2014.pdf]; W. Stroebe and F. Strack, "The Alleged Crisis and the Illusion of Exact Replication," *Perspectives on Psychological Science* 9 (2014): 59–71 [https://doi.org/10.1177/1745691613514450]. Dan published a response to these arguments: D. J. Simons, "The Value of Direct Replication," *Perspectives on Psychological Science* 9 (2014): 76–80 [https://doi .org/10.1177/1745691613514755].

14. We also noticed a surprising consistency in the two separate runs of the elderly priming experiment reported by Bargh and colleagues in their original 1996 paper. The primed participants took almost exactly the same time to walk to the elevator in both experiments, and the unprimed participants—those who did not read words about being old—were almost exactly one second faster in each experiment.

15. C. F. Chabris, P. R. Heck, J. Mandart, D. J. Benjamin, and D. J. Simons, "No Evidence That Experiencing Physical Warmth Promotes Interpersonal Warmth: Two Failures to Replicate Williams and Bargh (2008)," *Social Psychology* 50 (2019): 127–132 [https://doi.org/10.1027/1864-9335/a000361]. A separate team independently also failed to replicate the heat pack study: D. Lynott et al., "Replication of 'Experiencing Physical Warmth Promotes Interpersonal Warmth' by Williams and Bargh (2008)," *Social Psychology* 45 (2014): 216–222 [https://doi .org/10.1027/1864-9335/a000187].

16. Examples of large replication projects edited by Dan: M. O'Donnell et al., "Registered Replication Report: Dijksterhuis and van Knippenberg (1998)," *Perspectives on Psychological Science* 13 (2018): 268–294 [https://doi .org/10.1177/1745691618755704]; R. J. McCarthy et al., "Registered Replication Report on Srull and Wyer (1979)," *Advances in Methods and Practices in Psychological Science* 1 (2018): 321–336 [https://doi.org/10.1177/2515245918777487]; B. Verschuere et al., "Registered Replication Report on Mazar, Amir, and Ariely (2008)," *Advances in Methods and Practices in Psychological Science* 1 (2018): 299–317 [https://doi.org/10.1177/2515245918781032]. Srull and Wyer's study:

T. K. Srull and R. S. Wyer, "The Role of Category Accessibility in the Interpretation of Information About Persons: Some Determinants and Implications," *Journal of Personality and Social Psychology* 37 (1979): 1660–1672 [https://doi.org/10.1037/0022-3514.37.10.1660]. This paper was among the first to adopt the priming method of rearranging words and then evaluating how people rated a fictitious person as an outcome measure. It became one of the standard methods in later studies. The study's second author, Robert Wyer, told Dan that there might have been an error in how the original statistics were reported, but it's not clear what sort of error could yield this impossibly potent effect. Unfortunately, the reviewers and editor of the original journal article—and many of the thousands of authors who cited it in their own research—didn't notice how implausibly large the reported findings were. Ironically, on a second measure in the replication of the Srull and Wyer study, there was again no evidence of the predicted priming, but this time the small difference of 0.08 went in the opposite direction of the original result.

17. Schimmack's reanalysis: U. Schimmack, "Reconstruction of a Train Wreck: How Priming Research Went Off the Rails," Replicability-Index, February 2, 2017 [https://replicationindex.com/2017/02/02/reconstruction-of-a-train-wreck-how-priming-research-went-of-the-rails/]. Consistent with typical practices in this research area between about 1980 and 2010, these studies typically tested few participants and selectively or flexibly analyzed their results. Original "Lady Macbeth effect" study: S. Schnall, J. Benton, and S. Harvey, "With a Clean Conscience: Cleanliness Reduces the Severity of Moral Judgments," *Psychological Science* 19 (2008): 1219–1222 [https://doi.org/10.1111%2Fj.1467-9280.2008.02227.x]. Replication: F. Cheung and M. B. Donnellan, "Does Cleanliness Influence Moral Judgments? A Direct Replication of Schnall, Benton, and Harvey (2008)," *Social Psychology* 45 (2014): 209–215 [https://doi.org/10.1027/1864-9335/a000186]. Original "Ten Commandments" study: N. Mazar, O. Amir, and D. Ariely, "The Dishonesty of Honest People: A Theory of Self-Concept Maintenance," *Journal of Marketing Research* 45 (2008): 633–644 [https://doi.org/10.1509/jmkr.45.6.633]. Replication: B. Verschuere et al., "Registered Replication Report on Mazar, Amir, and Ariely (2008)," *Advances in Methods and Practices in Psychological Science* 1 (2018): 299–317 [https://doi.org/10.1177/2515245918781032]. Original money priming studies: K. D. Vohs, N. L. Mead, and M. R. Goode, "The Psychological Consequences of Money," *Science* 314 (2006): 1154–1156 [https://doi.org/10.1126/science.1132491]; E. M. Caruso, K. D. Vohs, B. Baxter, and A. Waytz, "Mere Exposure to Money Increases Endorsement of Free-Market Systems and Social Inequality," *Journal of Experimental Psychology: General* 142 (2013): 301–306 [https://doi.org/10.1037/a0029288]. Replication led by one of the researchers who had coauthored papers on this effect: E. M. Caruso, O. Shapira, and J. F. Landy, "Show Me the Money: A Systematic Exploration of Manipulations, Moderators,

and Mechanisms of Priming Effects," *Psychological Science* 28 (2017): 1148–1159 [https://doi.org/10.1177/0956797617706161].

18. Kahneman's reply was a comment on Replicability-Index [https://replicationindex.com/2017/02/02/reconstruction-of-a-train-wreck-how-priming-research-went-of-the-rails/comment-page-1/#comment-1454]. A. Tversky and D. Kahneman, "Belief in the Law of Small Numbers," *Psychological Bulletin* 76 (1971): 105–110 [https://doi.org/10.1037/h0031322].

19. J. Berger, M. Meredith, and S. C. Wheeler, "Contextual Priming: Where People Vote Affects How They Vote," *Proceedings of the National Academy of Sciences* 105 (2008): 8846–8849 [https://doi.org/10.1073/pnas.0711988105]. That paper first reported that actual Arizona voters assigned to vote in a school showed 2 percent greater support for a funding referendum than those assigned to vote in a church (56 percent support vs. 54 percent). The priming study had participants rate images that either did or didn't include school photos and then, in a later part of the study, "vote" for or against a school funding referendum. The calculation for warmth priming and charity is based on the size of the link between holding a hot object and prosociality in the second experiment (a correlation of $r = .28$): L. E. Williams and J. A. Bargh, "Experiencing Physical Warmth Promotes Interpersonal Warmth," *Science* 322 (2008): 606–607 [https://doi.org/10.1126/science.1162548]. The relationship between income and giving to secular charities ($r = .23$) was measured in this survey of 1,800 Americans: N. G. Choi and D. M. DiNitto, "Predictors of Time Volunteering, Religious Giving, and Secular Giving: Implications for Nonprofit Organizations," *Journal of Sociology and Social Welfare* 39 (2012): 93–120 [https://heinonline.org/HOL/LandingPage?handle=hein.journals/jrlsasw39&div=19&id=&page]. Squaring each to obtain the percentage of variance explained yields $(.28)^2 = .0784$ and $(.23)^2 = .0529$, forming a ratio of these two yields $.0784/.0529 = 1.482$, which represents a difference of 48.2 percent.

20. Appendices A–C of D. P. Green and A. S. Gerber, *Get Out the Vote!*, 3rd ed. (Washington, DC: Brookings Institution Press, 2015).

21. C. J. Bryan, G. M. Walton, T. Rogers, and C. S. Dweck, "Motivating Voter Turnout by Invoking the Self," *Proceedings of the National Academy of Sciences* 108 (2011): 12653–12656 [https://doi.org/10.1073/pnas.1103343108].

22. Voting was measured by examining public records, which in many states reveal who voted but not which candidates they voted for. We added the italics to the question wording ("*vote*" and "*be a voter*") to emphasize the subtle distinction.

23. A. S. Gerber, G. A. Huber, D. R. Biggers, and D. J. Hendry, "A Field Experiment Shows That Subtle Linguistic Cues Might Not Affect Voter Behavior," *Proceedings of the National Academy of Sciences* 113 (2016): 7112–7117 [https://doi.org/10.1073/pnas.1513727113].

24. The original verb tense study: W. Hart and D. Albarracín, "Learning About What Others Were Doing: Verb Aspect and Attributions of Mundane

and Criminal Intent for Past Actions," *Psychological Science* 22 (2011): 261–266 [https://doi.org/10.1177/0956797610395393]. The unsuccessful replication: A. Eerland et al., "Registered Replication Report: Hart and Albarracín (2011)," *Perspectives on Psychological Science* 11 (2016): 158–171 [https://doi.org/10.1177/1745691615605826]. Note: Just because an originally reported effect was too potent or isn't replicable doesn't mean it was fraudulent or that any misconduct was involved. Because publishing incentives favor significant and big findings, flukes in the direction of an overly potent effect tend to get published, but flukes in the opposite direction do not. The nature of chance means that flukes will happen even if researchers do nothing wrong.

25. G. M. Walton and G. L. Cohen, "A Brief Social-Belonging Intervention Improves Academic and Health Outcomes of Minority Students," *Science* 331 (2011): 1447–1451 [https://doi.org/10.1126/science.1198364]; G. D. Borman, J. Pyne, C. S. Rozek, and A. Schmidt, "A Replicable Identity-Based Intervention Reduces the Black-White Suspension Gap at Scale," *American Educational Research Journal* 59 (2022): 284–314 [https://doi.org/10.3102/00028312211042251].

26. If these interventions worked as promised, schools wouldn't continually abandon old ones for new ones as though keeping up with changing fashions. For discussion of these studies and the problems with them, see E. Yong, "A Worrying Trend for Psychology's 'Simple Little Tricks,'" *Atlantic*, September 9, 2016 [https://www.theatlantic.com/science/archive/2016/09/can-simple-tricks-mobilise-voters-and-help-students/499109/].

27. Original study: C. Green and D. Bavelier, "Action Video Game Modifies Visual Selective Attention," *Nature* 423 (2003): 534–537 [https://doi.org/10.1038/nature01647]. TED talk: [https://www.ted.com/talks/daphne_bavelier_your_brain_on_video_games]. Meta-analyses: G. Sala, K. S. Tatlidil, and F. Gobet, "Video Game Training Does Not Enhance Cognitive Ability: A Comprehensive Meta-Analytic Investigation," *Psychological Bulletin* 144 (2018): 111–139 [https://psycnet.apa.org/doi/10.1037/bul0000139]; J. Hilgard, G. Sala, W. R. Boot, and D. J. Simons, "Overestimation of Action-Game Training Effects: Publication Bias and Salami Slicing," *Collabra: Psychology* 5 (2019) [https://doi.org/10.1525/collabra.231].

28. Original study: D. R. Carney, A. J. Cuddy, and A. J. Yap, "Power Posing: Brief Nonverbal Displays Affect Neuroendocrine Levels and Risk Tolerance," *Psychological Science* 21 (2010): 1363–1368. TED talk: Amy Cuddy, "Your Body Language May Shape Who You Are," YouTube, October 1, 2012 [https://www.ted.com/talks/amy_cuddy_your_body_language_may_shape_who_you_are]. A failed replication: E. Ranehill, A. Dreber, M. Johannesson, S. Leiberg, S. Sul, and R. A. Weber, "Assessing the Robustness of Power Posing: No Effect on Hormones and Risk Tolerance in a Large Sample of Men and Women," *Psychological Science* 33 (2015): 1–4 [https://doi.org/10.1177/0956797614553946]. Statement from

the study's first author, Dana Carney: "My Position on 'Power Poses'" [https://faculty.haas.berkeley.edu/dana_carney/pdf_my%20position%20on%20power%20poses.pdf].

29. Summary of early work: C. S. Dweck, "Motivational Processes Affecting Learning," *American Psychologist* 41 (1986): 1040–1048 [https://doi.org/10.1037/0003-066X.41.10.1040]. Book: C. S. Dweck, *Mindset: The New Psychology of Success* (New York: Random House, 2006). TED talk: Carol Dweck, "The Power of Believing That You Can Improve," YouTube, December 17, 2014 [https://www.ted.com/talks/carol_dweck_the_power_of_believing_that_you_can_improve]. Stuart Ritchie's discussion: S. Ritchie, "How Growth Mindset Shrank," *Science Fictions*, October 11, 2022 [https://stuartritchie.substack.com/p/growth-mindset-decline]; S. Ritchie, *Science Fictions: How Fraud, Bias, Negligence, and Hype Undermine the Search for Truth* (New York: Metropolitan Books, 2020). Meta-analysis: B. N. Macnamara and A. P. Burgoyne, "Do Growth Mindset Interventions Impact Students' Academic Achievement? A Systematic Review and Meta-Analysis with Recommendations for Best Practices," *Psychological Bulletin* (2022), advance online publication [https://doi.org/10.1037/bul0000352].

30. For an analysis of the differences between evaluating options separately or comparatively, see M. H. Bazerman, D. A. Moore, A. E. Tenbrunsel, K. A. Wade-Benzoni, and S. Blount, "Explaining How Preferences Change Across Joint Versus Separate Evaluation," *Journal of Economic Behavior and Organization* 39 (1999): 41–58 [https://doi.org/10.1016/s0167-2681(99)00025-6].

31. We considered the panic around the notion that computer and Internet tools are decreasing our cognitive abilities in this essay: C. F. Chabris and D. J. Simons, "Digital Alarmists Are Wrong," *Los Angeles Times*, July 25, 2010 [https://www.latimes.com/archives/la-xpm-2010-jul-25-la-oe-chabris-computers-brain-20100725-story.html]. Even the noble crossword was once decried by the *New York Times*, which editorialized in 1924 that "no exercise could possibly be worse than working on these puzzles" but in the twenty-first century came to rely on word games for a substantial part of its business. And in Plato's *Phaedrus*, Socrates criticizes the view that written information "was at all better than knowledge and recollection of the same matters." See N. Carr, *The Shallows: What the Internet Is Doing to Our Brains* (New York: W. W. Norton, 2010), 54–55; N. Carr, "Is Google Making Us Stoopid?," *Atlantic*, July 1, 2008 [https://www.theatlantic.com/magazine/archive/2008/07/is-google-making-us-stupid/306868/] (the spelling "stoopid" was used on the cover of the magazine).

32. The same is true for studies of the benefits of "brain training." Almost all such studies measure performance in arbitrary, computer-based laboratory tasks, and few if any look at actual real-world benefits or costs. See D. J. Simons et al., "Do 'Brain-Training' Programs Work?," *Psychological Science in the Public Interest* 17 (2016): 103–186 [https://doi.org/10.1177%2F1529100616661983].

33. J. Hilgard, "Maximal Positive Controls: A Method for Estimating the Largest Plausible Effect Size," *Journal of Experimental Social Psychology* 93 (2021): 104082 [https://doi.org/10.1016/j.jesp.2020.104082]. The original study Hilgard reevaluated: Y. Hasan, L. Bègue, M. Scharkow, and B. J. Bushman, "The More You Play, the More Aggressive You Become: A Long-Term Experimental Study of Cumulative Violent Video Game Effects on Hostile Expectations and Aggressive Behavior," *Journal of Experimental Social Psychology* 49 (2013): 224–227 [https://doi.org/10.1016/j.jesp.2012.10.016]. The senior author of this paper, Brad Bushman, is a leading researcher in the field of aggression. According to the Retraction Watch database, as of September 2022, he also has been the senior author on three papers that have been retracted—one for duplicate publication, one for misconduct attributed to a student, and one over concerns about the data and nonreproducible results.

34. Comparing actual performance to the ideal or maximal performance can also reveal excessive consistency of the sort we discussed earlier. In a related paper, Hilgard reexamined another study that measured aggression as the amount of hot sauce someone poured for another participant to consume. In the experiment, participants who played a video game as the villain poured substantially more hot sauce, on average, than those who played the hero. But all of the people playing villains poured remarkably similar amounts of hot sauce (as did those playing heroes). Without a pipette, pouring a consistent amount of hot sauce is hard. Hilgard repeated the hot-sauce task, but without having people play video games first. Instead, he just picked an amount of hot sauce in advance and instructed each participant to pour exactly that much. They couldn't do it. In fact, their attempts to pour a consistent amount varied more than did the amounts reportedly poured by participants in the aggression study! The huge effects in the original study were due to implausibly consistent responses. J. Hilgard, "Comment on Yoon and Vargas (2014): An Implausibly Large Effect from Implausibly Invariant Data," *Psychological Science* 30 (2019): 1099–1102 [https://doi.org/10.1177/0956797618815434].

35. "Perceptions of Science in America," American Academy of Arts and Sciences, 2018 [https://www.amacad.org/sites/default/files/publication/downloads/PFoS-Perceptions-Science-America.pdf]; C. Funk, M. Heffernon, B. Kennedy, and C. Johnson, "Trust and Mistrust in Americans' Views of Scientific Experts," Pew Research Center, August 2, 2019 [https://www.pewresearch.org/science/2019/08/02/trust-and-mistrust-in-americans-views-of-scientific-experts/].

Conclusion: Somebody's Fool

1. H. G. Frankfurt, *On Bullshit* (Princeton, NJ: Princeton University Press, 2005). The original version was published in the *Raritan Review* in 1985 [http://www2.csudh.edu/ccauthen/576f12/frankfurt__harry_-_on_bullshit.pdf].

2. G. Pennycook, J. A. Cheyne, N. Barr, D. J. Koehler, and J. A. Fugelsang, "On the Reception and Detection of Pseudo-Profound Bullshit," *Judgment and Decision Making* 10 (2015): 549–563 [http://journal.sjdm.org/15/15923a/jdm15923a .pdf]. The Chopraism generators used in this study were "Wisdom of Chopra" [http://wisdomofchopra.com/] and "New Age Bullshit Generator" [http:// sebpearce.com/bullshit/].

3. D. J. Simons and C. F. Chabris, "What People Believe About How Memory Works: A Representative Survey of the US Population," *PLoS ONE* 6 (2011): e22757 [https://doi.org/10.1371/journal.pone.0022757]; D. J. Simons and C. F. Chabris, "Common (Mis)Beliefs About Memory: A Replication and Comparison of Telephone and Mechanical Turk Survey Methods," *PLoS ONE* 7 (2012): e51876 [https://doi.org/10.1371/journal.pone.0051876].

4. Questions about the veracity and completeness of Doug Bruce's story are raised in these articles: D. Segal, "A Trip down Memory Lane: Did Doug Bruce Forget It All, or Just the Boring Truth?," *Washington Post*, March 22, 2006 [https:// www.washingtonpost.com/archive/lifestyle/2006/03/22/a-trip-down-memory -lane-span-classbankheaddid-doug-bruce-forget-it-all-or-just-the-boring -truthspan/f5b3d8da-7aa3-4f7f-a3a8-3b6077433f7f/]; R. Ebert, "Is This Documentary a Fake?," RogerEbert.com, February 19, 2006 [https://www.rogerebert .com/roger-ebert/is-this-documentary-a-fake]; M. Dargis, "Mysteries, If Not Sunshine, of Another Spotless Mind," *New York Times*, February 24, 2006 [https:// www.nytimes.com/2006/02/24/movies/mysteries-if-not-sunshine-of-another -spotless-mind.html].

5. T. Drew, M. L. H. Võ, and J. M. Wolfe, "The Invisible Gorilla Strikes Again: Sustained Inattentional Blindness in Expert Observers," *Psychological Science* 24 (2013): 1848–1853 [https://doi.org/10.1177%2F0956797613479386].

6. G. Marcus, "Horse Rides Astronaut," *The Road to AI We Can Trust*, May 28, 2022 [https://garymarcus.substack.com/p/horse-rides-astronaut]. Marcus notes that such models do not truly "understand" the relations between objects, so they can produce output that looks downright silly when given novel prompts that mismatch their training set in important ways. For example, he shows that when prompted with "a horse riding an astronaut," the Imagen model produces an image of an astronaut riding a horse. In essence, it gets the "man bites dog" story backward because that story didn't occur (often) in its training set. The limitations of AI and the gap between performance and hype, as of 2019, are documented well in G. Marcus and E. Davis, *Rebooting AI: Building Artificial Intelligence We Can Trust* (New York: Pantheon, 2019), ch. 1. A representative example of the hype around incremental improvements in constrained text-processing tasks is this report of a press release by the Chinese technology company Alibaba: A. Cuthbertson, "Robots Can Now Read Better Than Humans, Putting Millions of Jobs at Risk," *Newsweek*, January 15, 2018 [https://www.newsweek.com

/robots-can-now-read-better-humans-putting-millions-jobs-risk-781393]. Discussion of Blake Lemoine's claim that Google's LaMDA is sentient: N. Tiku, "The Google Engineer Who Thinks the Company's AI Has Come to Life," *Washington Post*, June 11, 2022 [https://www.washingtonpost.com/technology/2022/06/11 /google-ai-lamda-blake-lemoine/]. Gary Marcus responds with this better description of what LaMDA does: "It just tries to be the best version of autocomplete it can be, by predicting what words best fit a given context": "Nonsense on Stilts," *The Road to AI We Can Trust* [https://garymarcus.substack.com/p /nonsense-on-stilts]. Some people were similarly taken in by the pioneering 1970s chatbot ELIZA, which pretended to be a psychotherapist by parrying statements like "I don't get along well with my mother" with responses like "Tell me more about your mother." Joseph Weizenbaum, creator of ELIZA, was surprised by how seriously people took the bot's banter and how emotionally they reacted to it: "I had not realized . . . that extremely short exposures to a relatively simple computer program could induce powerful delusional thinking in quite normal people." See J. Weizenbaum, *Computer Power and Human Reason: From Judgment to Calculation* (San Francisco: W. H. Freeman, 1976), 7. More information about ELIZA and screenshots of conversations with it are in "ELIZA," Wikipedia [https://en .wikipedia.org/wiki/ELIZA].

7. Captain Mbote victim: M. Zuckoff, "The Perfect Mark," *New Yorker*, May 15, 2006 [https://www.newyorker.com/magazine/2006/05/15/the-perfect -mark]. Advance fee fraud takings: "Advance-Fee Fraud Scams Rise Dramatically in 2009," Ultrascan AGI [https://ultrascan-agi.com/Advance-fee%20 Fraud%20Scams%20Rise%20Dramatically%20in%202009.html]. A more recent estimate suggests that these scams still take in over $700,000 each year: M. Leonhardt, "'Nigerian Prince' Email Scams Still Rake in over $700,000 a Year—Here's How to Protect Yourself," CNBC, April 18, 2019 [https://www .cnbc.com/2019/04/18/nigerian-prince-scams-still-rake-in-over-700000 -dollars-a-year.html]. We wrote an essay on the "Nigerian scam": C. Chabris and D. Simons, "Why We Should Scam the Scammers," *Wall Street Journal*, August 3, 2012 [https://www.wsj.com/articles/SB10000872396390443931404577 548813973954518]; some of the prose in this section is adapted from that article. Most scammers are never caught or prosecuted, although an American who laundered money as part of a "Nigerian Prince" scam was indicted on 269 counts of various federal crimes in 2017. In a further irony, he apparently was lured into this role via a romance scam perpetrated by actual scammers from Nigeria, to two of whom he forwarded the scam's proceeds. See B. Warren, "'Nigerian Prince' and Online Romance Scams Raked in at Least $250,000, Slidell Police Say," NOLA.com, January 2, 2018 [https://www.nola.com/news/northshore /article_f7f6f13d-6d5a-55de-99c8-1a3f48b46a40.html]; C. Caron, "Louisiana Man Charged in 'Nigerian Prince' Scheme." *New York Times*, December 31, 2017

[https://www.nytimes.com/2017/12/31/us/nigerian-prince-fraud.html]; L. Vaas, "Your Nigerian Prince Is a 67 Year Old from Louisiana," *Naked Security*, January 3, 2018 [https://nakedsecurity.sophos.com/2018/01/03/your-nigerian-prince-is -a-67-year-old-from-louisiana/]. A recent advance-fee fraud from the Netherlands appeals to nationalistic sentiment: If you are a Dutch "sovereign citizen," the government is said to have put €1.5 million in trust for you, and the first step to access it is to pay €100 to join a club: A. Kouwenhoven and W. Heck, "Separated from the Netherlands, with 1.5 Million Euros Added," NRC, April 21, 2022 [https:// www.nrc.nl/nieuws/2022/04/21/losgemaakt-van-nederland-met-15-miljoen -euro-toe-a4116891].

8. C. Herley, "Why Do Nigerian Scammers Say They Are from Nigeria?," *Proceedings of the Workshop on Information Security*, Berlin, June 25–26, 2012 [https:// www.microsoft.com/en-us/research/wp-content/uploads/2016/02/WhyFrom Nigeria.pdf].

9. G. B. Trudeau, *Doonesbury*, January 27, 1985 [https://www.gocomics.com /doonesbury/1985/01/27].

10. Raniere was sentenced to 120 years in prison after convictions for racketeering, racketeering conspiracy, sex trafficking, attempted sex trafficking, sex trafficking conspiracy, forced labor conspiracy, and wire fraud conspiracy [https://www.justice.gov/usao-edny/pr/nxivm-leader-keith-raniere-sentenced -120-years-prison-racketeering-and-sex-trafficking]. The NXIVM case is detailed in several sources, including the 2020–2022 HBO documentary series *The Vow* [https://www.hbo.com/the-vow], Season 1 (2018) of the CBC investigative podcast *Uncover* [https://www.cbc.ca/radio/uncover], and a series of *New York Times* articles starting with B. Meier, "Inside a Secretive Group Where Women Are Branded," *New York Times*, October 17, 2017 [https://www.nytimes .com/2017/10/17/nyregion/nxivm-women-branded-albany.html]. Toni Natalie's memoir of her membership in the group (written with Chet Hardin) is *The Program: Inside the Mind of Keith Raniere and the Rise of NXIVM* (New York: Grand Central Publishing, 2019); her quotation is from p. 10. Note that multilevel marketing organizations are often described as pyramid schemes, which are commonly associated with deceptive business practices.

11. Similar tactics have been employed to interfere with online recruiters for terrorist organizations. Perhaps the scam baiters could ultimately be replaced by bots powered by machine-learning language models that could do all the work without spending any human time. If you hear only about the "success stories" of scammers who work outlandish swindles, you might imagine they must be persuasive geniuses—it was said of the famous con artist Gilbert Chikli that if you gave him a phone, he could talk anyone into anything—but the bigger and least noticed part of their formula for success is the hard work in contacting dozens of potential victims for each one who is willing to go all the way

to handing over money. If you wanted to get into this business but gave up after the first five, ten, or one hundred potential marks hung up on you, you weren't cut out for it.

12. This hypothetical scenario is based on a company called Fine Art Treasures, which auctioned art on satellite television networks every weekend for a few years in the early 2000s. This organization specialized in giclée prints, which are limited-edition prints made with ink-jet technology. These were advertised as signed, fully authorized pieces but in fact were often mass-produced without proper payment to the artists. Similar scams involved works of Picasso, Dalí, and other twentieth-century icons. Paintings were even sold on cruise ships to naïfs who aspired to build collections or open galleries of their own. That ruse sometimes revealed itself on their next cruise, when they saw the same paintings being offered again. See A. M. Amore, *The Art of the Con* (New York: Palgrave Macmillan, 2015). Three people pleaded guilty and were sentenced in connection with this fraudulent scheme: Kristine Eubanks; her husband, Gerald Sullivan; and James Mobley [https://www.justice.gov/archive/usao/cac/Pressroom/pr2010/060 .html]; [https://www.justice.gov/archive/usao/cac/Pressroom/pr2010/158.html].

13. G. Klein, "Performing a Project Premortem," *Harvard Business Review* 85 (2007): 18–19.

14. H. Schofield, "The Fake French Minister in a Silicone Mask Who Stole Millions," BBC News, June 19, 2019 [https://www.bbc.com/news/world-europe -48510027]; see also the *Persona: The French Deception* podcast.

15. D. Mangan and B. Schwartz, "Jeffrey Epstein 'Misappropriated Vast Sums of Money from Me,' Les Wexner Says," CNBC, August 7, 2019 [https://www.cnbc.com/2019/08/07/jeffrey-epstein-misappropriated-vast -sums-les-wexner-says.html]; G. Sherman, "The Mogul and the Monster: Inside Jeffrey Epstein's Decades-Long Relationship with His Biggest Client," *Vanity Fair*, July–August 2021 [https://www.vanityfair.com/news/2021/06/inside -jeffrey-epsteins-decades-long-relationship-with-his-biggest-client].

16. Blagojevich was convicted of eighteen felonies and sentenced to fourteen years in prison [https://www.justice.gov/archive/usao/iln/chicago/2011 /pr1207_01.pdf]. The ethics reform signing: Illinois State Bar Association, "Ethics Corner: Blagojevich Signs Ethics Reform into Law," *Public Servant*, March 2004. Details about the ethics training are online: "Services," Office of Executive Inspector General, Illinois.gov [https://www2.illinois.gov/oeig/ethics/Pages/Ethics Training.aspx].

17. The answer to whether the training prevents deliberate misconduct apparently is no, at least in Blagojevich's case, since he did take the course as governor: D. Baron, "Did Indicted Illinois Ex-Governor Skip the Online Ethics Training That He Mandated for All State Employees?," *The Web of Language*, December 10, 2008 [https://blogs.illinois.edu/view/25/5658]. People determined to game the system

will do so whether or not they were "trained," and those miscreants likely account for the big-ticket, Blagojevichian misconduct among state employees. If the main benefit is to make it less likely that a small fraction of employees cheat a tiny bit on their time cards, it's likely a bad investment.

18. Jamie Petrone pleaded guilty and was sentenced to nine years in prison [https://www.justice.gov/usao-ct/pr/former-yale-med-school-employee-who -stole-40-million-electronics-sentenced-9-years-prison].

19. US regulations on structuring: "4.26.13 Structuring," Internal Revenue Service, April 10, 2020 [https://www.irs.gov/irm/part4/irm_04-026-013].

20. L. Tompkins, "To Avoid Quarantining Students, a School District Tries Moving Them Around Every 15 Minutes," *New York Times*, October 20, 2020 [https://www.nytimes.com/2020/10/20/us/billings-schools-montana-covid .html].

21. A good history of doping and detection practices in cycling is at "Doping at the Tour de France," Wikipedia [https://en.wikipedia.org/wiki/Doping _at_the_Tour_de_France].

INDEX

Nature, 146, 199, 219
Nelson, Leif, 62, 286n33
Netflix, 164
neuroscience, 39
New Republic, 254n18
New York Post, 53
New York Times, 6, 94, 108, 165, 308n31
New Yorker, 232
Ng, Roger, 290n12
Nigerian prince scam, 14, 231–233, 235, 311n7
Nigrini, Mark, 67–68
Nikola, 39–40, 161, 260n23
No One Would Listen (Markopolos), 282n10
noise: absence of, 136–137, 140–141; in data, 131, 136, 194; in financial markets, 136, 141, 192, 282n11; in human behavior, 137, 140, 186; in judicial system, 283n15; as problematic, 140; in sports performances, 140–141
Noise (Kahneman, Sibony, and Sunstein), 140
Nolan, Sydney, 294n31
nonanswers: accepting as real, 120–121; "here's a list of stuff that supports our claim," 122–123; "it's been validated," 122; "it's been vetted or authenticated," 122; "originals have been lost," 123; phrases to signal quality, 124; "we did our due diligence," 121–122; "we have multiple sources," 124
Norton, Michael, 121
nudging, 217, 292n19
Nunes, Claudio, 145

O, 38
Obama, Barack, 49, 55, 221, 239
Ocean's Eleven (film), 10
Ocrant, Michael, 9
odometer study, 61–63, 266n30
Ólafsson, Helgi, 97–98
Olson, Jay, 64
Olsson, Andreas, 81
one-hit wonders, 32
one-pixel attacks, 27, 257n7
O'Neal, Shaquille, 75, 76
Operation Varsity Blues, 10

opinion, work required to have, 278n32
opportunity cost, 105–106, 276n12, 293n24
options, asking for better, 126
orchestra, fake, 110–114
Orient Paper Ltd., 119, 279n33
Orlando Museum of Art, 93–94
Orlando Sentinel, 158
O'Sullivan, Chris, 158

paper mill, 149
paranoid delusions, 78
passwords: phishing for, 171–173; recovery questions, 237
Paul, Rand, 183–185
PBS, 112
peanut butter brands, 75, 76
Pearl, Minnie, 159
peer review, 88–90, 114, 230
Penn and Teller Fool Us (series), 85
penny-auction industry, 102–104
Pennycook, Gordon, 7, 226, 253n12
perception, metaphorical priming and, 59
personality typologies, 186
perspective, 181, 184
persuasion: by potency, 205; by precision, 186
Petrone, Jamie, 240, 314n18
Petrosian, Tigran L., 282n14
Pew Research, 80
Phaedrus (Plato), 308n31
Phinney, Tom, 261n3
phishing, 170–173, 232, 293n26, 293n28
photographers, influence of expectations on, 57–58
The Picture of Dorian Gray (Wilde), 159
pitch, evaluation of, 177–178
placebic information, 121, 279n36
placebo effects, 208
plagiarism, 176, 255n20, 256n22
Plato, 308n31
Podesta, John, 171
poker, 92, 104, 142–144, 284n20
policy shifts, 137
political disinformation, 4
political polling, 193–195, 298n19, 298n21
Pollock, Jackson, 106–108

Daniel Simons is a professor in the Department of Psychology at the University of Illinois, where he directs the Visual Cognition Laboratory. He lives in Champaign, Illinois.

Christopher Chabris is a cognitive scientist who has taught at Union College and Harvard University. He lives in Lewisburg, Pennsylvania.